the men who want to make their workplaces work better for everyone! Andie and Al's advice is practical without asking women to be something other than who they are, which is why it will also be effective for those who utilize it."

—Dr. **Arin Reeves, author of** *One Size Never Fits All: Business Development Strategies for Women (and Most Men)* **and** *The Next IQ: The Next Generation of Intelligence for 21st Century Leaders*

"Breaking Through Bias serves as a wake-up call for senior business leaders. The book explores common gender stereotypes and discusses the discriminatory bias that result. Based on my own work on culture change over the past five years, I am convinced that bias in the workplace is real. Things aren't equal. I can't allow myself to be satisfied with an environment where female employees have to expend energy combatting bias, so culture change is necessary—but it is slow work. This book offers insights and practical approaches to help women manage the environment as it exists. It is essential reading for modern businesspeople of either gender."

—**Lee Richard Tschanz, Global Vice President Enterprise Accounts CPG & LS, Rockwell Automation**

"The medical profession is no more free of gender bias than all other professions that make up our economy. From the early stages of training to achieving the attending physician status, bias exists at every level. Thus, I am enthusiastically recommending that women medical students, residents, and fellow colleagues read and reread *Breaking Through Bias*."

—**Neelum T. Aggarwal, MD, Chief Diversity Officer of American Medical Women's Association; Chair of Mentors, Advisors and Peers Committee, Women in Bio (Chicago); Associate Professor, Departments of Neurological Sciences and Rush Alzheimer's Disease Center**

Praise for

Breaking Through Bias
and Andrea S. Kramer and Alton B. Harris

"According to spouses Kramer and Harris, 'Women don't need to be fixed,' but society does, and quickly. The authors proceed to identify a serious advancement problem for women, who make up 45 percent of entry-level professionals but only 17 percent of C-suite executives. They blame this gap on the pervasiveness of gender stereotypes, which lead to a kind of 'benevolent sexism' that's as damaging as it is unintentional. Kramer and Harris acknowledge that systemic change is important, but it takes time, which leaves current would-be executives in the dust. The authors discuss managing perceptions, being aware of body language, crafting communications, and using anger to its best effect…a well-organized, well-thought-out call to action." **—Publishers Weekly**

"Of the structural barriers to women's advancement in the workplace, none seem more intractable than gender stereotypes held by career gatekeepers, often unconsciously. *Breaking Through Bias* is an indispensable guide to overcoming these barriers—a practical system of 'attuned gender communication' enabling women to achieve their career goals while simultaneously transforming American organizations. This is an important book for women, and for all those who seek to create a better workplace."
**—Frederick M. Lawrence, Secretary and CEO,
The Phi Beta Kappa Society, Distinguished Lecturer in
Law, Georgetown University Law Center**

"Women are more qualified, educated, and prepared for leadership roles in every field—business, law, politics, and technology—than ever before. Yet, well into the twenty-first century, we still encounter the old barriers of prejudice and gender bias. *Breaking Through Bias* provides women with hugely impactful tools that can be put to use right now to confront gender issues and, yes, partner with enlightened men to promote our advancement."
—Jan Schakowsky, Congresswoman, Ninth District of Illinois

"Change cannot come fast enough in the pursuit of gender equality in the workplace. In *Breaking Through Bias,* Andie and Al provide strategies that allow women—and men—to create their own change by teaching us to communicate in a way that overcomes biases and stereotypes. This information is invaluable for all professionals looking to accelerate within inclusive workplaces around the globe."

—Deborah Gillis, Former President & CEO, Catalyst

"It is exciting to see the ideas that Andie has been using for so long to personally mentor women now being made available on a broad scale in this terrific book. A great read for any woman who wants to take control of her career and be seen as the smart, capable woman she is."

—Julie Howard, Former Chairman & CEO,
Navigant Consulting, Inc.

"Andie and Al tackle the all-important subject of gender-correlated communication styles in the workplace from a fresh perspective. Combining their own real-life experiences (as a woman and as a man) with solid research, *Breaking Through Bias* is a highly readable book. Offering both practical advice for women and essential knowledge to the men who want to support them, this is a book to read and to share with others."

—Carol Frohlinger, President, Negotiating Women, Inc.

"Barriers to gender equality persist. This groundbreaking book encourages talented women to persevere on the road to achieving the success they seek. This book should be mandatory reading for women both at the onset of their careers and on the path to the top of their profession."

—Laurel G. Bellows, Managing Principal, The Bellows Law Group,
P.C., and Past President, American Bar Association

"Andie has worked tirelessly on the advancement of women in workplaces for so many years, and the wisdom and insights from that work are elegantly captured in this book! *Breaking Through Bias* is a great resource for women navigating the realities of workplace gender bias and

Breaking Through Bias

Communication Techniques for Women to
Succeed at Work

Second Edition

ANDREA S. KRAMER
ALTON B. HARRIS

NICHOLAS BREALEY
PUBLISHING

BOSTON · LONDON

First edition published by Bibliomotion, Inc., in 2016
This edition published in 2020 by Nicholas Brealey Publishing
An imprint of John Murray Press

A Hachette company

25 24 23 22 21 20   1 2 3 4 5 6 7 8 9 10

Image credit: page 179. Reproduced with permission of Punch Cartoon Library / TopFoto

A CIP catalogue record for this title is available from the British Library

Library of Congress Control Number: 2020931277

ISBN 978-1-5293-1729-9
US eBook ISBN 978-1-5293-1732-9
UK eBook ISBN 978-1-529-31731-2

Printed and bound in the United States of America

John Murray Press policy is to use papers that are natural, renewable, and recyclable products and made from wood grown in sustainable forests. The logging and manufacturing processes are expected to conform to the environmental regulations of the country of origin.

John Murray Press Ltd
Carmelite House
50 Victoria Embankment
London EC4Y 0DZ
Tel: 020 3122 6000

Nicholas Brealey Publishing
Hachette Book Group
53 State Street
Boston, MA 02109, USA
Tel: (617) 523 3801

www.nbuspublishing.com

For Cynthia, whose persistence, brilliance, and astonishing accomplishments remain a continuing inspiration to us.

CONTENTS

ANDIE'S PREFACE TO SECOND EDITION

Since the first edition of this book was published, my husband, Al, and I have watched dramatic changes—some positive, some negative—in the discussions about and treatment of women in gender-biased workplaces. One area where there has been little improvement is in the critical mass of women moving into the leadership ranks of workplaces in America and around the world. This second edition reflects our efforts to include changes since the first edition was published, to update the information and advice we provide throughout the book, and to refine and modify some of the communication techniques to deal with today's workplaces.

My journey to helping women succeed in gendered workplaces began many years ago. When I graduated from law school I was fortunate to have a number of job offers, but two in particular interested me. One was from a large and highly prestigious law firm; the other was from a small, three-year-old firm with only seven lawyers, hardly any reputation, and no national prestige. The large firm promised me a place in a prominent, highly respected, and nationally recognized tax department; the opportunity to earn a great deal of money; and immediate personal and professional status. At the small firm I would be the only tax lawyer but the partners told me they would give me whatever resources and support I needed and send me to whatever classes I thought would be useful. Although the partners had great hopes for the future, they made it clear that the firm's prospects were not certain. I was young, undoubtedly foolish, and certainly without fear of failure; I accepted the small firm's job offer.

The decision was right for me. I spent almost 15 years at that firm and two characteristics are most memorable. First, the partners kept all of their promises to me, and I learned how to be a real lawyer. I became an equity partner, brought in my own clients, and chaired the firm's tax group, which had seven lawyers in it by the time I left.

Second, and much more importantly, my being a woman had nothing to do with my professional development or advancement. I worked with a group of senior lawyers, all of whom were men, not one of whom, not once, not even for an instant, made me feel that being a woman made a whit of difference to my career opportunities, acceptance into the senior leadership ranks, or my becoming a great lawyer. Growing as a lawyer is never smooth sailing, but my being a woman was never the cause of the rough waters I encountered.

Because of the opportunities that firm gave me, the time came when I needed the resources of a much bigger law firm to meet the needs of my clients. When I left, I was apprehensive. I expected many differences, but the most disturbing one I encountered was the one I least expected: gender bias. At my new firm—and at all of the other very large law firms and businesses I interacted with—I saw obstacles in the way of women's career paths. I saw inconsistencies in the opportunities made available to women as opposed to men, and I found unfair demands placed on fabulous women trying to become good lawyers while they simultaneously raised children.

It all reminded me of the career advice I received in my teens. I was told then that there is a difference between being a "lawyer" and a "lady lawyer." Lawyers could be successful and happy; lady lawyers could never be both. Well, I was a lawyer (a successful one at that), I was a lady, and I was happy. I knew that other women could be just as successful and happy as I was. I was damned if I was going to sit back and watch law firms and other professional and business organizations discriminate against women; force them to choose between success and happiness; or hinder their likelihood of attaining successful, satisfying careers.

Coming face-to-face with the reality of gender bias after not seeing it at the start of my career taught me several things. First, I learned that there are truly gender-neutral workplaces, but these are a precious few. By and large, we live in a society of gendered workplaces, where men run most organizations and make most of the career advancement decisions. As a result, those career decisions are often affected by gender bias (conscious and unconscious).

Second, I learned that if women are going to advance as we aspire to—and all of the research shows that young women are just as ambitious as young men, if not more so—we cannot passively accept the current gender-skewed environment. In addition, we cannot wait for our workplaces to become gender-neutral. Women need to recognize and purposefully counter the gender stereotypes and biases present in our workplaces. Women can use communication techniques to overcome or avoid gender bias.

Third, I realized that successful women deal with gender stereotypes through nuanced and carefully honed communication skills. Al and I call these skills "attuned gender communication," and these techniques remain the subject of this book's second edition.

Close to 30 years ago, I made a commitment to myself to do everything in my power to help other women be successful *and* happy in their careers—so they might come as close as possible to experiencing the gender-neutral path I had been lucky enough to follow when I first started my career. I have been trying to make good on that commitment ever since.

Since joining my current law firm, I founded its Gender Diversity Committee, launched its LGBT Committee, and served on both its Management Committee and Compensation Committee. I am pleased to have participated in many of its efforts to successfully increase gender diversity and inclusion. We've been named one of the best law firms for women, a top 10 female- and family-friendly firm, and one of the 10 best Big Law firms for female attorneys. We exceed industry averages in the advancement and promotion of women into our leadership ranks, and our market-leading policies and procedures have been adopted and followed by other professional organizations. I'm very proud of my firm, my personal contributions to its gender diversity efforts, and the ways in which my female colleagues have successfully advanced in their careers.

In the early 2000s, I began to speak publicly about how women can confront the difficulties they face in their careers because of gender bias. I have spoken on this topic before hundreds of groups; written hundreds of articles, blog posts, and guides; and led more than a hundred workshops aimed at helping women advance in their careers. In 2005, I cofounded the Women's Leadership and Mentoring Alliance (WLMA), a not-for-profit corporation that provides a national mentorship program for women across industries and professions, and I continue to serve as WLMA's board chair.

Al and I wrote the first edition of this book after I realized that my techniques for overcoming gender stereotypes and bias had struck a chord. We knew that Al's male perspective was invaluable and provided a unique addition to my views. In combining social science research, stories from women we have mentored and interviewed, as well as our own experiences and perspectives, we provide women and men with a clearer understanding of the operation of gender stereotypes and bias.

In collaborating again on this second edition, Al and I hope to continue to offer helpful and immediately actionable advice about ways in which women can communicate to avoid or overcome the career-disrupting effects of stereotypes and bias. We both believe that women can take control of their own careers in gender-biased workplaces and achieve the success and satisfaction they desire and to which they are entitled. Women do not need to wait until their organizations become more gender neutral. With this second edition, we update and expand communication tools women can use to ensure that gender bias does not prevent them from going as far and as fast in their careers as their talents will allow.

Andie Kramer
Chicago, IL

AL'S PREFACE TO
SECOND EDITION

I was a founding partner of that small law firm where Andie started her career. I am proud that we were able to give her the bias-free opportunities and support she needed to develop into the superb and successful lawyer she is today. Andie's experience at our firm, however, is not the whole story. In early 2015, after growing to well over 100 lawyers, that law firm merged with a much larger national law firm. Sometime before that merger, I began to reflect on our history and consider what we had done right and what we had done wrong. We had consciously tried to create a workplace that would allow women and men to thrive equally. Nevertheless, although many women, including Andie, did thrive and succeed marvelously, there had been serious disparities in the career achievements of our women and our men. We had hired women and men in almost equal numbers, but we had lost far more women than men. By the time we merged, a mere 15 percent of our top partnership rank were women. What had gone wrong? Why weren't the women in our firm staying with their careers as long as the men or being elevated to equity partner as frequently as the men?

Most certainly it was not because our female attorneys lacked the talent or ambition of our male attorneys; these women were without exception not only bright and well trained, but enthusiastic about practicing law and committed to having long and successful careers. After several years, too many of these fabulously talented women would leave. Sometimes, they left for more prestigious positions, but as I later learned, many left because they felt a lack of tangible career satisfaction and success.

They believed they had little support or career-enhancing opportunities, they interacted with few female role models, and they experienced a sense of being excluded from the ingroup. In other words, women left because they did not have the same positive career experience as their male counterparts.

Our failure to retain and advance women on a basis comparable to men was hardly unique. Rather, it reflected a broader national pattern in the legal profession and the business world generally. *I always thought* we were different; *I always thought* women were not disadvantaged; and *I always thought* we were a place where each of our attorneys could find happiness and career success. I was wrong on all counts.

As I reflected on our firm's failure to become a place of true gender equality, I became convinced that our problem lay in the fact that our workplace—just like the workplaces in most other businesses throughout the United States—was gendered. Gendered workplaces are led and dominated by men and structured to expect conformity with masculine norms, values, and expectations. In gendered workplaces, two powerful yet generally (but not always) implicit or unconscious biases create serious obstacles to women's advancement into senior leadership: affinity bias and gender bias. Affinity bias is the instinctive preference to associate with and advocate for people who are similar to oneself, so a man may decide to support and promote a man because they "think" the same way. Gender bias—the stereotype-driven expectation that men will be superior to women when facing career challenges—may prevent a man in leadership from considering offering a career-enhancing project to a woman. As a result of these biases, often (but not always) without consciously discriminatory intent, women face hurdles, potholes, and dangerous curves on their career paths not on men's paths.

I now realize that there were a great many things our firm should have done—and that modern organizations can do now—to clear these discriminatory obstacles from women's career paths. I also realize, as a result of working with Andie and many other talented women who have successfully moved into senior leadership positions, that there are a great many things women can do for themselves to avoid or overcome the discriminatory consequences of affinity and gender biases. With the right information, tools, and techniques, ambitious, talented, hardworking women can do much to end the shameful disparity in women's and men's career achievements. Women do not need to wait for gendered workplaces to become gender neutral, nor do they need to start acting more like men. Women, just as they are, with the right information and tools can claim their rightful seats at the leadership table and speak with voices that will be acknowledged, listened to, and respected.

This brings me to the reasons I originally wrote this book with Andie and why we have updated it together for this second edition.

First, the bias-driven dynamics of gendered workplaces cause high-potential, once-eager women to drop out of their careers or choose to move to less intense, less interesting, and less financially rewarding positions. They often do this because they find their professional lives unfulfilling, frustrating, or oppressive. Many women are not prepared for these dynamics, much less how to navigate them successfully. I believe, however, that with an understanding of affinity and gender bias, women can transform these frustrating, negative dynamics into positive work experiences. With concrete, effective, practical advice about how to cope with these discriminatory obstacles, women can achieve full and satisfying careers. I have written and revised this book with Andie to provide women with that information and advice.

My second reason is that women can benefit from a male perspective on what women can and should do to achieve career success. While Andie and I share similar views about how women can deal with affinity and gender biases, our views are not identical. By bringing our perspectives together, we hope women will gain a clearer picture of how workplaces look from both a female and a male point of view. Moreover, I hope that our dual perspectives will provide women with original, practical, and effective advice to aid them in advancing in their careers.

My third reason is that most senior men don't realize how much harder it is for a woman to advance in a career than it is for men. Too many men are, *just as I was*, convinced they are totally without bias and that their organizations are perfect meritocracies. They are wrong on both counts. This book is obviously for women: it is addressed to women, talks about problems that are unique to women, and offers communication strategies and techniques tailored specifically for women. But I believe that men—particularly men in senior leadership positions—also need to read this book. They need to read it to understand how and why affinity and gender biases discriminate against women as they compete with men for career advancement. They need to read this book to recognize that their own unconscious biases are often directly contrary to their conscious beliefs and values. They need to read this book to realize how important it is to become active participants in the effort to diversify their organizations' senior leadership. Men need to offer a helping hand to the women with whom they work; to mentor and sponsor the women around them; and to make sure the women who work for them are challenged, coached, trained, encouraged, compensated, and promoted in the same way and to the same extent as men. Thus, my hope is that men will read this book and recognize the need to increase the number of women leaders in their own organizations.

The final reason is for our daughter, Cynthia. She is an incredibly talented, ambitious, and personable young woman. At the time this book was first published, she was in medical school and firmly believed the world was a meritocracy, that women and men were equal not only in their abilities but also in their opportunities, and that nothing would hold her back in her medical career except her own shortcomings and mistakes. This book was originally intended in part as a gift to Cynthia of the advice I believed she would need when she found that the world is not a meritocracy, that women's and men's career opportunities are not equal, and that her career could be impeded for reasons that had nothing to do with her talent but everything to do with her being a woman. She is now an MD, has seen the working world in all its unfairness and absurdity, and has used much of the advice we offer in this book to advance successfully despite such biases and unfairness. This second edition is for

Cynthia as well. In many ways, her continuing career success has been her gift to us; to see so much of what Andie and I have tried to convey put to work and to make a real, concrete difference. There cannot be a better reason to have written and revised this book than that.

Al Harris
Chicago, IL

INTRODUCTION TO
SECOND EDITION

There is a wide disparity in women's and men's career achievements. This book is about how you as a woman with—or about to begin—a career can avoid falling victim to this disparity. It is about how you—right now, just the way you are—can advance as far and as fast as your talent, hard work, and commitment will take you. Achieving such success depends on your understanding of the nature, causes, and operation of gender stereotypes; how they foster biases; and how these biases operate to hold women back. It also depends on your willingness to use the communication techniques that will allow you to avoid or overcome these biases. Before jumping directly into these matters, let's look closely at the extent of the persistent and vexing disparities between women's and men's representation in senior leadership.

Disparities in Women's and Men's Career Achievements

In corporate America, women make up 48 percent of entry-level career employees but only 38 percent of first-tier managers, 34 percent of senior managers, 30 percent of vice presidents, 26 percent of senior vice presidents, and 21 percent of executives in the C-suite.[1] In Fortune 500 companies, women make up only 9.5 percent of the top earners,[2] constitute only 12.5 percent of CFOs,[3] only 6.6 percent of CEOs,[4] and only 22.5 percent of board members.[5] Outside of corporate America, women fare no better. They make up 47 percent of law firm associates but only 20 percent of equity partners.[6] Women are over 50 percent of medical students[7] but only 25 percent of full professors, 18 percent of department chairs, and 16 percent of deans at medical schools.[8] Women are just 27 percent of tenure track professors at four-year colleges and universities,[9] despite making up 54 percent of full-time students.[10] With respect to political office, women make up only 24 percent of the members of the US House of Representatives, 23 percent of US senators, 28 percent of state legislators, 18 percent of state governors, and 23 percent of the mayors of the 100 largest American cities.[11] Of the 250 top-grossing Hollywood films of 2017, women made up just 18 percent of the directors, executive producers, producers, writers, cinematographers, and editors.[12]

Many more similar statistics are available, but the point should be clear enough: women are not moving into senior leadership positions in business, the professions, academia, government, and entertainment in numbers anywhere near comparable to men. And discouragingly, women have made virtually no progress in changing this situation since the 1990s. As this graph from the US Census Bureau dramatically

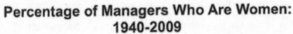

Percentage of Managers Who Are Women: 1940-2009

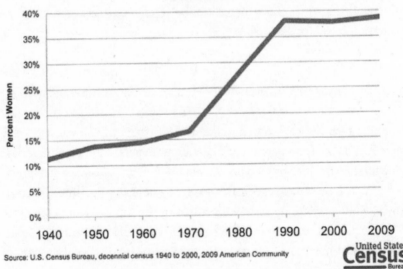

Source: U.S. Census Bureau, decennial census 1940 to 2000, 2009 American Community

United States Census Bureau

illustrates, between 1970 and 1990 women made steady and rapid progress, increasing their representation among corporate managers from about 16 percent to more than 35 percent. Since then, however, women's progress has been nonexistent.[13]

The US Census Bureau graph stops at 2009, but the Bureau of Labor Statistics reports that things had not significantly improved by 2016,[14] and the 2019 LeanIn and McKinsey study on women in the workplace makes clear that there has been no progress since then.[15] Indeed, as LeanIn and McKinsey concluded in their 2018 report, "Progress isn't just slow. It's stalled."[16]

Perhaps equally troubling as women's lack of increased representation in senior leadership ranks is the fact that when women do gain access to those ranks, they are largely concentrated in "feminized" positions such as human resources. And regardless of the type of management position they hold, women are paid less than men in similar positions.[17]

Why the Achievement Disparity?

The difference in women's and men's career achievements is often explained by claiming that women prefer to spend time with their children rather than pursuing career success; they don't ask (or don't want) to move up to senior leadership positions; and they lack the ambition, confidence, and core competencies needed to successfully compete against men. These claims, however, are all patently false.

A growing body of research makes clear that women are just as talented, ambitious, and committed to career advancement as men. For example, a 2017 study by the Boston Consulting Group found "on average, women entered the workforce with the same—or higher—levels of ambition as men, in terms of their desire to hold leadership positions or be promoted.... [I]t is also unequivocal: having children does not affect women's desire to lead. The ambition levels of women with children and women without children track each other almost exactly over time."[18] Moreover, recent psychological research finds that "one's sex has little or no bearing on personality, cognition and leadership."[19] Indeed, as a review of hundreds of studies on cognitive performance (such as math ability), personality and social behaviors (such as leadership), and psychological well-being (such as self-esteem) found, there are more similarities than differences between men and women.[20]

Writing in the *Harvard Business Review*, Catherine Tinsley and Robin Ely conclude that "on average, the sexes are far more similar in their inclinations, attitudes, and skills than popular opinion would have us believe. [There are] sex differences in various settings, including the workplace—but those differences are not rooted in fixed gender traits. Rather, they stem from organizational structures, company practices, and patterns of interaction that position men and women differently, creating systematically different experiences for them."[21] This is confirmed by a 2011 report by Catalyst which found that even when women do everything they are told to do to get ahead, they still fail to advance as far and as fast as men.[22] In other words, women with high ambition, terrific abilities, can-do attitudes, and appropriate behavioral characteristics are systematically disadvantaged in relation to men in their pursuit of career advancement.

So what is the problem? Why are women at such a disadvantage in comparison to men when it comes to career achievement? A recent American Bar Association (ABA) report on why experienced women lawyers leave the legal profession provides a key insight. This ABA report concludes, "It is clear that women lawyers on average do not advance along the same trajectory as men," for they "have far less access to the building blocks for success than men."[23] Indeed, the ABA found that "women report being four to eight times more likely to be overlooked for advancement, denied a salary increase or bonus, treated as a token representative for diversity, lack access to business development opportunities, perceived as less committed to their career, and lack access to sponsors." Thus, women's *experience* in the pursuit of career success in large law firms is very different from that of their male counterparts. Our research makes clear that this sharply differentiated workplace experience of women and men is also found in virtually all other professions, business settings, academia, and politics.[24]

Gender Bias

The question is: what accounts for women's and men's very different workplace experiences and their divergent representation in senior leadership? The answer to that question is the focus of this book: pervasive, persistent gender stereotypes and the biases that flow from them. We first discuss what these stereotypes and biases are, why they are most pronounced in workplaces led and dominated by men with decidedly masculine cultures, and how these stereotypes and biases operate to create obstacles to women's career advancement. Most importantly, we then go on to spell out in detail the concrete, practical, effective steps women can take to avoid or overcome these discriminatory obstacles. In other words, this book is about the myriad ways in which gender stereotypes and their ensuing biases hold women back and how women can break through these biases to achieve career success *and* satisfaction.

Implicit Gender Bias

A person holds an implicit gender bias when she or he unconsciously— that is, without any conscious awareness—assumes, expects, or anticipates that men will be better than women at critical workplace tasks, that women are better at and have a greater responsibility for childcare than men, that women and men are best suited for different societal roles, and that men should play leadership roles and women should play supporting roles. Implicit gender bias has numerous variants: motherhood bias (mothers pursuing careers are hurting their small children), self-limiting bias (women's assumption that certain careers, positions, and tasks are not appropriate for women), agentic bias (discomfort with women who do not conform to traditional feminine behavior norms), negative bias (communal women are not cut out for leadership roles), and affinity bias (a preference for associating with and supporting people who are like you).

Implicit gender bias and its variants affect people's actions, decisions, and judgments. They influence how people relate to women and men, decide what assignments and projects to give them, evaluate their performance, and provide them with feedback. Although implicit gender bias and its variants adversely affect women's career advancement, these concepts do not involve bad intentions or malevolent motivations. Implicit biases result not from consciously held beliefs, but from deep-seated, long-established stereotypes we have acquired simply by growing up in this society and being exposed to contemporary media, entertainment, politics, and education.

Explicit Gender Bias

In writing the first edition of this book, we focused almost exclusively on implicit gender bias. We assumed that explicit gender bias—the open, intentional, aggressive, and hostile expression of sexist and misogynistic views[25]—was so socially unacceptable that it did not pose a serious threat to women's careers. While that assumption may have been justified in late 2015 when we submitted our manuscript, Donald Trump's presidential campaign and election have made it apparent that that assumption is no longer justified. Beginning with Trump's campaign, the media has been flooded with crude, angry, and mean-spirited criticisms of women. Indeed, explicit gender bias has now become so prevalent that we are convinced it poses a real and very severe threat to women's career advancement. Our change of heart is nicely captured by Cheryl Strayed when she writes:

> I've never been under the illusion that sexism had vanished, [but] before Trump was elected there was a history-lesson element to the stories I told of my first consciousness about what it meant to be female in America, a quality that had made the sexism I

experienced as a girl seem antiquated and nearly extinct. The message was: *This is the way it used to be! Isn't that amazing?* In witnessing the presidential campaign and Trump's eventual election, I've concluded that I had it wrong. This isn't how it used to be. It is the way it is . . . . This election wasn't simply a political contest. It was a referendum on how much America still hates [strong, ambitious] women.[26]

Explicit gender bias exists on a continuum of discriminatory gender-specific behaviors that includes implicit gender bias, incivility to and microaggressions against women, inappropriate sexual comments, unwelcomed touching, actionable sexual harassment, and criminal sexual assault. As we wrote in the *Harvard Business Review*, because these discriminatory behaviors are all related and interconnected, they need to be "addressed collectively, because sexual harassment [and other forms of explicit gender bias are] far more likely in organizations that experience offenses on the 'less severe' end of the spectrum than in those that don't."[27] As a consequence, this book's continuing focus on implicit gender bias remains highly relevant. Misogynistic criticism of women striving to achieve true gender equality is tolerated only when there is a pervasive, unconscious assumption that women are somehow less capable, less qualified, and less entitled to play leadership roles than men. Therefore, to effectively attack such explicit gender bias, implicit gender bias must also be attacked. And that, of course, is precisely the objective of this book.

Approach

Given the overwhelming evidence of the adverse career consequences for women of gender bias, it might be thought appropriate for us to focus all our attention on the legal and institutional reforms needed to rid American workplaces of the discriminatory consequences of such bias. Unquestionably, this reform is necessary, and there are many sensible and persuasive advocates working toward that goal.[28] In fact, in our book *It's Not You, It's the Workplace*, we present a comprehensive program for achieving true gender diversity in organizations' senior leadership ranks. Our focus in this book, however, remains on what women can do on their own *right now, today*, to improve their career prospects *despite* the presence of gender bias. Ambitious, talented women should not have to wait for large-scale structural or organizational changes to achieve career success. Therefore, our focus is on the great many things women can do *now* to avoid or overcome the discriminatory consequences of gender bias. Accordingly, we lay out tools and techniques women can use *despite gender bias* to make their own careers more successful, satisfying, and sustainable. Effective use of these tools and techniques depends on women's ability to identify the stereotypes and biases held by the people who maintain the checkpoints and gatehouses on their career paths. By managing the ways in which women interact with their career gatekeepers—managing the impressions they have through what we call attuned gender communication—women can avoid, disarm, or overcome—break through—gender bias.

It's important to note that the communication techniques we present in this book have nothing to do with women learning to act more like men. We believe women are just fine the way they are. Women's attitudes, abilities, and behaviors are as suitable for the boardroom as they are for the nursery. Consequently, we make no attempt to teach women to be different from the way they are now. Our goal is to help women become better at identifying the presence of gender stereotypes, more sensitive to how these stereotypes foster gender biases, and more skillful at managing the impressions they make in order to avoid or overcome these biases. With these abilities, women can take control of their own careers and advance on terms comparable to those of the men with whom they work and compete.

Many self-help books for women argue that women are responsible for their failure to advance in the workplace because of the way they speak. These books argue that women are holding themselves back because their speech patterns are either too assertive or not assertive enough. Either way, these books argue that women need in some way to be fixed in order to succeed in their careers.

Again, we want to be very clear that we don't think women need to be fixed. We agree with linguist Cecilia Ford that a negative response to a woman when she speaks is "based first and foremost on the fact that she is speaking from a woman's body: speaking not 'like' a woman but 'as' a woman . . . [She is] penalized because she is *speaking while being a woman*."[29] In other words, the problem is not *the way women speak* but that women are speaking while being women. The reason this is a problem is because of the stereotypes their audience ascribes to them simply because they are women. The objective, therefore, is not for women to be fixed so they communicate more "like" someone else; rather, the objective is for women to communicate in such a way that they can avoid or overcome the discriminatory consequences of these stereotypes. This means providing women with tools and techniques to allow them to communicate—using their voice, posture, movement, words, and attitudes—in such a way that they are listened to; seen as competent, confident, socially sensitive leaders; and not penalized for being women. In other words, to master attuned gender communication.

Attuned Gender Communication and Impression Management

Attuned gender communication involves four elements:

1. The cultivation and active use of the key attitudes needed for career success: grit, a positive perspective on your abilities, a coping sense of humor, and a confident self-image.
2. A high degree of self-awareness or self-monitoring.
3. A keen awareness of the impressions you are making on the people with whom you deal in your career.
4. An ability to use a variety of communication techniques to manage and change those impressions in order to avoid or overcome

the biases arising from the gender stereotypes that are so pervasive in gendered workplaces.

You communicate through spoken and written words, but you also communicate through your attitudes, facial expressions, gestures, postures, touches, use of personal space, dress, punctuality, responsiveness, and so on. You communicate with every aspect of your behavior, and the whole of your behavior shapes everything other people think of you, from their first impression of you to your ability to lead, influence, inspire, and motivate them. Therefore, the heart of attuned gender communication is managing the impressions you make by controlling the totality of your behavior. By managing how and what you communicate, you can shape the impressions other people have of you. This is hardly a new concept. Philosopher and historian David Hume made the point in the 1770s:

> An orator addresses himself to a particular audience, and must have a regard to their particular genius, interests, opinions, passions, and prejudices; otherwise he hopes in vain to govern their resolutions, and inflame their affections. Should they ever have entertained some prepossessions against him, however unreasonable, he must not overlook this disadvantage; but, before he enters upon the subject, must endeavor to conciliate their affection, and acquire their good graces.[30]

If we replaced "orator" with "woman in a business situation" and modernized Hume's language, we have the essence of attuned gender communication in two sentences.

Our Audience

This book is addressed to talented, ambitious women who are prepared to compete vigorously for career advancement and don't want to be held back simply because they are women. In virtually every segment of our economy, and certainly in every traditionally male segment, the playing field for career advancement is decidedly tilted against women. Women's success depends on their being able to find ways to level this playing field. Attuned gender communication involves a series of practical, real-world communication techniques that women can use to do this. Moreover, it is important to recognize that by working for their individual advancement, women can do a great deal to positively affect the organizational changes that will make it increasingly easier for other women to achieve *their* career success.

Men

Throughout this book, we address our comments and advice to women. It would be a great mistake, however, for men to think this book is not relevant for them. Men, particularly men who play senior leadership roles in business and the professions, most definitely should read this book. Unfortunately, most men believe that they are free of biases against women and that the organizations in which they work treat women and men equally. By reading this book, men will quickly realize that both of these beliefs are false and that it is far harder for women to advance in their careers than it is for men. The importance of such a realization lies in the fact that when men become aware of the extent and consequences of gender bias, they also become aware of the importance of their full participation in diversity and inclusion.[31] We also believe that if senior-level men read this book, they are likely to become active mentors and sponsors of women, call out their colleagues who behave in biased and exclusionary ways, and support initiatives to ensure that women receive a fair shot at getting to the top. The more men become aware of how much work needs to be done to achieve gender equality, why achieving such equality is so important, and how hard it is to do, the easier it will become for women to advance in their careers.

What Is to Follow

This book is divided into four parts. In part I, "Understanding Gender Stereotypes," we discuss the common gender stereotypes that both sexes have about women, men, families, career, and leadership. We explain why these stereotypes are at the root of the disparity in career achievement between women and men, and we discuss how they operate as scripts for discriminatory behavior. We explore why women so often think stereotypically about themselves, their careers, and their families and why women who buy into these stereotypes accept career-limiting roles. We also specifically address explicit gender bias through an examination of the consequences of Trump's public misogynistic behavior and the revelations resulting from the #MeToo movement.

In part II, "Conversations with Yourself," we address the conversations you, as a woman, need to have with yourself about yourself and your career. These conversations are about key career attitudes: grit, mind-set, humor, and self-image, and the importance of managing the impressions you make as you interact with others. These are conversations about how you, like Hume's orator, can win the "affection" of the people with whom you are dealing and "acquire their good graces."

Part III, "Conversations with Others," is about how you can effectively communicate with the people with whom you deal in your work life. Your communication must be designed to make an impression of competence, confidence, and social sensitivity. It should avoid impressions that trigger or reinforce hurtful gender stereotypes. We address what is commonly called women's double bind: the adverse career consequences women often suffer whether they behave communally—being seen as likable but not a leader—or agentically—being seen as competent but not likable. We refer to this double bind as the Goldilocks Dilemma: women's risk of appearing to be too soft or too hard but rarely as just right.

In part IV, "Communicating in Difficult Situations," we examine in several chapters how you can effectively advocate for yourself without running afoul of the common expectation that women should be modest and not self-promoting. We end with a chapter focused on the key choices in your life away from work that play a critical role in your ability to maintain the career commitment that is essential to success. We discuss why "work-life balance" and "having it all" are gender stereotypes that will not help you achieve satisfaction either in your career or in the other aspects of your life. We also explain the importance of sensibly choosing what you actually want to have in your life.

PART I

Understanding Gender Stereotypes

Chapter 1

The Elephant in the Room

IN THE INTRODUCTION, WE DISCUSSED the wide and persistent gap between women's and men's overall career achievements. We also made clear that this gap is not due to women being less ambitious, competent, or committed to their careers than men. Indeed, the important takeaway is that gender has little or no bearing on leadership ability, career ambition, or commitment.[1] Another misconception about the reason for the achievement gap is because of rigid workplace practices. It is often argued that if American workplaces demanded less "face time," allowed more flextime, permitted more telecommuting, provided more generous paid maternity leave, and created more welcoming reentry programs, women would advance in their careers in a manner comparable to men.

Although these (and other) structural workplace changes are sensible, desirable, and much needed, we seriously doubt that—by themselves—they would do much to end the disparity in women's and men's career achievements. The reason is that the fundamental phenomenon holding women back is not structural but psychological: the elephant in the room of the disparity in women's and men's career achievement is gender bias. This bias flows from the multitude of stereotypes that the people controlling women's careers hold about women, men, families, competitiveness, ambition, commitment, and leadership. Unless we recognize the pervasiveness of these stereotypes and find ways to avoid or overcome the biases that flow from them, women will continue to encounter serious obstacles to their career advancement regardless of much-needed structural changes that should be made to workplace practices.

Gender Bias

Gender bias is manifested in the systematic depreciation of women's competence in relation to men's. Gender bias can be explicit—consciously motivated, open, and hostile disparagement of women—or implicit—unconsciously motivated, even at odds with a person's strongly held conscious beliefs. We address explicit gender bias in chapter 3. In this chapter, we focus exclusively on implicit gender bias. Implicit bias is the direct result of the stereotypes people exhibiting such bias hold; therefore, we need to carefully examine those stereotypes.

Gender Stereotypes

Stereotypes are reflexive, automatic, unconscious beliefs, expectations, and preconceptions about the capacities, behavior, and characteristics of various sorts of people. The stereotypes about women and men are based on inescapable biological and physiological characteristics. Sex characteristics are unique among a person's other characteristics, however, for at least four reasons:

1. Identifying a person as either female or male is not optional; everyone does it automatically with respect to everyone— including themselves. There is no escaping that categorization.
2. Once we identify a person as of one sex or the other, we tend to categorize them as a woman or a man, and it is extremely difficult to alter that characterization. That person is a she or he, period. (Sexual identity and transgender issues blur this point, but its basic thrust remains valid.)

3. We sort people by sex as soon as we hear or see them, and we usually know immediately whether the person is a woman or a man (if we don't, we are likely to be thrown off balance).
4. A person's sex cuts across all other categories. No matter what other social identities about another person we use to sort them—occupation, status, personality, race, age, or something else—we always sort that person by her or his sex.

Sorting people by sex is, in itself, largely benign, and some researchers suggest this probably has an evolutionary value. But this sorting does not stop with the biological division of the population. Once we have sorted people by sex, we then ascribe to them certain socially constructed roles, behaviors, norms, attitudes, activities, and characteristics we believe are appropriate for women and men. In this way, we turn a person's sex into their gender. And despite the enormous changes in women's activities and opportunities over the past 50 years, these socially constructed gender characteristics—the gender stereotypes highlighted throughout this book—have hardly changed at all.

The Bem Sex Role Inventory (BSRI), developed in 1974, and an extensive 2004 study of gender stereotypes both identified virtually identical sets of characteristics associated with women and with men. According to the BSRI, people expect women to be affectionate, sensitive, warm, and concerned with making others feel more at ease. Men are expected to be aggressive, competent, forceful, and independent leaders.[2] The 2004 study found that people still expected women to be affectionate, sensitive, warm, and friendly, while people still expected men to be aggressive, competent, independent, tough, and achievement oriented.[3] All of these stereotypes remain operative today. Men are still assumed to be characterized by traits of action, competence, and independence, which are often called "agentic" qualities.[4] Women, in contrast, are still assumed to be characterized by traits of sensitivity, warmth, and caregiving, which are often called "communal" qualities.[5]

Perniciousness of Gender Stereotypes

Why are we making such a big deal about gender stereotypes? If most people think that women are warm rather than assertive and that men are aggressive rather than sensitive, what is the harm? The harm in the workplace is that the traits associated with women are also associated with home and caregiving, while the traits associated with men are also associated with leadership and power. When a woman is assumed to be communal simply because she is a woman, she is also assumed to be suited for "feminine" jobs (such as a nurse, teacher, or administrative assistant) and not for "masculine" jobs (such as an investment banker, line manager, or CEO). This means that women are more likely to be tracked into personnel or assistant roles seen to require warmth and a sensitivity to the needs of others, while men are more likely to be tracked into leadership roles seen to require forceful, competent, and competitive behavior.[6]

Because of gender stereotypes, most people—women *and* men—tend to think "men" when they see words such as boss, CEO, and director, and to think "women" when they see words such as assistant, attendant, and secretary. People often have these associations because "it is easier for people to capture and understand information about unknown others that is consistent with the gender stereotype (she is a nurse) than counter-stereotypical information (she is a mechanic)."[7]

Gender stereotypes create a fundamental incongruity between general expectations of roles and behaviors of women and those of leaders. Thus, people think (perhaps unconsciously) that women should be caring, while leaders should be decisive; women should be modest, while leaders should be assertive; women should be helpful, while leaders should be independent. In other words, gender stereotypes contribute to the idea that women are less appropriate leaders than men—and when women behave in ways thought to be appropriate for leaders, they are often subject to backlash in the form of criticism—not praise or recognition.[8]

Ridding Ourselves of Gender Stereotypes

Of course, gender stereotypes do not reflect reality. As we have made clear, women and men are *not* inherently different in significant nonbiological ways. Why then can't we simply end gender bias by telling ourselves to stop thinking in terms of these misleading stereotypes? After all, the only reason anyone unconsciously discriminates against women in making career-affecting decisions such as assigning challenging projects to men rather than women is because the stereotypes he (or she) unconsciously holds led him (or her) to expect that men would perform the projects better than the women. Therefore, if we—all of us—would just stop allowing stereotypes to influence our career-affecting decisions, we would be free of implicit gender bias and workplace discrimination against women would end. Wouldn't that be nice! Unfortunately, eliminating gender bias is not so simple.

To understand why, it is useful to draw on an analogy with the Muller-Lyer optical illusion with which many readers may be familiar:

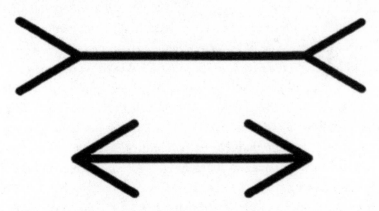

In looking at the two lines, we—all of us—see the top line as longer than the bottom one. It does not matter that we are told the two lines are exactly equal in length or that we measure the lines to confirm they are equal. Regardless of *consciously knowing* the lines are equal, *we don't see them* as equal. The same thing is true of gender stereotypes. It doesn't matter that we consciously know women and men are fundamentally equal with respect to ambition, talent, commitment, and competitiveness. Because of gender stereotypes we don't see them as equal in these respects.

That is not to say that women cannot do a great deal to avoid or overcome the discriminatory consequences of gender stereotypes—precisely the focus of this book—or that organizations cannot do a great deal to prevent gender stereotypes from having a discriminatory impact on the decisions affecting women's careers—precisely the focus of the last chapter of our book *It's Not You, It's the Workplace.*[9] But it is to say that we cannot break through bias by simply telling ourselves to stop thinking in terms of gender stereotypes.

Gender Stereotypes Are Scripts for Discriminatory Behavior

Stereotypes operate both as sorting mechanisms and behavioral guides. Thus stereotypes "help us" assign people to particular categories (friend, foe; desirable, undesirable; forceful, deferential; competent, incompetent). And thus once we have sorted them, stereotypes also "tell" us how we should relate to the people we have assigned to those categories.

To put this a different way, stereotypes are generalizations: all people who are X are like Y and, therefore, they should be treated like Z. Because not all people who are X are like Y, we are prone to misjudge particular individuals' actual characteristics, abilities, and potentials. And as a result, because we have mischaracterized certain people who are X as being Y, when we act like Z toward then, we are likely to behave toward them in inappropriate and discriminatory ways. For example, managers may well pick an all-male negotiating team because they (unconsciously) believe that "men are more competitive than women," even though if they had examined each individual's actual characteristics, it would have been quite apparent to the managers that several of the women were better negotiators than the men they actually selected.

People generally believe they don't make such discriminatory decisions, that they do not rely on stereotypes in judging other people, and that they are free of the biases these stereotypes foster. Psychological and sociological studies, however, make it clear that virtually all of us have implicit biases. As Mahzanin Banaji and her colleagues point out, "Most of us believe that we are ethical and unbiased. We imagine we're good decision-makers, able to objectively size up a job candidate or a business deal and reach a fair and rational conclusion that is in our, and our organization's, best interests. [More than two decades of research, however,] confirms that, in reality, most of us fall woefully short of our inflated self-perception. We're deluded by…the illusion of objectivity, the notion that we are free of the very biases we are so quick to recognize in others.…The prevalence of these biases suggests that even the most well-meaning person unwittingly allows unconscious thoughts and feelings to influence seemingly objective decisions."[10]

Al: On a recent flight from Chicago to Washington, DC, an airline employee sat next to me on her way home. The weather had been terrible, flights had been canceled over the past two days, and I was pleased my flight had boarded. The airline employee said she was flying home after having been called up at 1:00 a.m. for an early flight to Chicago. She was now flying back to her base in DC and then to her home in Roanoke, Virginia. I thought to myself, "Why would the airline call up a flight attendant as far away from DC as Roanoke?" I then turned to really look at my seatmate for the first time and saw she had stripes on the sleeves of her jacket and a hat in her lap. She was a pilot.

My unconscious stereotypes had been at work: women in uniforms on airplanes are almost always flight attendants; men in uniforms are pilots. Now, while it may have been statistically unlikely for her to be a pilot, I had clearly categorized her incorrectly, albeit relatively harmlessly in this case. But would it have been harmless if I had been in charge of hiring airline pilots and

(Continued)

a woman had applied for the job? Would that woman have had a
harder time getting my endorsement than a man would have had?
I hope not, but I think about that female pilot every time I find
myself about to make a categorization of a person based on gender,
race, age, or another social identity.

How Gender Stereotypes Lead to Discrimination
against Women

Women pursuing careers in gendered workplaces are subject to particularly discriminatory stereotypes. Because of traditional gender stereotypes, both women and men are twice as likely to hire a male candidate
than an equally qualified woman.[11] Women are 25 to 46 percent more
likely to be hired if their gender is not disclosed.[12] In addition, almost
half of women (42 percent) report having faced discrimination on the job
because of their gender; and women with postgraduate degrees report
gender discrimination at an even higher rate of 57 percent.[13]

The biases fostered by gender stereotypes typically function among
men in tandem with their sense of male privilege. Such a sense of privilege involves the (usually unconscious) assumption that they are superior
to women at valued workplace roles, tasks, and challenges; are entitled to
preference over women with respect to career opportunities, resources,
and sponsorships; and are immune from criticism for anger, aggressiveness, and self-promotion—conduct that is severely criticized when displayed by women. Because of this implicit sense of privilege, 62 percent
of men believe women are well represented in leadership when only one
in three managers is a woman, and 44 percent of men think women are
well represented in senior leadership when only 10 percent of an organization's senior leaders are women.[14]

We can get a clearer picture of the biased behavior resulting from
gender stereotypes by separating this behavior into negative or hostile
behavior and benevolent or kindly behavior.

Negative or Hostile Gender Bias

Traditional gender stereotypes lead people (women as well as men) to have a negative view of women in comparison to men when considering their fitness for high-pressure, competitive leadership tasks. A telling and troubling example is revealed in a 2012 Yale University study of the attitudes of science professors toward women's potential as future scientists.[15] The researchers surveyed a broad, nationwide sample of biology, chemistry, and physics professors, asking them to evaluate an undergraduate science student who had applied for a position as a laboratory manager. All of the professors received exactly the same materials about the applicant, except that 50 percent of the professors received an application purportedly from a woman and 50 percent purportedly from a man. The professors were asked to rate the student's competence and "hireability," suggest an appropriate starting salary, and indicate the amount of mentoring they would be willing to offer the student. Both the female and male professors consistently judged the female student as less competent and less suitable to be hired than an identically credentialed male student. When the professors offered a job to the female student, they offered her a lower salary and less career mentoring than they offered male students.[16] The pervasive gender bias revealed by this study is not limited to academic science.

Al: Consider the story of Kim O'Grady. O'Grady was an accomplished consultant with considerable experience and a proven track record of successful engagements. He was so confident of the strength of his résumé that when he grew dissatisfied with the firm he was working for, he quit without first lining up another job. When he started his job search, he was baffled that he was not getting any interviews—that is, until he added *Mr.* before his name. After making this simple change, he quickly landed a new job. He wrote about his experience in a Tumblr blog post, "How I Discovered Gender Discrimination," that went viral.[17]

Because of the gender stereotypes that career gatekeepers hold, they tend to have low expectations about women's performance capabilities and potential.[18] Too frequently, the mind-set of these gatekeepers is that *this* job requires *these* characteristics, and women just don't have *these* characteristics. In such cases, it doesn't matter what a woman's actual characteristics are. If the job doesn't fit the communal stereotype, then a woman might not even have the chance to demonstrate her ability to do it.

In 2005 the nonprofit organization Catalyst, whose goal is to create more inclusive workplaces, surveyed 296 senior corporate executives (168 women and 128 men).[19] Catalyst asked these executives to rate the effectiveness of women and men on 10 different leadership behaviors. Both the female and male executives rated women more effective at traditionally feminine tasks, such as caregiving, and rated men more effective at traditionally masculine tasks, such as leadership.[20]

Andie: I am often told that this or that organization would gladly have more women in leadership and management positions, but it can't find any women who are qualified for these jobs. I seriously doubt this ever to be true. More likely, the leaders of these organizations don't think that women are qualified, and therefore they have not seriously evaluated the abilities of particular women in their organizations. I know qualified women in a variety of organizations all across the country who are consistently overlooked for advancement to positions for which they are clearly qualified. What is most heartbreaking for me is to watch these women grow cynical and resigned to their current positions after management has failed to recognize their ambition, talent, and capability.

One of the most ironic situations I have personally encountered involved a female general counsel who had frequently expressed a concern that too few women in her medical services company were being promoted to important, executive-level positions. A friend of

(Continued)

mine recommended that she talk with me. I visited the company, spent several hours with her, and presented a proposal for a workshop on gender bias for her senior management team—a workshop that had proven highly successful at several other companies. After our meeting, I never heard anything further from her. I asked my friend what had happened, and he told me she decided she needed a man to head the training program because a man would be more effective than a woman in presenting the case for greater participation by women in company leadership.

When I first heard this, I didn't know whether to laugh or cry. I did realize, however, that if I had ever thought that the discriminatory operation of gender stereotypes was limited to men, I had been seriously wrong.

Another example of gender stereotyping is reflected in the controversy over Viking-era remains discovered in Birka, Sweden, in the late 1800s. The remains, named Bj 581, had been buried as an elite, wealthy warrior and strategist.[21] Because of Bj 581's accomplished warrior status, scientists assumed the remains were male. When 2017 DNA analysis confirmed that the remains were female, some scientists immediately argued that Bj 581 couldn't possibly have been a warrior. Others suggested there must have been an undiscovered set of male remains in that grave to have warranted such a significant burial.[22] Despite scientific evidence supporting the existence of the female warrior, some critics still argue that these remains were of a servant or a housewife—buried with no domestic items—in the grave of a man whose remains are absent.[23]

The controversy over Bj 581 demonstrated how even scientists—people we *want* to believe are highly rational empiricists—struggled to accept that a woman might have been a powerful leader or strategic warrior. With this example, we can see why gender stereotypes create such an issue: in the case of the Bj 581 warrior at Birka, gender stereotypes risk rewriting history to reinforce current stereotypes. In the case of the modern dynamic woman—these stereotypes may cause someone to dismiss your value and skill set, thus limiting your career opportunities.

The Goldilocks Dilemma

Negative gender bias is a coin with two sides. When a woman conforms to the most basic communal stereotypes—being warm, caring, and sensitive to others' feelings—she is most often viewed as pleasant and likable but not particularly competent or a leader. On the other hand, if she acts contrary to these stereotypes by displaying agentic characteristics—forcefully advocating a point of view, doggedly pursuing a competitive objective, or frequently exhibiting a fierce commitment to performance excellence—she is likely to face a backlash and be viewed as competent but socially insensitive, "bitter, quarrelsome, selfish, deceitful, devious, and unlikable."[24]

Andie: A personal experience might help illustrate the difficult and insidious problem that is created by the tension between a woman's need to be agentic to move ahead and her need to be communal to be liked. When I was about 12, I already knew I wanted to be a lawyer. My parents had one friend who was a lawyer, so they arranged for me to have lunch with him. He spent our entire meal telling me why I didn't want to be a lawyer. He told me that there was a difference between "lawyers" and "lady lawyers." Lawyers can be happy and successful, but lady lawyers can never be both. If I became a lawyer, no one would ever love me. I would never get married. I would never have a family. I would not have any friends. I would be lonely.

What was going on? Why would this grown man say such things to a young girl? Looking back, I think he was clumsily trying to alert me to the dilemma the workplace still poses for women. My parents' friend saw that the female lawyers he knew needed to choose between success and likability. I think he recognized that

(Continued)

a woman who wants real career success and is willing to compete hard to achieve it runs the risk of social isolation. We discuss impression management later in this book, but whatever negative thoughts I had then of my lunch companion, I see now that he was on to something and not just being unkind.

The double bind—that women need to be communal to be liked but agentic to advance in their career[25]—is what we call the Goldilocks Dilemma. Whether they behave communally or agentically, women can suffer negative consequences. Indeed, women often feel they are damned if they do and damned if they don't. As a result, many women try to play it safe by appearing a little less agentic so they can be seen as a little more likable.[26]

Defensive behavior of this sort can take several forms.[27] One of the most common is illustrated by a 2011 study of students at the Harvard Business School (HBS). The women and men in the study started at HBS with essentially equal academic and career achievements. Yet despite this rough comparability, the study found that, compared to the men, the women prepared more but participated less in class; they received significantly fewer academic honors; and after graduation, they judged their HBS experiences as far less positive.[28]

In seeking an explanation of why women and men responded to their HBS experience in such different ways, Harvard found that two principal factors adversely affected women during their time at the business school. First, there was an obvious clannishness on the part of male professors and male students that isolated the women. HBS took immediate steps to correct this problem. But Harvard also uncovered a far subtler and more intractable problem: the women were "self-editing in the classroom to manage their out-of-classroom image[s]."[29] The women felt less comfortable participating in class discussions because of the penalties they believed they would face if they violated traditional communal stereotypes. They were consciously trying not to appear (too) forceful or aggressive in the classroom so they would not be viewed as unlikable outside of class. Harvard found there were a large number of extraordinarily talented women holding themselves back academically because they were worried they would not be viewed positively or accepted socially if they were seen as competing "too hard." These women were trying to have it both ways: to succeed (a little less), but to be liked (a little more).

The behavior of the HBS women is entirely understandable if you think about how exactly the same agentic behaviors are likely to be viewed when exhibited by a woman and by a man:

- She's pushy; he's determined.
- She's bossy; he's a leader.
- She's a self-promoter, show off, and a braggart; he knows his own worth.
- She's abrasive; he's incisive.
- She's a harpy; he's tenacious.
- She's selfish; he's too busy to pitch in.
- She's aggressive; he's a go-getter.
- She's rude; he's direct and to the point.

Al: My friend Dan told me about a recent board meeting at his condominium association. Tiffany, who had just been elected to the board, raised some of the same concerns Dan had expressed at an earlier board meeting, which she had not attended. The board president, a white man in his late 50s, interrupted Tiffany and in a loud voice asked, "Why are you being so aggressive?" Tiffany tried to continue, but the president interrupted her again, asking, "Is it your intention to come to every meeting and be so critical?"

At that point, Dan stood up and pointed out that Tiffany was only saying what he had said several meetings earlier and that her tone of voice was far less "aggressive" than the president's tone. Dan stated that Tiffany was being businesslike and that it was refreshing

(Continued)

to have a board member prepared to raise important issues in such a straightforward way. The board president asked Tiffany to continue and never again attempted to criticize her for being "aggressive."

When I think about Dan's story, I consider whether the board president would have backed down if Dan hadn't spoken up—or if another woman had defended Tiffany instead. A woman can always use male allies, but sometimes they can be especially valuable in dealing with particularly difficult senior men.

Motherhood Bias

Let's shift gears slightly and look at the Goldilocks Dilemma in another context: motherhood. Women with children face particularly severe career penalties. On the "too soft" side of the dilemma, gender stereotypes suggest—and gender bias assumes—that these women need to be available to their children at all times, perpetuating the misconception that they will be less available for career demands than women without children or than men (with or without children). On the "too hard" side, however, if women with children demonstrate that they *are* fully committed to their careers, gender stereotypes suggest—and gender bias assumes—they are bad mothers and not appropriately committed to their children. Indeed, women with children and a strong commitment to their careers are frequently seen as less warm, less likable, and more hostile than similarly committed women without children.

Al: Andie and I have both worked full time. When our daughter was growing up, we juggled our schedules so we could be home to have dinner as a family every night that we were not traveling. In order to be able to spend evenings and weekends with Cynthia, we frequently worked at home after she had gone to bed. And one of us was always present at her school and sporting events.

(Continued)

When Cynthia was about eight years old a friend's mother asked her, "What does your dad do for a living?" She replied, "He's a lawyer." The woman said, "That's great." Cynthia then expected to be asked about her mom's occupation. When that didn't happen, she proudly volunteered, "My mom's a lawyer too." But she did not get the same positive response she had received about her father. Instead, her friend's mother asked her in a very sympathetic tone, "How does it feel to be raised by a nanny?"

Because of stereotypes about mothers, women with careers and children often face an organizational backlash: they are less likely to be hired and more likely to be offered lower salaries than their childless female coworkers, despite being acknowledged to be equally competent.[30] Indeed, one well-known 2005 study found that mothers were 79 percent less likely to be hired, 100 percent less likely to be promoted, offered an average of $11,000 less in salary, and held to higher performance and punctuality standards than women without children.[31]

Andie: When I joined my current law firm, our daughter was two years old. Shortly after I got there, I mentioned something in passing about her to a male partner I was working with. After that, he started leaving voicemail messages asking me in a condescending tone whether I could talk about our project at 5:00 p.m. if I'd "still be around." I never made myself available at 5:00 p.m., but I always offered to talk to him that same night any time after 6:00 p.m., or to meet with him the next day any time after 6:00 a.m.. He never took me up on any of my suggested meeting times. He really wasn't interested in meeting, only in showing his commitment and what he assumed was my lack of it. When it became apparent to him that I was committed to both my child and my career, he stopped asking to talk at 5:00 P.M. Many years later, I mentioned this experience to

(Continued)

> him in the context of a gender diversity discussion. He told me that this never would have happened if he had known at the time how hard I worked. Because I was a mother, he had assumed I was not committed to my career. In his eyes, he was just doing his job of "identifying uncommitted members of the project team."

Having a career and raising children at the same time requires resources, assistance, and careful planning under the best of circumstances. We discuss dealing with these challenges in chapter 11, "Your Career and the Rest of Your Life." The point we want to make here is that working mothers—and particularly mothers who are stereotypically seen as working by "choice" because they have successful working partners—not only must perform a high-wire juggling act to raise their children *and* advance in their careers, but they also must find ways to cope with the discriminatory biases that result from the stereotypes about mothers with careers. A recent small-scale study found that because of these stereotypes, mothers experienced normative discrimination at work; 57 percent of non-self-employed mothers suffered wage inequality; 59.1 percent of mothers have felt a desire to opt out of the workforce; and 67 percent had changed their jobs due to their status as mothers.[32] Academic research confirms the results of this survey. Participants in another study were shown a video of a woman interacting with others in a work scenario. The participants rated a woman lower with respect to performance and work commitment when she appeared to be pregnant as compared to an otherwise identical video in which the same woman did not appear to be pregnant.[33]

Another study found in a sample of female and male workers that only mothers were viewed as less capable than all other workers.[34] A third study found that mothers were held to stricter standards than fathers and disadvantaged in hiring and promotion.[35] As a classic paper on the motherhood penalty concludes, "Female participants in our study... held highly successful mothers to stricter standards and penalized them on recommendations for promotion, hire, and salary. Importantly, the penalties for highly successful mothers were not explained by the competence and commitment ratings. Instead, a substantial proportion of the penalty was mediated by the perception that successful mothers were interpersonally deficient."[36]

Aging Out of Negative Gender Bias

It is tempting to think that gender stereotypes will lose much of their discriminatory force when the current crop of business, professional, government, and scientific leaders retire and a younger, more open-minded group replaces them. Millennials, those Americans now roughly between 20 and 40 years old, are often assumed to be ushering in a new era of enlightened interpersonal relations. For example, in 2013 *Time* predicted Millennials would "save us all" because they are "more accepting of differences . . . in everyone."[37] That same year, the *Atlantic* stated that Millennials hold the "historically unprecedented belief that there are no inherently male or female roles in society."[38] And in 2015 the *Huffington Post* wrote that Millennial men are "likely to see women as equals."[39]

If these characterizations are even close to accurate, then we should expect the pervasive, damaging negative biases against women leaders to diminish substantially, if not end entirely, once Millennials assume positions of economic, academic, and political power.

Before we start celebrating a coming age of gender parity, however, we need to ask whether there is any truth to these rosy predictions. Do Millennials really believe there are no inherently female or male roles in society? Do Millennial men really "see women as equals"? Unfortunately, the best information we have indicates the answer to both questions is no. In a 2014 survey of more than 2,000 US adults, Harris Poll found that young men were less open to accepting women leaders than were older men.[40] Only 41 percent of Millennial men were comfortable with women engineers, compared to 65 percent of men 65 or older. Likewise, only 43 percent of Millennial men were comfortable with women being US senators, compared to 64 percent of Americans overall. (The numbers were 39 percent versus 61 percent for women being CEOs of Fortune 500 companies, and 35 percent versus 57 percent for president of the United States.)

Given these findings, it would be a serious mistake to assume that with the Millennial generation we will "age" into gender-neutral workplaces.

Benevolent Gender Bias

Many women work for (typically but not always) male supervisors who treat them in ways that appear to be kind and considerate. Such benevolent behavior often takes the form of frequent expressions of concern for a woman's welfare, solicitousness as to her domestic responsibilities, and "extra" assistance with her job responsibilities. Too often, however, this behavior results from a form of traditional sexism, an assumption that women need to be protected, directed, and assisted by men.[41] We discuss a woman's temptation to buy into benevolent bias in chapter 2, "The Apple in the Room."

Al: Kelly, a senior manager at a large corporation based in New York City, told me that when she was first out of college she had applied to be a flight attendant working out of New York City. The male interviewer said, "I would worry about a nice girl like you living alone in a dangerous city like New York." She told him she was a native New Yorker, walked out of the interview, and enrolled in business school.

Supervisors with benevolent sexist attitudes often praise women highly for their performance but assign them to devalued projects. If supervisors (unconsciously) think that women are emotional, weak, and sensitive, they are likely to give them easy assignments, "protecting" them from the difficulties and struggles inherent in challenging, competitive work. This is *not* the kind of help women need.

A 2012 study of a New York law firm's performance evaluations of its associates provides a classic illustration of benevolent sexism. The researchers found that the women received more positive comments

(Excellent! Stellar! Terrific!) than the men did, but only 6 percent of the women, compared with 15 percent of the men, were mentioned as potential partner material.[42]

Al: Dara, a senior IT manager at a major manufacturing company, was about to roll out a new computer system for several departments and outside vendors. As the launch date approached, she ran a series of tests and concluded that the system was not ready to go live. She delayed the start-up date and explained the reasons to her boss. She was shocked to discover he believed the delay was really because she lacked the confidence to go forward on schedule. He told her he understood that she needed more time to "get comfortable" with the rollout and that he would support the delay until she "felt ready." Although her boss might have pushed a man to go forward with the launch anyway (if he truly believed the problem was simply a lack of confidence), he dealt with her "sympathetically," asking frequently if she needed more help. Dara later learned that after she had delayed the launch, he made a series of personnel changes that weakened her status and authority.

The dangers a woman faces in a benevolent biased environment can best be understood by looking at a normal career advancement path. Moving up depends upon your professional development: acquiring the knowledge, skills, and organizational savvy to be recognized as a person of competence, confidence, and potential. The only way you can acquire these traits is to be exposed to challenging work experiences that allow—and force—you to learn, develop, and prove yourself.

A challenging work experience is difficult, stimulating, and unfamiliar. It stretches your abilities and tests your determination. Undertaking such an experience helps you gain substantive knowledge and deeper insights into the complexities of your job. Experiences of this sort also help you gain self-confidence, which in turn encourages you to seek out and volunteer for even more challenging projects in the future. Not surprisingly, the frequency, quantity, variety, and difficulty of your work experiences predict the pace and extent of your career advancement.[43] When you are engaged in a challenging project, you are in the spotlight and your supervisors are watching closely. Therefore, these sorts of projects provide you the chance to demonstrate that you are ready to move up to the next rung of the career ladder.[44]

If instead of giving you challenging projects (or forcing you to take them on) your supervisors help you with your work or protect you from this sort of experience, you will never develop the skills, resilience, and confidence you need to realize your career aspirations. You will lack the experience needed when the time comes for the next round of promotions. You will not be seriously considered if you are excluded from high-profile projects and projects that involve extensive travel or long hours, if you are given special breaks and a bit of extra help because you are a mother, if you are criticized less than comparably situated men for the same sort of job performance, or if you are encouraged to leave when others stay late or to not take on extra work.

Andie: More than 15 years ago at my current law firm, we found that at promotion time many women did not have the same depth and breadth of experience as did the men with the same years of legal experience. As a result, the men were getting promoted and the women were not. This was an unacceptable result, so we changed the process by which assignments were made. Each practice group was required to identify skills that lawyers were expected to have developed by the end of each year of practice. The objective was to ensure that all lawyers received the same types of assignments and development opportunities. Senior lawyers, most of whom were men, could no longer give the plum assignments to their favored male associates while giving the grunt projects and "easy stuff" to women.

(Continued)

It worked! In recent years, women at our firm have been promoted to partner at rates substantially higher than the legal profession average. This is a substantial change from where we were
before we started this program. But as I keep reminding myself,
the change did not come about voluntarily; it required someone to
build the business case for change and a commitment on the part
of senior management to actually make the change and enforce it.

All of this should be obvious enough: to advance in your career you
need to develop broad and deep career-relevant skills, and to do this
you need to push yourself and be pushed by your supervisors. You need
more—not fewer—challenges at work. But if you are put on a pedestal,
so to speak, because you are thought to have a mild and sensitive nature,
then you will not be exposed to the rough-and-tumble competitive struggles that are characteristic of high-pressure executive and professional
lives. Therefore, you need to be wary of supervisors and career gatekeepers who exhibit respectful, caring, concerned, and protective attitudes,
or who express a solicitous concern for your personal welfare. You need
to be encouraged, not protected; you need to be thrown into the game,
not kept safely on the sidelines. Kindness shown toward you that is not
also shown toward comparably situated men is sexism, plain and simple,
and its consequences are anything but benevolent.

KEY TAKEAWAYS

- *Figure out your own biases.* Before you can effectively cope with
  other people's gender stereotypes, you need to know your own.
  Take the Implicit Association Test (IAT) at Harvard University's
  Project Implicit webpage: https://implicit.harvard.edu/implicit/.
- *Identify your feminine and masculine traits.* Review the Bem
  Stereotypes. You should consider the relative strengths of your
  communal and agentic traits—and which ones you will need to

strengthen—because both sets of traits are important to advance in your career.

- *Be on the lookout for benevolent sexism.* Solicitous and patronizing behavior can be just as hurtful to your career as overt negative bias. Demand challenging assignments; refuse special help or privileges; and if your male colleagues are traveling or working late, make sure you are traveling and working late too. Review our discussion in <u>chapter 2</u>.

- *Likability is important but overrated,* and as we stress throughout this book, you need to develop attuned gender communication skills that encourage it. But likability can be highly overrated. There are great advantages if the people you work with like you, but if they don't, that's not the end of the world, much less your career.

Chapter 2

The Apple in the Room

A s we've explained in <u>CHAPTER 1</u>, the stereotypes that career gate-keepers have about women, men, leaders, family, and work often cause them to discriminate against women as they pursue their careers. Yet it is also important to recognize that women frequently hold stereotypes about themselves *because they are women*. These stereotypes often operate to color their attitudes about their talents, capacities, resources, and appropriate objectives and activities. Because of these stereotypes, women often *choose* "gender appropriate" college majors, jobs, and assignments. They *choose* to take on a greater share of family and domestic responsibilities than their male partners, and *choose* to accept career-limiting gender roles in their workplaces. The stereotypes women hold about themselves and other women also affect the ways in which they interact with other women at work.

We call this chapter "The Apple in the Room," referring to women's (conscious or unconscious) temptation to accept traditional gender stereotypes and apply them to themselves. Women who have eaten the apple of stereotype temptation might think:

- "I am a woman so I am not good at math, not suited for high-pressure consulting work, and not able to negotiate successfully against men."

- "I am a woman, so I will be happier working part-time and putting my family responsibilities ahead of my career."
- "I am a woman, so I need to be caring, sympathetic, and modest, not forceful, assertive, and self-promoting."

These attitudes are tempting because adhering to them promises interpersonal interactions with less conflict, less frustration, and less disappointment than openly violating them. We have known far too many women who have been their own worst enemies because they believe that because they are women they are not able to do X or are not supposed to do Y, when a comparably situated man would not believe such a thing.

Stereotype Threat

When you choose to avoid a task because you believe (consciously or unconsciously) that being a woman prevents you from performing that task, you are reacting to what is often referred to as "stereotype threat." When you become anxious, uncomfortable, or uncertain about your ability to perform up to your capabilities in situations in which your gender is highly salient, that is stereotype threat. And when you fear you will perform poorly at tasks that are closely associated with masculine stereotypes, that is also stereotype threat. Stereotype threat is a particularly treacherous minefield because success in business and the professions—being perceived as a leader, effective negotiator, strong advocate, and keen evaluator—involves performing tasks associated with positive masculine stereotypes and, hence, are assumed to be tasks at which women are not particularly good.

Women, of course, are not the only group to experience stereotype threat. It has also been documented among African Americans,[1] Latinos, and people from low socioeconomic backgrounds.[2] Even high-status white men perform worse on social sensitivity tests—tests of their ability to decode others' nonverbal cues—when they are told women typically score better on these tests than men.[3]

Examples of situations in which stereotype threat often prevent women from playing at the top of their game include:

1. When a woman feels *her* performance will reflect on other women, she may become excessively concerned about failure. She may become overly anxious, which diverts her attention from the task at hand.[4]
2. In problem-solving situations in which women are stereotypically expected to perform poorly, a woman can become excessively concerned about trying to disprove the stereotype. This can drain resources from her working memory, which impairs her ability to perform at her best.[5]
3. If a woman is aware of a negative stereotype regarding women's ability to perform a specific task, she may lose confidence in her ability to perform that task. Successful performance requires skill *and* confidence. If her self-confidence suffers, her performance suffers.[6]

A classic experiment to demonstrate the effect of stereotype threat involves giving women a math test after reminding them of the traditional stereotype that women are not as good at math as men.[7] Under these conditions, women consistently perform below their potential. (Women who are not primed to think about gender gaps in math perform just as well as men do.) Other experiments showing stereotype threat have included activities as different as playing chess[8] and driving a car. A good example of this phenomenon is negotiation.[9] In one study, female and male MBA students were paired and asked to negotiate the supposed purchase of a biotechnology plant.[10] Half of the negotiating pairs were given the information that women are often not effective negotiators because they are not assertive, rational, decisive, forceful, and unemotional. The other half were given neutral information. Women in the stereotype threat group confirmed the stereotypes by performing worse than the men, while women negotiating without being primed for stereotype threat performed as well as the men.

Stereotype threat is debilitating because it reduces the working memory available to perform a specific task—and the availability of working memory is one of the strongest correlates with general intelligence.[11] In other words, when women experience stereotype threat, they expend mental resources in an effort to disprove the stereotype, thereby reducing their mental resources for performing the task at hand. Stereotype threat thus creates a vicious cycle of stress, anxiety, and reduced performance that maintains and exacerbates the underrepresentation of women in senior leadership positions.

In situations involving stereotype threat, therefore, the key to women performing well is their being able to disregard the threatening stereotype. You need to see opportunity, not threat; find sharper focus, not distraction; and maintain your self-confidence, not succumb to self-doubt. So how can you do this?

The answer is not to *try* to dismiss the stereotypes. It is self-defeating to seek to avoid the effects of stereotype threat by trying not to be anxious, not to have feelings of self-doubt, and not to pay attention to negative gender stereotypes. Such efforts further deplete the cognitive resources you otherwise have available for successfully performing workplace tasks.[12] *Trying* to not be affected by stereotype threat can only make the situation worse.

This is not to say that trying to avoid performance impairment due to stereotype threat is pointless. Rather, you need to do it in a smarter way. One technique is suggested by a 2008 research study in which women were asked to complete a math problem. Before they began the task, half the participants were told that their performance would not be impaired—and could even be improved—by any anxiety they might experience due to the common stereotype that women are less proficient in mathematics than men. The other half were told nothing. The women who heard the "no impairment" statement performed up to their full potential; the other women did not.[13]

The takeaway from this study is simple: in situations that pose a potential stereotype threat for you, try telling yourself that the anxiety you may experience has nothing to do with your actual ability to perform that task.

In other words, you need to give yourself a "no impairment" message. When you do this and believe what you are telling yourself, you transform your anxiety from an indication of self-doubt to something more akin to stage fright, a source of adrenaline, energy, and an outlet for that energy.

Another technique to use in situations that pose a stereotype threat is to view yourself through a nongender lens. Don't think, "I am the only woman in this meeting," or, "The men will try to take advantage of me because I am a woman." Instead, try to think something like, "I am one of only two MBAs in this meeting," or, "I am the only one involved in this transaction who has gone through a major acquisition before." In other words, in situations where gender is highly salient and stereotype threat is likely, make a concerted effort to think about your strengths, experiences, and potential instead of your gender.

A particularly effective technique for preventing stereotypes from impairing your performance is to stop thinking that your performance of a traditionally male task will reflect your true, fixed, and permanent abilities. Rather, think of your performance as an opportunity to improve your abilities through effort and challenge. Situations of stereotype threat should be seen as opportunities to grow, expand your experience, and gain confidence. Indeed, stereotype threat situations often involve senior male evaluators and career gatekeepers, precisely the audience you *need* to witness your competence, confidence, and potential.

A fourth technique for dealing with stereotype threat is to use a coping sense of humor. By bringing humor to bear on difficult and stressful situations caused by stereotype threat, you can diminish your negative emotional reactions and increase your performance capabilities. Humor also allows you to change your perspective on the excessive external or internal demands that stereotype threat might otherwise create. Using humor to cope with stereotype threat is not about laughing out loud, but about cultivating an attitude that gender stereotypes aren't just infuriating but frequently ridiculous. While we believe that the human brain is flexible enough to simultaneously recognize that gender stereotypes are seriously harmful, there is something somewhat laughable about people really believing that women are poor negotiators, lack ambition, and cannot be effective leaders. When you can see the absurdity of gender stereotypes, you can reimagine stereotype threat as a challenge, not a danger. You can use humor to put emotional distance between you and the threat. You can increase your self-confidence as you expose yourself to potentially unpleasant personal situations, especially those likely to involve an evaluation of your performance. Humor of this sort allows you to put difficult problems, people, and situations in a much less threatening perspective. A coping sense of humor helps you avoid the anxiety, confusion, uncertainty, and inhibition that can undermine your performance.[14] We discuss the value of a coping sense of humor in chapter 5, "Your Attitudes Matter."

"Gender Appropriate" Behavior

The belief that certain activities and careers are "appropriate" for women while certain other careers are not is the result of stereotype threat, pure and simple. If you believe women are good at psychology but not computer science, you are more likely to major in psychology than computer science. If you believe women are good at personal relationships but not finance, you are more likely to seek a job in human resources than accounting or investment banking. And if you believe women are not good at negotiating but are good at administrative tasks, you are not likely to volunteer for a major merger or acquisition and more likely to offer to develop a new filing system.

The entire subject of gender-appropriate activities is a highly sensitive one. For instance, pointing out the gender segregation in college majors and occupations (such as 85 percent of health service majors are female but only 19 percent of engineering majors are; 80 percent of social workers are female but only 15 percent of computer programmers are) can quickly be interpreted as a form of "blaming the victim." Similarly, pointing out gender segregation in careers can be taken as an attempt to hold women responsible for having lower status and lower-paying jobs than men.

So before we begin to discuss this subject, we want to make clear that we don't think some college majors are better for women than others, that some occupations are better than others, or that some career roles are better than others. There are multiple factors affecting women's decisions with respect to all of these areas, and we have no interest in making judgments about anyone's actual choices. We are, however, interested in increasing your awareness of the gender segregation that pervades America's college majors, occupations, and career responsibilities. We believe that if you are sensitive to this segregation, you will be less likely to place limitations and restraints on your own work-related attitudes, choices, and behavior simply because you are a woman. As we have said, we don't want you to be more like a man, but we do want you to believe and behave as though you can do anything in your career that a man can do—and do it just as well, if not better.

To achieve gender parity across all US occupations, 40 percent of college-educated women and men would need to change their careers. This occupational gender segregation is most often attributed to "demand-side" influences: employers' decisions about who they will hire and who they will make feel welcome. There is some evidence, however, that "supply-side" factors also play a role. This means that women's and men's personal decisions about where (and at what) they want to work contribute to this segregation.

Researchers from McGill University and the Wharton School of the University of Pennsylvania looked at the jobs comparably qualified women and men applied for after attending an elite, one-year international MBA program.[15] Their study focused on three factors influencing a person's choice of a job: how the applicant values the specific rewards offered by the job, whether the applicant identifies with the job, and whether the applicant expects that applying for that job will result in a job offer. The researchers examined how each of these factors affected women's and men's applications to work in the fields of finance, consulting, and general management.

The researchers found no differences in the monetary and other values women and men assigned to these jobs. Nevertheless, the women were far less likely than the men to apply for jobs in finance and consulting and were far more likely to apply for general management positions.

The researchers found that this gender disparity was due almost entirely to women not "identifying" with finance jobs because of the strong masculine stereotypes associated with them; similarly, the women did not "identify" with consulting jobs because of anticipated difficulties with "work-life balance." The researchers concluded that the low number of women in the fields of finance and consulting is largely the result of women's "gender role socialization": the stereotypes they hold about themselves and particular careers. The researchers also concluded, however, that when a woman can overcome exceptionally high barriers to female participation early in her career, this may actually reduce her gendered behavior in subsequent stages of her career.[16]

Gendered behavior is shaped or caused by gender stereotypes. Take one well-documented phenomenon: men typically apply for jobs when they meet 60 percent of the job criteria, but women typically don't apply until they feel they meet at least 100 percent of the criteria.[17] This is gendered behavior, pure and simple. It is due in all likelihood to the two elements of stereotype threat: (1) women's belief that they are just not as good at particular tasks as men, and (2) their consequent fear that if they are not *fully* qualified for a potential job, they are likely to fail. This same fear too frequently causes some women to choose assignments and positions that involve less risk, lower visibility, fewer challenges, less responsibility, and less external pressure than the ones their male colleagues typically choose.[18]

If you work in a gendered workplace, there are lots of people and situations that will hold you back simply because you are a woman. You are likely to be as talented, prepared, and capable as the men, so be your own best fan: avoid negativity and self-doubt, and trust that you are competent and capable. We discuss advocating for yourself in chapter 10.

Benevolent Sexism

We discussed the dangers of benevolent sexism in the last chapter, but we did not say anything there about a woman's temptation to accept traditional gender stereotypes when they are wrapped in apparent benevolence. Praise is a good example of this sort of packaging. When you receive praise and compliments, it is tempting not to look behind them to assess whether they are truly warranted. More importantly, when you receive enthusiastic praise, you may not bother to think about whether your compensation and promotion progression are consistent with what you are being told. Too many women find themselves in situations in which they receive a lot of praise but only slight career advancement. If you find yourself in such a situation, it might be a sign that your supervisors think you are a nice person but not suitable for a leadership role. If this pattern continues for any significant period of time, your skills will dull, your self-doubt will increase, and your ambition will diminish.[19]

Being "taken care of" is another example of how benevolent sexism can create a temptation for a woman to incorporate traditional gender stereotypes into her thinking about herself. In a gendered workplace, a woman can easily feel exposed and vulnerable. When she receives care, attention, and protection from a "kind" typically (but not always) male superior, she can be tempted to welcome it, put herself under his "wing," and be guided by his preferences. By praising her positive traits—her warmth, niceness, and communal attitudes—and offering her support and special dispensations, a supervisor can hide the realities of workplace gender inequality. In other words, in a gendered workplace, being taken care of by a powerful (typically) male supervisor can provide a woman with a sense of security and safety.

Benevolent sexist supervisors can also package traditional gender stereotypes in a tempting way by making it clear that embracing these stereotypes will enhance your subjective life satisfaction. Benevolent sexism is about the maintenance of traditional gender roles: kind, vulnerable women and strong, protective men. This type of sexism promotes these traditional gender roles as if they are appropriate, fair, and desirable. When a woman sees her workplace as functioning fairly with balanced, complementary, but unequal gender roles, she is far more likely to find her job comfortable and less stressful than she would if she stepped out of traditional gender roles and exhibited her strong agentic qualities.

The temptation to accept and enjoy benevolent sexism is very real. But the apple that is being offered is truly a poisoned fruit. If you buy your sense of psychological satisfaction at the cost of believing a discriminatory work environment is appropriate, you will have also bought yourself decreased self-esteem, increased depression, and less confidence and proactivity.[20] Beware of benevolent supervisors who want to help you manage work and family; they come bearing gifts that may not lead to an ultimately fulfilling career.

Women Working with Women

Another gender stereotype that tempts many women is the view that women don't work well with one another. At our workshops we are frequently asked some variation of this: "Why are the women I work for so mean [critical, hostile, nasty, unhelpful] to me?" This is puzzling because it flies in the face of the empirical evidence. For example, a 2012 Catalyst study of the career experiences of female and male MBA graduates found that these graduates received more support, mentoring, and sponsorship from senior women than they did from senior men. In addition, women were far more likely than senior men to mentor the female graduates. Indeed, Catalyst concluded that senior women are more likely to support other women than to undermine them or block their career advancement.[21]

But if the Catalyst study correctly describes the workplace reality—and we believe it does—then why are many women so concerned about the problem of women working with other women? Much of this concern arises, we believe, because of the gender stereotypes women have about other women: women should be warm, caring, supportive, and sensitive to *me*. As a result of these stereotypes, when a woman works for an agentic senior woman who is decisive, critical, forceful, opinionated, and apparently uninterested in the junior woman's feelings, the junior woman is likely to view her as unlikable, difficult, or unbending—perhaps even a bitch.

Andie: At workshops on gender stereotypes, I often mention that senior female leaders can be criticized by junior women for exhibiting the same sort of agentic behavior that senior men exhibit. I typically point out that junior women often expect senior women to be kind, solicitous, and helpful—in effect, to act very much as they expect from their mothers or sisters. In one workshop, Tara (a junior bank officer five years out of graduate school) spoke up to say she has always found working for the men at her bank far easier than working for the women. Indeed, the only person she has ever hated working for is Adrian, a woman with whom she is now forced to work closely. Tara said she dreads Adrian's assignments, characterizing Adrian as hostile, unfeeling, and unreasonable.

I asked Tara to describe for the group precisely how Adrian acted in ways that were different from the ways Tara's male superiors acted. Tara hesitated. She reflected for a minute and then said that Adrian acted much the same way as the men. Tara said that on reflection, she had wanted Adrian to be her friend, not a distant, direct, and forceful supervisor. When pressed, Tara acknowledged she did not expect this same relationship from the men she worked with.

As the group started to discuss this situation, several women said they had similar reactions to many of the senior women for whom they worked. One woman suggested that junior women hold senior women to different standards than the ones they apply to senior men. The group consensus was that women often want other women to be communal: warm, understanding, and supportive of their unique situations. They don't want other women to be demanding, goal oriented, and abrupt—agentic characteristics they willingly accept in the men for whom they work. Conversations like this one prompted Al and me to research and write our new book, *It's Not You, It's the Workplace.*

A second stereotype that women often have about senior women is that they must have gotten to where they are for reasons other than talent—tokenism, appearance, sucking up to the senior men, seductiveness, or any number of other reasons unrelated to their talent. This view is the reciprocal of the preceding "my female boss is a bitch" view. When a senior woman is seen as too agentic, she is a bitch, but when she is not agentic enough, she is seen as unqualified for a leadership role.

A third stereotype that women often have about the women for whom they work is that they are duplicitous, selfish, and concerned only about themselves. This view often arises when a senior woman praises a female subordinate for the quality of her work yet she does not see her career advancing: no salary increases, no promotions, no formal recognition. In such situations, the problem often is not that the female supervisor is disingenuous but that she is not powerful enough to push effectively for her subordinates. If you are working for a woman who compliments your work but you don't see tangible rewards, discuss your concerns with her. Ask her about the compensation and promotion process. Ask who makes the decisions, who has meaningful input, and to whom she makes *her* recommendations. You may not get what you want, but assuming she has your best interests at heart, you will get a clearer picture of what you are up against—and a better appreciation of what she might be up against too.

The last gender stereotype is that senior women are bullies. While there certainly are women bullies—just as there are men who are bullies[22]—a critical, highly demanding female supervisor is often seen as a bully when the same conduct by a man is accepted as an effective leadership style.

Al: I read with interest the news articles about the firing of Lt. Col. Kate Germano. She had led the only all-female marine recruit battalion for about a year. When Germano took over command of her unit, she found that the women in boot camp were kept separate from the male recruits and that their performance at

(Continued)

non-strength-related skills, such as shooting, were lower than the scores of the men. The Marine Corps' mind-set at that time held female recruits to lower performance standards than the men. According to the reports, Germano was determined to change this. In her short tenure, Germano stopped many of the separate training protocols, resulting in improved performance by the women in her unit in almost all categories. Germano was, nevertheless, fired because of complaints of a "toxic," and "hostile, unprofessional, and abusive" leadership style. Her supporters claim that she had been "firm but fair" and that she had only been trying to make the unit better by holding the women to tougher standards. Germano's supporters claim that there would have been no objection to her conduct if she had been a man. Germano was publicly criticized by fellow officers as being "too aggressive," "too blunt," and "too direct."

I am certainly not in a position to say whether Germano was actually a bully, but I doubt it. A bully does not care about the good of the organization or the people who work for her, but Germano did.[23]

There is a clear difference between a highly critical, demanding boss and a bully. A bully is not interested in getting a good result; a bully is only interested in humiliating, undermining, excluding, and driving other people out of the organization. Being bullied by a woman puts you in a very difficult situation. If you stick up for yourself and fight back, your conflict can be seen as a catfight, a stereotypical view of female behavior as hostile and bitter, and a stereotypical confirmation that women can't work with other women. On the other hand, if you don't stick up for yourself, you can suffer adverse career consequences.

If you are being bullied, whether by a woman or a man, you need help. Go to human resources, the head of your department, or a senior person in your organization. Real bullying creates a hostile work environment; it is illegal and should be responded to in the same way you would respond to illegal discrimination and sexual harassment.

All of these stereotypes can make women's workplace relationships with other women difficult. Precisely because of these difficulties, however, women need to understand the way gender stereotypes operate. Women should give other women the benefit of the doubt, see the workplace through their eyes, and understand the jobs that other women are expected to do. They should also be attentive to *actual* differences between women's and men's behaviors, attitudes, and language, not buying into gender stereotypes.

Authenticity

Women often tell us they need to be authentic and that authenticity requires them to be true to their one true self. Any suggestions that they modify their communication styles to avoid or overcome the gender bias they face in the workplace is often met with "I can't be a phony." This idea that authenticity suggests that you only have one true self, one way of being authentic, and one communication style is not only a gender stereotype—it ignores your dynamic nature as a woman. Nevertheless, workplaces are suffused with gender bias; women need to manage the impressions other people have of them. Women need to be able to call on a forceful, decisive communication style, an inclusive style, an empathetic style, a concerned style—and many other styles—to navigate gender bias. Just as you dress differently for different occasions, you need to call on different communication styles to accomplish your career objectives.

Authenticity relates to your communication style and focuses on remaining true to your core values. Bill George, who writes extensively on authenticity, defines authentic leaders as people who are "genuine and true to what they believe in. They understand the purpose of leadership, they lead with very consistent values, and with their heart, as well as their head. They have courage, compassion, empathy—qualities like that—and they build long-term connected relationships. And they have the personal self-discipline to deliver extraordinary results from their teams."[24] Authenticity does not mean you must communicate in exactly the same way no matter what the situation or context. As George says, authenticity is "not about style. It's the person inside of you."[25]

Just because a particular way of acting or communicating feels more comfortable doesn't mean it is more authentic than any other, nor does it mean this more comfortable style is a more useful tool in your communications tool kit. What's more, pulling from different communication styles doesn't mean that you are inauthentic or pandering to gender stereotypes. Rather, it is simply a skill every effective leader needs to accomplish the business objective at hand. In some situations, for example, you will be most effective if you are articulate and direct, while in other situations you will be most effective if you use softer expressions to connect with other people.

Judging Your Career Success

Another tempting stereotype is the idea that you can measure your career success by your progress in relation to that of other women. We all naturally compare our abilities and achievements to our peers' achievements.[26] But if you assume your only peers are other women, you can delude yourself into believing you are being treated fairly when you are not. According to recent research, most women are likely to acknowledge that women in general do not receive compensation and other career-related rewards comparable to that of similarly situated men, but they are also likely to deny that they personally are subject to any gender discrimination.[27] This myth of personal uniqueness—the belief that you are being treated fairly while the rest of the women in your organization are not—is perpetuated when you compare yourself only to other women. Unless you judge yourself in relation to your male counterparts, you will never really know—or have an incentive to do something about—whether you are being treated fairly.

Andie: Marie, a mechanical engineer and a successful senior executive at an international consulting company, asked my advice when she learned potentially devastating news about her career progress. Marie had been happy at work and knew her career progression compared

(Continued)

favorably with that of other senior women. Then, she learned by chance that several men who reported directly to her were making more money than she was. She investigated and learned that two of the three women at her responsibility level with whom she always compared herself to also had male direct reports who earned more than they did. Marie dug further and could not find a single man at her responsibility level with *any* direct reports who made more than they did. To make matters even worse, she also learned that *all* of the men at her responsibility level had substantially higher salaries and routinely received larger bonuses than she and the other women did.

After she told me all of this, Marie and I worked out a four-part plan of attack. First, she would request a "no-ifs-ands-or-buts" explanation from her supervisor of the pay disparity. Second, she would ask for her supervisor's written evaluation of her— something she had never received in a form she could compare with the evaluations she had given of her direct reports. Third, she would undertake a series of changes in her communication techniques to ensure she would be perceived as more important and valuable than she obviously was perceived at present. And fourth, she would develop a focused self-evaluation to be presented at her next annual evaluation.

Marie is in the midst of implementing her plan, but she reported back that while her supervisor had been surprised by her forceful demands, he had complimented her on her spunk and determination. He also assured Marie that the company did not want to lose her. I don't know much about her company's culture or structure, but I do know Marie. I believe she will be vigilant until she gets what she thinks is fair—or she will move on to her next career opportunity.

If you are not looking at the careers of the men in your organization when you are evaluating your own career, you need to expand your field of vision. When pursuing a career in a traditionally male career field, such as manufacturing, technology, consulting, finance, law, or medicine, you are competing primarily against men. The only way you can keep score—to know if you are being compensated and advanced as a competent, confident, high-potential person—is to compare yourself to comparably situated men. If you don't know comparably situated men who will share compensation information with you, start cultivating some new male friends. Study information about comparable organizations and positions on the internet. Ask your supervisor how you are doing relative to your male peers and demand straight answers. Finally, pay close attention to all reports of promotions and status changes, particularly to those involving people at your level.

Believing Work Is a Meritocracy

A stereotype that many women find irresistible is the notion that their organization is a true meritocracy. Believing their workplace is or is not a meritocracy poses a real dilemma for a woman. On the one hand, if she believes her workplace is unfair and that hard work and high-quality output will not necessarily result in her advancement, she may very well not try as hard as she otherwise would—creating a self-fulfilling prophecy. On the other hand, if she believes her workplace is fair and that she will be rewarded on the same basis and at the same rate as a man, she is likely to blame herself when she does not receive the same rewards. The problem, therefore, is that in gendered workplaces, women seem to lose no matter what they believe about whether their workplace is a meritocracy.[28]

Institutional and structural changes are certainly needed for our workplaces to become true meritocracies. But we are skeptical about the near-term (or far-term, for that matter) likelihood of these changes happening. The issue, therefore, is how you can advance in your career even in organizations that are not true meritocracies. Simply working harder, turning out high-quality deliverables, and evidencing your strong commitment to your job are necessary to achieve this objective, but they are not sufficient. If you are a woman in a gendered workplace,

your advancement depends on attracting the right kind of attention—
attention you draw because you are a savvy, dynamic person with confidence and competence who does not get tangled up in gender stereotypes. Attaining this sort of attention requires attuned gender communication: self-monitoring, impression management, the right attitudes, and a variety of communication techniques, all of which we begin to address in chapter 4. For now, however, keep in mind that workplace meritocracy is a myth, but with the right tools you can succeed just as though it were not.

Modesty

Another tempting stereotype for women is the idea that women should be modest. The modesty stereotype suggests that women are expected to be selfless and deferential. In this selflessness, women are expected to focus on facilitating the advancement of others, rather than themselves.[29] Accepting the modesty stereotype unnecessarily limits a woman's career choices and restricts her advancement opportunities. The modesty stereotype suggests that simply *because you are a woman*, you should be unassuming, self-effacing, and reluctant to put yourself forward. If you believe in this stereotype, you likely also believe that modesty and success in your career are perfectly compatible: if you just work hard enough and turn out work of high enough quality, your performance will be recognized and you will be compensated and promoted fairly and appropriately. Unfortunately, as we have just discussed, most workplaces are not meritocracies. You cannot just sit at your desk, do good work, and expect to advance in your career at the pace you want. To move up, you need to be *noticed* as being competent, confident, and capable of managing tasks and situations typically handled by people who are senior to you. To be noticed in this way, you need to promote yourself, advertise your abilities and accomplishments, and actively shape the impressions others have of you.

In other words, you need to remove your modesty veil. This can be difficult for many women. Since you were young, you have probably been told not to be boastful, self-assertive, or prideful. You have probably also been told to be reserved, respectful, and "ladylike." As a result, you may be reluctant to raise your hand, strongly compete for career-enhancing opportunities, or forcefully advocate for yourself. And you are hardly alone if you behave in this way. A 2014 study found that over half of working women believe they are overlooked for promotions because they are too modest, too reluctant to be clear and direct about their qualifications, and too concerned about being seen as arrogant, conceited, or aggressive.[30]

When you remain behind your modesty veil, you are likely to be seen as pleasant, warm, and likable—but not proactive, talented, or ready for leadership. Business and professional leaders come in a variety of flavors; modesty is not one of them. To escape the modesty trap that holds back so many women, you need to give yourself permission to advocate for yourself. You need to do for yourself what Google did for its women employees.

Google employees need to nominate themselves for a promotion in order to advance. When Google reviewed its promotion records, it found that women were nominating themselves far less frequently than the men, and thus, men were being promoted far more frequently than the women.[31] The women felt that nominating themselves would damage their relationships with their colleagues by making them appear immodest, disagreeable, and pushy. To overcome this, Google began a campaign to let women know they were *expected* to advocate for themselves, that doing so was appropriate and necessary, and that no one would think badly of them for doing so. In a short time, the gender differences in nominations for promotion disappeared. We discuss additional ways to advocate for yourself in chapter 10.

If you are uncomfortable with self-promotion, start with some small steps. The next time someone tells you that you did a great job on a project you worked hard to complete, don't say, "Oh, it was nothing," or, "I got a lot of help." Instead, say, "Thanks. It was a lot of work," or, "Thanks, your recognition makes my effort doubly worthwhile." You don't want to wallow in the compliments you receive, but you don't want to brush them off either. Proudly accept acknowledgments of your contributions—and don't stop with the small stuff. Career advancement depends on being noticed as ambitious, competent, and confident. This means, in addition to performing first-rate work, you must present your qualifications at appropriate times in a forceful, direct way—while still coming across as warm, inclusive, and socially sensitive. Removing your modesty veil doesn't mean you are suddenly no longer communal. By claiming your rightful achievements and accepting recognition for your contributions, you are in a better position in your workplace to seek greater organizational change and reduce gender bias. By helping other women advance, you can demonstrate that communal characteristics to support others do not require modesty.

But for a woman, this sort of self-promotion—as necessary as it may be for career advancement—carries the risk of provoking a negative reaction because you are not being modest and unassertive in the way that other people stereotypically think *women should be*. The key to managing this sort of backlash is using attuned gender communication—displaying competence and power while also being perceived as pleasant and inclusive. Mastering the art of attuned gender communication is what we address in part II.

KEY TAKEAWAYS

- *Watch out for stereotype threat and choose your assignments carefully.* Understand if and when stereotype threat is triggered for you, and practice the techniques we suggest to avoid it. Don't hold yourself back by letting yourself think you are not as talented, prepared, and capable as the men with whom you are competing. Give yourself a "no impairment" message so that your anxiety will not affect your ability to perform, and work to develop your coping sense of humor.
- *Think about your achievement goals.* Are you pursuing jobs or assignments because they are "gender appropriate" or because they are what you dream of doing?

- *Move out of your comfort zone.* Career advancement requires you to complete challenging, high-risk projects and assignments. Make sure you seek them out.
- *Beware of benevolent sexism.* Praise without advancement plays into traditional gender stereotypes. Take and keep taking a hard look at how your career is advancing. Ask yourself these questions from the Catalyst report "Good Intentions, Imperfect Execution? Women Get Fewer of the 'Hot Jobs' Needed to Advance":[32]

  1. Are you aware of the size and scope of your projects relative to those of others?
  2. Are you strategically working toward getting assigned to large and visible projects?
  3. Do you step forward and volunteer to take on important assignments?
  4. Have you participated in a formal leadership development program? Do you need to?
  5. Are you planning for your next development opportunity? Do you have a clear idea of how to get it?

- *Glowing reviews don't translate into promotions.* Promotion requires you to be noticed by your supervisors as a person with the ambition, competence, and potential to perform successfully at the next level. You need to demonstrate that you have the potential to succeed if promoted, not simply that you can perform competently in your current position.
- *Consider your relationships with other women at work.* Remember that women adopt stereotypes about themselves and other women.
- *Advocating for yourself does not mean you are violating communal stereotypes.* Advocating for yourself can provide you with the ability to advocate for other women and support organizational change.

Chapter 3

The Vipers in the Room

S INCE THE FIRST EDITION OF this book was released in 2016, America has seen an astonishing increase in open, hostile, mean-spirited criticism of successful, ambitious women. It has also seen revelations of the predatory sexual practices of many prominent and powerful men. These verbal and physical attacks against women are both forms of explicit gender bias: conscious, purposeful behavior designed to intimidate, silence, and demean women. We call this chapter "The Vipers in the Room" because the people who engage in such explicit gender bias are dangerous and treacherous, just like members of that venomous snake family, the viper (*Viperidae*).

A (Very) Short History of Explicit Gender Bias

Explicit gender bias, whether in the form of verbal or physical attacks on women, is hardly a new phenomenon. Indeed, at the very beginning of Western civilization we have a striking example of a man forcefully silencing a woman who is attempting to assert herself in public.[1] In Book 1 of Homer's *Odyssey*, Penelope, Odysseus's wife and Telemachus's mother, comes down from her private quarters and enters the great hall where a bard is singing about the difficulties the Greek heroes, including her husband, are having returning home from the Trojan War. In front of Telemachus and her many suitors, Penelope tells the bard to "stop this upsetting song that always breaks my heart." Telemachus immediately rebukes her, ordering her to "go in and do your work. Stick to your loom and distaff....It is for men to talk, especially me. I am the master." Whereupon Penelope returns to her room weeping.[2]

The Homeric view of women's and men's proper public roles has prevailed throughout most of subsequent Western history. As Susan B. Anthony wrote in 1900,

> No advanced step taken by women has been so bitterly contested as that of speaking in public. For nothing which they have attempted, not even to secure the suffrage, have they been so abused, condemned and antagonized. In this they were defying not only the prejudice of the ages, but also what the world had been taught as a divine command... "I suffer not a woman to speak in public." This was the law and gospel enforced by man.[3]

The vigorous condemnation of the suffragettes who were speaking in public was common and often extreme during the decade leading up to the passage of the Nineteenth Amendment, granting women the right to vote. These women were openly and repeatedly criticized for publicly advocating for women's right to vote and thereby seeking to destroy the very fabric of civil society. Newspapers described these women as "undesirable militants," "unwomanly," "shameless," "pathological," and "dangerous." A well-known theologian at that time even described women who sought to perform "men's functions" as "monstrosities of nature."[4]

With the emergence in the 1960s and 1970s of second-wave feminism and the modern women's movement, such blatant public criticism of women who were active in the public arena seemed to have lost its social acceptability. Indeed, misogynistic attacks were muted, if they were voiced at all, when Sandra Day O'Connor was appointed to the Supreme Court as its first woman justice; Shirley Chisholm and Pat Schroeder ran for their party's presidential nomination; and Geraldine Ferraro and Sarah Palin were selected as their party's vice presidential nominees. And apart from the frequency of the ranting of anonymous social media trolls, in recent years there seems to have been a moratorium on public expressions of misogynistic views that are not anonymous. This moratorium came to an abrupt end in 2016 with the campaign and election of Donald Trump. Crude, open, and hostile attacks on publicly active and visible women came roaring back as a powerful social force.[5]

Sexual harassment and assault, like verbal attacks against women who assert themselves publicly, are hardly a recent phenomenon. Indeed, Roman mythology celebrates the forcible abduction of women from the Sabine tribe in a violent encounter that was led by Romulus himself. The "Rape of the Sabine Women" was celebrated throughout Roman history and was the subject of much artistic expression during and after the Renaissance.[6]

While rape was condemned and punished as a crime during much of Western history, until the #MeToo movement, rape received little mainstream attention and was not generally regarded as a major societal problem. This lack of widespread concern was not because there were no efforts to awaken public recognition of how serious a problem was posed by the pervasive nature of rape and sexual harassment. During the 1970s, for example, a number of prominent feminists forcefully spoke and wrote about the physical, emotional, and societal harm inflicted on a great many women by sexual harassment and violence. Kate Millett's *Sexual Politics*,[7] Shulamith Firestone's *The Dialectic of Sex*,[8] and Susan Brownmiller's *Against Our Will*[9] all attempted to call attention to the terrible toll that rape and sexual violence were extracting from women. Of the 1970s feminists, Andrea Dworkin is perhaps the most clearheaded and insightful writer on sexual violence.[10] Dworkin saw such violence as an "atrocity" being waged against women. She derided the 1970s vogue of encouraging men to get in touch with their feminine qualities. As she wrote, "Men who want to support women in our struggle for freedom and justice should understand that it is not terrifically important to us that they learn to cry; it is important to us that they stop the crimes of violence against us."[11] Dworkin was one of the first commentators to recognize that "rape is not committed by psychopaths"; rather she saw clearly that "rape is committed by normal men." And precisely because of their normality, "rapists and their defenders…not only go unpunished; they remain influential arbiters of morality; they have high and esteemed places in society; they are priests, lawyers, judges, lawmakers, politicians, doctors, artists, corporate executives, psychiatrists, and teachers."[12] As Michelle Goldberg, a *New York Times* columnist, wrote in February 2019, "Dworkin, so profoundly out of fashion just a few years ago, certainly [now] seems prophetic."[13]

Despite the insightfulness and vigor of Dworkin's—and other feminists'—exposure and denunciation of sexual violence, their work did not receive widespread public attention, and nothing seemed to change with respect to the public's concern about sexual harassment and violence. Yet the world did change in 2017: when women collectively came forward under the banner of #MeToo to expose the predatory behavior of a great many well-known and powerful men, sexual harassment become a matter of broad and serious concern.

After this (very) brief history of explicit gender bias, we now turn to the recent manifestations of explicit gender bias—both verbal and physical—by examining the consequences of Trump's crude, public misogynistic behavior and the revelations and consequences of the #MeToo movement.

Trump

During the 2016 presidential campaign, Trump waged a relentless, sexist attack against Hillary Clinton, calling her "unbalanced," "unstable," a "pathological liar,"[14] "a nasty woman,"[15] and "crooked."[16] Apart from the disturbing fact that these comments occurred in the context of a battle to become president of the United States—presumably a dignified and highly consequential position—this outpouring of misogynistic hostility from Trump should not have been surprising given his past behavior.

Shock jock Howard Stern, for example, described Trump as someone who "always talked in a misogynistic, sexist kind of way…proudly and out in the open. Trump's comments about women reflect exactly 'who Trump is.'"[17] Trump's penchant for demeaning women with whom he is at odds is reflected in his calling Bette Midler "ugly";[18] tweeting that Arianna Huffington "is unattractive both inside and out";[19] sending Gail Collins one of her newspaper columns with her picture circled and a note saying "the face of a dog";[20] calling Alicia Machado, a former Miss Universe, "Miss Piggy";[21] and characterizing Omarosa Manigault Newman, a former White House aide, as "that dog" and a "crazed, crying lowlife."[22]

But Trump's insulting comments about individual women do not provide a complete picture of his misogyny. In 1991, Trump had this to say about a recent bout of bad press: "You know, it really doesn't matter what they write as long as you've got a young and beautiful piece of ass. But she's got to be young and beautiful."[23] On the set of *The Apprentice*, Trump talked openly about women's breast sizes, discussed which contestants he'd want to have sex with, and asked male contestants to rate the women based on their sexual desirability.[24] And in the now infamous *Access Hollywood* video, he bragged about grabbing women "by the pussy."[25]

"Halo of Crudeness"

As offensive as Trump's language and behavior may be, if he were simply one individual, however prominent, whose misogynistic comments and behavior were generally condemned, he might be seen as highly offensive but ultimately aberrational and irrelevant. But Trump is neither aberrational nor irrelevant. As Katy Tur, the NBC correspondent who covered Trump during the 2016 presidential campaign, writes, "Trump is crude, and in his halo of crudeness other people get to be crude as well."[26]

This crudeness was on full display at Trump's rallies during the 2016 campaign, where two of the milder T-shirt messages were "Trump That Bitch" and "Trump 2016: Finally Someone With Balls."[27] At Trump's current rallies, chants of "Lock her up" are still heard.[28] Criticism of Democratic Congresswoman Ilhan Omar has been met with cries of "Send her back," despite the fact that she is a naturalized US citizen.[29] One of Omar's Republican challengers has been banned from Twitter for life after tweeting out a link to a conspiracy theory "backed by zero evidence," calling for Omar to be tried for treason and hanged.[30] And in

October 2019, Donald Trump Jr. stated on Twitter that Kamala Harris is "the most disingenuous person in politics…after Hillary."[31] Republican operative Stuart Stevens summarizes: "Trump is the worst within us, and he markets that worst as admirable.…He appeals to our darkest angels, not our better angels." [32]

Misogyny Is Now on Full Display

In Trump's "halo of crudeness" a large number of women and men seem to have been granted permission to give vent to their own misogynistic views. This widespread hostility toward—and even open anger with—women who challenge traditional gender roles was on full display in voter attitudes in the 2016 election. Three studies of these attitudes in the 2016 election—where 58 percent of white voters (62 percent of white male voters and 53 percent of white female voters) supported Trump[33]—all found that racism and "hostile sexism," that is, misogyny, were fundamental motivating factors in voter support for Trump.

In the first of these studies, "Mobilizing Sexism: The Interaction of Emotion and Gender Attitudes in the 2016 US Presidential Election," the researchers looked at survey data collected before the election in June of 2016.[34] They asked potential voters four questions designed to measure the degree of their hostile sexism. The answers were collapsed into a single number; the higher the number, the more hostile the respondent's attitude toward ambitious women. The researchers found that 54 percent of men who scored high in hostile sexism (above the median score) planned to vote for Trump, but only 23 percent of men low in hostile sexism planned to do so. Significantly, the relationship between hostile sexism and voter choice was nearly as strong for women as men: 47 percent of women who were high in hostile sexism planned to vote for Trump, but only 20 percent of women low in hostile sexism planned to do so.

The researchers found "in the late primary period of June 2016 that sexism was strongly associated with support for Trump." They found this significant because sexism had not been a significant factor in identifying voters who supported the Republican candidate in 2004, 2008, or 2012.[35] As to why sexist attitudes came to be so important in 2016, the researchers concluded that the answer "revolves centrally around the reactions Trump supporters had not only to Clinton's gender and outspoken feminism but also to Trump's sexist comments and behavior before and during the campaign. While sexism is only one of many forces to be considered... it is a powerful one without recent historical precedent."

The second of the studies, "Understanding White Polarization in the 2016 Vote for President: The Sobering Role of Racism and Sexism,"[36] looked specifically at the attitudes of white people who voted in the election. This study found two striking patterns. First, there was an unprecedented gap between the presidential vote preferences of college-educated and non-college-educated white voters. Among whites with a college degree, Trump had only a four-point margin over Clinton (10 points less than Mitt Romney's margin over Barack Obama in 2012). Among non-college-educated white voters, however, Trump had a nearly 40-point margin. In fact, Trump won more than 70 percent of the two-party vote among whites without a college degree, "easily exceeding the performance of any Republican going back to at least 1980."

Second, while economic considerations played an important role in Trump's victory, racial attitudes and hostile sexism were even more strongly correlated with voter support for Trump. In the case of hostile sexism, moving from people with the least to the most sexist views coincided with an increase in support for Trump of about 30 points.

In an analysis of these two voting patterns, the researchers found that very little of the dramatic polarization of the voting choices of white people with different educational attainments could be explained by the greater economic difficulties that less-educated whites might face in comparison with more-educated whites. Rather, the researchers found that most of the divide was associated with sexism and racism. The researchers concluded that Trump's explicit sexist and racist appeals hurt his position with more-educated whites, but won him even greater support from less-educated white voters.

The third study, "Why Did Women Vote for Donald Trump?"[37] found that "female voters, like their male counterparts, were most powerfully influenced by the degree to which they hold racially resentful and sexist attitudes." Indeed, the researchers found that female Trump supporters were almost as sexist as his male supporters. Women with "the highest levels of sexism were 50 percentage points (that is, 70 percent versus 20 percent) more likely to support Trump than those who expressed no sexist attitudes." Thus, the researchers concluded that women who voted for Trump held "sexist and racially resentful attitudes" more similar to the men supporting Trump than to the women who supported the other candidates.

Why Are So Many Women Misogynists?

Taken together, these three studies make it clear that many women—as well as a great many men—are extremely hostile to other women's attempts to promote or achieve gender equality. But why? Why are so many women opposed to efforts to ensure that women's economic, social, and legal status is the same as men's? Undoubtedly, the answers to this question are complex and differ for different women, but Rebecca Solnit provides a keen insight when she writes

> To be a feminist you have to believe in your equality and rights, which can make your life unpleasant and dangerous if you live in a marriage, a family, a community, a church, a state that does not agree with you about this. For many women it's safer not to have those thoughts in this country. And those thoughts are not so available in a country where feminism is forever being demonized and distorted.[38]

Combating Hostile, Verbal Attacks on Women

Trump did not create the explicit gender bias that is now on such distasteful display, but his public comments have provided cover for other people to publicly express their own hostile, angry, aggressive misogyny without fear of general condemnation. Because of this, the tone and character of our public discourse about gender equality, women's appropriate societal roles, and the value of gender diversity in America's economic and political leadership have been radically transformed since 2016. As a result, the tools and techniques for avoiding and overcoming implicit gender bias need to be supplemented by active, vigorous condemnation of all public expressions of sexist and misogynistic views. We must be vigilant in ensuring that explicit gender bias is called out as reprehensible and not to be tolerated. This is not always easy to do, but it must be accomplished if we are ever to find a way to return to a time of civil, respectful discourse about women, men, power, gender roles, and equality.

#MeToo

Sexual harassment and assault are express forms of explicit gender bias. As an Appellate Panel of the New York State Supreme Court ruled in late 2019,[39] "coerced sexual activity is dehumanizing and fear inducing. Malice or ill will based on gender is apparent from the alleged commission of the act itself." The court's ruling came in an opinion upholding the conviction of movie producer Paul Haggis under a New York City law prohibiting "animus based on the victim's gender." Haggis had argued that the law did not apply to him because there was no evidence of hatred against women as a group. Significantly and quite correctly, the court ruled that plaintiffs can use the law to pursue sexual assault even if there is no other evidence that the defendant has shown hatred of the victim's gender. In other words, the very act of rape or sexual assault is conclusive evidence of explicit gender bias under New York City law.

The same thing is true of other lesser forms of offensive sexual behavior specifically directed against women (such as "locker room talk," off-color jokes, unwelcome attention or touching, and inappropriate comments about appearance or behavior). All such hostile sexual activities are manifestations of explicit gender bias and are designed primarily to intimidate, silence, and put women down—rather than to initiate intimate sexual relationships. These forms of explicit gender bias are of a piece with implicit gender bias, and because these biased attitudes and behaviors are interconnected, as we asserted in the *Harvard Business Review*, these attitudes and behaviors need to be "addressed collectively, because sexual harassment [and other forms of explicit gender bias are] far more likely in organizations that experience offenses on the 'less severe' [implicit bias] end of the spectrum than in those that don't."[40]

Obviously, the behavioral forms of explicit gender bias did not become a serious societal issue in just the last four years. Since the initial publication of this book in 2016, however, such behavior has become the subject of much greater public attention and concern—in large part because of the women who have bravely come forward under the #MeToo banner to recount their own stories of sexual harassment and assault. The question is, *Why did this happen now? Why did the #MeToo movement arise in 2017 and not earlier?* As we pointed out earlier in this chapter, women had been vigorously speaking out about sexual harassment and violence well before 2017, so why did the dam burst then?

2017

On January 21, 2017, the day after the presidential inauguration, the largest single-day, globally coordinated public gathering in history occurred in the form of the Women's March.[41] On April 1, 2017, Bill O'Reilly's sexual harassment of multiple women was reported,[42] and shortly thereafter he was fired by Fox News. On October 5, 2017, the *New York Times* broke the story of Harvey Weinstein's sexual predations,[43] and the *New Yorker* followed suit with even more details on October 10, 2017.[44] Then on October 15, 2017, the actor Alyssa Milano tweeted a request to her followers: "If you've been sexually harassed or assaulted write 'me too' as a reply to this tweet."[45] The next morning she had 55,000 replies, and over the next 45 days, #MeToo was posted 85 million times on Facebook.[46]

Activist Tarana Burke had coined the phrase MeToo in 1997,[47] but it was not until 2017 that the floodgates of women's outrage opened. But again, why? Why was 2017 the year of #MeToo?

It certainly was not because sexual harassment and sexual violence had become more prevalent or serious than it had been in the 1970s when

Dworkin was railing against its pervasiveness. Nor was it because the men who were engaged in sexual misconduct had become more powerful or prominent. After all, Weinstein and Roger Ailes, the longtime head of Fox News, had been engaging in outrageous sexual misconduct for decades before they were brought down in 2017.

In her book *Reckoning: The Epic Battle against Sexual Abuse and Harassment,* Linda Hirshman argues, "No social movement arises in an instant," and #MeToo was no exception, resting as it does "on a long history of organization and activism."[48] Undoubtedly, there is a great deal of truth to Hirshman's claim—but something changed in 2017, and we think Milano has put her finger on it when she writes that the movement would never "have turned into what it is if [Trump] wasn't in office."[49] Her view is echoed by Ashwini Tambe, a professor of women's studies at the University of Maryland, who stated on National Public Radio, "The election of Donald Trump has served as a trigger [for the #MeToo movement], and it has provoked a great deal of fury and impatience because [Trump] represents, for many people, the ultimate unpunished predator."[50] Indeed, as the *New York Times* has reported, Trump's 2016 campaign and election sparked "a fervor [that] has swept the country, promoting women's marches, a record number of female candidates running for office and an outcry about sexual assault at all levels of society."[51]

There may well be other factors besides Trump's campaign and election that helped ignite women's collective campaign against sexual harassment and assault: a collective sense that enough is enough; a sufficient number of courageous women coming forward to encourage others to do the same; and the media's new willingness to finally treat sexual harassment as the serious problem it is.[52] Whatever the ultimate reasons for the explosion of women's anger, after the exposure of O'Reilly, Weinstein, and Ailes, scores of women publicly spoke out about being the victims of inappropriate sexual behavior by well-known and powerful men. Matt Lauer, Sean Hannity, Charles Payne, Leon Wieseltier, Tavis Smiley, Mark Halperin, Les Moonves, Charlie Rose, and many more have now been called out and brought down for their crude, hurtful, and illegal sexual conduct.

Temin and Company, a management consulting firm that has tracked public reports of serious sexual misconduct since comedian Bill Cosby's arrest in December 2015, found that through May of 2019 there had been 1,227 high-profile accusations (that is, accusations reported in at least 7 media sources) of sexual harassment by public figures.[53] Such accusations averaged just 6 per month in the period between the accusations against Cosby and Weinstein, but after Weinstein's exposure, accusations jumped to 78 in October 2017, 119 in November, and 103 in December. Such accusations averaged over 40 per month in 2018, and while the number of accusations decreased in 2019, it was still higher than it had been before allegations first surfaced against Weinstein.[54]

Just the Tip of the Iceberg

From the perspective of the 1970s and the antiviolence crusade that Dworkin and other feminists were then waging, the fall of so many prominent men in recent years is truly astonishing. Given what we know about the scope of the sexual harassment problem, however, #MeToo has only exposed the tip of the proverbial iceberg. An online survey by Stop Street Harassment, for example, found that 38 percent of women report having experienced sexual harassment in their workplaces.[55] Since 76 million women work outside their homes,[56] if this estimate is correct, approximately 29 million American women have been sexually harassed at work. And this number may be far too low. According to the Equal Employment Opportunity Commission, between 60 and 70 percent of women "have been on the receiving end of sexual harassment on the job at some point during their careers."[57]

Optimistic Signs

There are reasons to be optimistic that the #MeToo movement will bring about meaningful change with respect to the prevalence of workplace sexual harassment and violence.[58] First, the movement has clearly resulted in a major shift in public attitudes. In 1998, only 34 percent of

Americans thought sexual harassment was a serious problem. By late 2017, roughly 75 percent of Americans believed that sexual harassment and assault "were very important" issues for the country. Moreover, 66 percent of adults now say allegations of sexual harassment "mainly reflect widespread problems in society,"—with only 28 percent attributing them primarily to individual misconduct—and 86 percent of Americans now endorse a "zero tolerance" policy toward sexual harassment.[59]

Beyond the shift in societal attitudes, since 2017 there have been concrete substantive legal changes as well. In a June 2019 report, the National Women's Law Center reported that 15 states had passed new laws designed to provide employees with more protection against sexual harassment and gender discrimination.[60] These laws have included extending the statute of limitations to bring lawsuit, removing the requirement that harassment be "severe or pervasive" to create a hostile work environment, and mandating antiharassment training.

Given the massive attention being paid to sexual harassment and assault because of #MeToo,[61] these positive developments are not surprising. Nevertheless, much more needs to be done to reform the ways in which workplace sexual harassment and assault are reported, adjudicated, and punished. Even with enactment of the most progressive reforms imaginable (a highly unlikely development), unless our workplace cultures change, the ultimate goal of assuring that women can thrive in all career fields without fear for their safety or of unwelcome comments or conduct will not be realized. In other words, the focus of #MeToo must expand from outing bad actors to reforming workplace cultures so that all forms of inappropriate sexual conduct are condemned.

Toxic Workplace Cultures

The need for cultural reform is apparent from a brief review of the cultures of the organizations in which some of the most powerful and prominent harassers worked and thrived.

After Lauer, the host of *The Today Show*, was fired by NBC for sexual misconduct, it was revealed that the behind-the-scenes environment of that show resembled a "boys' club": jokes about women's appearance were routine; men would play a crude game in which they would identify the women they would prefer "to marry, kill, or have sex with"; and inappropriate sexual comments about women were routine.[62]

At Weinstein's companies, sexual harassment was so prevalent that one woman advised a peer to wear a parka as an additional layer of protection against unwelcome advances from Weinstein.[63] Professional meetings were often "little more than pretexts for sexual advances on young actresses and models." In fact, predatory sexual behavior was so widespread that employees described "a culture of complicity... with numerous people... fully aware of [Weinstein's] behavior but either abetting it or looking the other way."[64]

After Rose was dropped by CBS, PBS, and Bloomberg TV for his crude sexual advances spanning many years, current and former employees of *The Charlie Rose Show* described a "hostile work environment, with no human resource department and Rose essentially running his own fief."[65] At CBS, the former network CEO Les Moonves, morning show anchor Rose, and *60 Minutes* executive producer Jeff Fager were all fired because of sexual misconduct. Outside investigators found a pattern of "harassment and violation," noting that the claims against Moonves "were a reflection of the culture at CBS."[66]

At Fox News, former commentator O'Reilly was fired after multiple allegations of sexual harassment and disclosure of settlement agreements of approximately $45 million with numerous accusers.[67] Nevertheless, O'Reilly left Fox News with a $20 million severance payment.[68] Ailes was forced out of Fox News after more than two dozen women accused him of sexual harassment. Like O'Reilly, Ailes left with a severance payment; in his case $40 million.[69] *New York* magazine reported that Fox News's "grotesque abuses of power has left even its liberal critics stunned.... [The] women who have come forward to accuse Ailes of sexual harassment... have exposed a culture of misogyny and one of corruption and surveillance, smear campaigns and hush money with implications reaching far wider than one disturbed man at the top."[70]

Workplace Cultures Generally

Although we doubt that more than a small fraction of American workplaces have cultures as toxic as Fox News and Weinstein's companies, nevertheless most workplace cultures are hostile to or biased against ambitious women. For example, while researchers found that between 2016 and 2018 actual sexual coercion (being bribed or pressured to engage in sexual behavior) and unwanted sexual attention (being the object of staring, leering, ogling, or unwanted sexual touching) had declined; they also found an *increase* in "gender harassment," the negative treatment of women through incivility, exclusion, or crude comments.[71] Indeed, the percentage of women reporting gender harassment grew from 76 percent in 2016 to 92 percent in 2018.

Based on this increase in gender harassment, the researchers concluded, "while blatant sexual harassment—experiences that drive many women out of their careers—might be declining, workplaces may be seeing a 'backlash effect,' or an increase in hostility toward women.... Constant exposure to [such] gender harassment can be just as damaging to women as the most egregious forms of sexual harassment."[72]

This study's finding of an increase in workplace hostility is confirmed by a 2018 Gallup survey[73] that found that only 48 percent of US women believe women are treated with respect and dignity, a 14-point decline from 2017. Of all 21 industrialized countries across Western Europe, the US, and Canada, the US received the lowest rating with respect to women's sense of being treated with dignity and respect.[74] The US also had the largest gap (22 percentage points) between the views of women and men about how women are treated. In the US, 70 percent of men—but only 48 percent of women—think women are treated with dignity and respect. Comparable figures for Canada are 90 percent of men and 87 percent of women, and for the United Kingdom the percentages are 86 and 83.

The increase in gender harassment, the low percentage of women who feel they are treated with dignity and respect, and the serious disconnect between the way in which *women feel* they are treated and the way *men think* women are treated combine to depict a highly troubling reality. As we noted earlier, explicit gender bias in the forms of verbal and physical attacks on women is far more likely in workplaces in which women are not treated with dignity and respect than in workplaces where they are.[75] Even though reported sexual harassment has declined between 2016 and 2018, it continues to thrive in workplaces where women feel unwelcome or disrespected. As Joanna Grossman, a law professor at Southern Methodist University, points out, workplaces where women are not viewed as having equal talent and leadership potential are rife with "opportunity structures" for sexual harassment.[76] This is the same point we made in the *Harvard Business Review* article we mentioned earlier. Gender bias in all of its forms—implicit, explicit, sexual, nonsexual—is of a piece, and if it is to be addressed comprehensively, workplace cultures must be the target. A workplace with a culture that is free of implicit gender bias is also likely to be free of gender harassment and explicit gender bias in the form of sexual harassment and assault. Until women are seen as equal participants with men as they pursue their careers, however, there is little hope of making significant progress against explicit gender bias.

Increasing Women in Senior Leadership

The most effective way to assure women are treated with dignity and respect in the workplace is to significantly increase the number of women in senior leadership positions. Increased female leadership not only advances individual women but also benefits the organization as a whole by fostering cultural change. For example, in a study of 81 Texas-based Fortune 100 companies with a total of 5,679 discrete workplaces,[77] researchers found that greater representation of women in leadership positions at both the corporate level (executive officers and board members) and at the workplace level (managers) is significantly associated with less gender segregation in an organization's nonmanagerial workforce. In other words, women's presence at the top of organizations and as managers reduces gender segregation among subordinates.

Moreover, and most significantly, there is a positive and significant correlation between the percentage of women who are corporate executives and the percentage of women who are managers. Thus, if a significant number of women can become corporate executives, more women will thus become managers—fostering a self-reinforcing process of increasing female participation in leadership.

When a critical mass of women attain senior leadership status in a given organization, the culture and nature of the workplaces in those organizations is likely to change. For example, in a qualitative study of 255 senior executives at 19 Australian organizations where women constituted about 30 percent of the top three executive leadership levels, researchers found that "both women and men clearly agreed that the presence of women in senior roles had changed management cultures and influenced methods of decision-making."[78] As one male executive commented, women's presence in senior leadership "has broken down the male clubbing. So that's so much less a feature of business in this organization than it used to be."[79] The researchers also found that both women and men welcomed what they considered to be more friendly and collegial work environments brought about by women in senior leadership. Overall, the researchers concluded, "the consequences for managerial culture arising from the presence of women in a critical mass is a closer alignment with the ideals of contemporary leadership [that] should be seen as desirable. The women. . . actively sought to create work environments that sustained them, simultaneously enacting a range of [changes to] cultural norms, [that were] accepted by their male colleagues."[80]

We don't want to minimize the challenge posed by achieving a critical mass of women in an organization's senior leadership. In this book, we lay out clear, practical, effective steps that individual women can take to become senior leaders. With a sufficient number of ambitious and committed women willing to take these steps, a critical mass of women in an organization's senior leadership becomes a realistic possibility. Once that critical mass is in place, explicit gender bias—both verbal and physical—should become a thing of the past.

PART II

Conversations
with Yourself

Chapter 4

The Importance of Impression Management

Your career success depends on a variety of factors, not the least of which is just plain luck. Among the factors within your control, the most important are social presence, organizational intelligence, political savvy, and impressive job performance. These skills are just as important for a man's career success as they are for yours. Unlike a man, however, you need two additional skills: the ability to recognize the operation of gender stereotypes in your workplace and to avoid or overcome the discriminatory obstacles they place in your career path. Thus, you need to be able to read the preconceptions and expectations of the gatekeepers to your career advancement and to manage the impressions they have of you so you can disprove those preconceptions and expectations when they involve gender bias.

Stereotypes ascribed to you because you are a woman—and the impression you make on people through your verbal and nonverbal behavior—influence how other people view you and react to you. When that view or reaction is not what you want it to be, you must also be able to change your behavior in such a way that changes their view or expectation. You are not likely to be able to change *their* stereotypes on the spot. Put most simply, your career success depends to a great degree on your ability to manage your impressions.

Why Impression Management?

Imagine a typical mixed-gender business meeting. Whatever the purpose of the meeting, the participants are likely to hold at least three stereotypes. First, they will expect the men to be agentic (that is, tough-minded, aggressive, confident, competent, independent, and assertive). Second, they will expect the women to be communal (that is, friendly, unselfish, warm, kind, compassionate, supportive, and nurturing). And third, they will expect anyone capable of leading the meeting to be agentic. Given these stereotypes, if one of the women at the mixed-gender meeting attempts to exercise a leadership role, one of two scenarios is likely to play out. If she attempts to lead without behaving in an agentic manner, she will likely be ignored. If she attempts to lead by adopting agentic characteristics, she will likely be seen as unfeminine, unpleasant, and unlikable. Either way, she is likely to suffer backlash resulting in negative career consequences.

This double bind can be very difficult for ambitious women to avoid; they can become frustrated and discouraged, concluding that they will never have the chance to exhibit their leadership ability and hence their competence, confidence, and potential. For such women, the only hope seems to be for the stereotypes in their workplaces to be eliminated. When these stereotypes remain (since elimination is not likely to happen in a timely manner), these women often drop out of the career advancement game altogether or resign themselves to a workplace reality of little opportunity and much disappointment.

Al: Bethany, a lawyer in another city, read an earlier draft of this chapter. After she reached the sentence "these women often drop out of the career advancement game altogether or resign themselves to a workplace reality of little opportunity and much disappointment," she sent me the following email:

(Continued)

I circled that sentence and wrote "ME" beside it. In all of the major corporations where I have worked, younger, less experienced, not-as-talented men have been promoted over me. Men in power pick younger men who remind them of themselves; it takes a special man to recognize that diversity of thinking in a business and the C-suite is beneficial. Sadly, the men who would like to help women are often afraid that doing so will make them look weak. It is easier for them to just keep finding "mini-me's" to promote so they don't have to deal with fallout from their male colleagues.

My current boss recently told me he was considering promoting a new hotshot male lawyer, two years out of law school with no law license (he has never taken the bar exam), to be assistant general counsel because he has "the right characteristics." I expressed my concern that this young man was not nearly ready and didn't have the experience (or law license) for such a position. My boss got very angry and said to me, "I have every confidence in my ability to pick the right people to hire and promote." And, of course, he has the power to do whatever he wants.

I could go on for hours, days, weeks, and years. I am just angry, bitter, and disappointed. Despite how frequently I tell myself "just do your time in Folsom Prison," I can't shut off my ambition and strong desire to succeed. But, when success doesn't come, I just get more angry and bitter. As I have gotten older, I have gotten better at just "doing my time," but when I do this, I feel I am letting down the other professional women in the organization. I just don't seem to be able to win.

Bethany's frustrated ambition and dashed dreams are heartbreaking. Sadly, we know of far too many women with similar stories. Fortunately, we believe there is a way forward for Bethany and other women—a way for them to be seen as leaders without being viewed as either pushy, unlikable bitches *or* sweet but "not competent enough to move up" women.

Let's return to our example of a mixed-gender business meeting. As we pointed out, a woman at such a meeting attempting to play a leadership role while exhibiting *exclusively* communal or *exclusively* agentic traits is likely to face the classic lose/lose double bind. But what if she selectively and appropriately uses both sets of traits—in other words, what if she is able to manage the impressions she is making so that people with whom she is dealing don't see her as just communal or just agentic but "just right" to be a competent, effective leader? In fact, when a woman can dial up or down both her communal and agentic characteristics as needed she stands a good chance of minimizing or escaping the discriminatory consequences of being seen as either "too soft" or "too hard."[1]

We recognize that simply recommending you use a combination of agentic and communal communication styles to avoid getting caught in a double bind is hardly helpful. It leaves unanswered a whole host of practical questions about the nature of these different communication styles, how to use them most effectively, and when they are most appropriate. The chapters that follow address these questions in considerable detail. But before we get there, we want to make clear why your ability to control your communication style and the impressions you make is so critical for your career success.

How to Manage Impressions

Impression management is a simple concept: it is the conscious control of what and how you communicate in an effort to shape the impressions other people have of you.[2] You are continually seeking rewards in the course of your career: respect, recognition, opportunities, support, increased compensation, and advancement. If you can shape the impressions that the people who control these rewards have of you, you can also shape (to a great extent) the ways in which they treat, evaluate, and talk about you. When you control the impressions you make, you greatly increase the likelihood that you will receive the career rewards you seek—and to which you are entitled.

There are many factors that influence when, why, and how you seek to manage your impressions. Two key factors, however, underlie all effective impression management. The first is a high degree of self-awareness, or what social science literature often calls high self-monitoring. This is an awareness of *what* you are communicating—not just the substantive content of what you are saying, but everything you are conveying about yourself as a result of the totality of your behavior. In other words, your being attuned to *whether* the impressions you are making as a result of your communications are the ones you want to be making. The second key factor is an ability to use a variety of communication techniques to change the impressions you are making.

Thus, effective impression management depends on both acute self-awareness and a facility for nuanced verbal and nonverbal behavior. Much of the remainder of this book is devoted to how you can acquire and use both skills.

Andie: Simone is an experienced lawyer with an impressive record of achievements. She is smart and very, very intense. Simone recently assumed a new position within a corporate legal department and is now the only woman participating in extensive drafting sessions in preparation for a major acquisition. Simone told me she is not uncomfortable being the lone woman in these sessions, but she has been struggling with the dynamics of her professional relationship with Matt, the senior man on the project.

As Simone explained the problem to me, Matt will listen to her ideas but then turn to her colleague Chuck to discuss the points exclusively. Matt physically turns his body away from her and toward Chuck. Simone asked for my advice about how she could get Matt to interact directly with her. When I asked Simone if she felt that her intensity, her unrelieved focus on making her points, and her lack of friendly banter could be making Matt uncomfortable, she acknowledged that this was possible. She also said, however, "My intensity is what has gotten me to where I am. Surely

(Continued)

that's a positive aspect of who I am. I can't change that." I pointed out that Matt was not going to engage with her unless and until he felt comfortable doing so. If he found her intensity hard to take, she would either have to dial it down or accept the status quo. So she grudgingly said, "Okay," and we discussed a number of behavioral changes she could try that would allow her to come across as more relaxed, approachable, and engaging.

Simone got back to me the very next day in an email: "I talked slower and tried to appear relaxed, pleasant, and interested in Matt's life away from the office. I was careful to watch Matt's reactions, and when he seemed to be getting uncomfortable. I tried to lighten things up. Well, it worked; he interacted directly with me and only once tried to engage Chuck. I think I am on the right track."

Let's return to the claim that by using both communal and agentic communication styles you can effectively avoid or overcome the gender biases arising from the leadership double bind. In a recent study, researchers tracked 132 female and male MBA graduates over an eight-year period.[3] Some—but by no means all—of the women in this group were highly self-aware and comfortable using both agentic and communal communication techniques as appropriate. These high-self-monitoring women received 1.5 times as many promotions as agentic men, 1.5 times as many promotions as communal women, 2 times as many promotions as communal men, and 3 times as many promotions as agentic women.[4]

Women and Authenticity

The results of the study of MBA graduates constitute a strong argument for why women should manage their impressions through a combination of agentic and communal communication techniques. Nevertheless, many women strongly resist the notion that they need to manage their impressions. They tell us such things as, "That wouldn't be me," "I'd feel like a phony trying to manipulate what people think of me," or "I am who I am, and I am not going to change." The reactions are understandable but misguided. Impression management does not involve being other than yourself, but it does involve drawing on a variety of the aspects of that self. And unless you are willing to utilize the totality of your characteristics, capacities, and emotional resources, you are effectively saying, "I am going to play the competitive promotion game with one hand tied behind my back."

We all have forceful, decisive aspects to our personalities and empathic, concerned aspects to our personalities. Just as we go to our closet in the morning and take out the clothes that will be appropriate for that day's activities, impression management involves going to our personality closet and taking out those characteristics that will be needed to get each particular job done. If decisiveness is called for, you must provide it. When a sense of inclusiveness and warmth is needed, that's up to you, too. This has nothing to do with being inauthentic and everything to do with accomplishing what needs to be accomplished to advance in your career.

If you need someone with skills or experiences you don't have, you wouldn't hesitate bringing her or him on to a project where needed to get the job done. Likewise, when the job to be done is to advance your own career, you shouldn't hesitate to bring to that project different aspects of your personality—and different communication styles—if that is what it will take for you to get *that* job done.

But doesn't doing this require you to be inauthentic, a phony, and not true to yourself? No, no, and no. Managing the impressions you make requires you to be the very opposite of inauthentic. To do it effectively, you need to be deeply connected to your own feelings, capacities, and potentials; it requires you to be able to draw on the many different characteristics and qualities that make you who you are. Managing your impressions is about making sure that the message you convey *about yourself* through the totality of your behavior is the most appropriate and effective for that particular situation.[5] Impression management does not require you to be inauthentic. Authenticity is staying true to your core values and being "genuine and true to what [you] believe in."[6] It has nothing to do with limiting your ability to draw on different aspects of your personality or using only one communication style. The objective of impression management is to present the right aspects of *your personality* at the right time and place. This requires high self-monitoring and the use of varied communication techniques—not playacting or being a phony. Putting those skills together may not be easy, but it certainly is not being inauthentic.

Women may also resist impression management because they misunderstand what impression management requires and think it will force them to present themselves in stereotypically male ways, and they find this offensive. Managing the impressions you make does not require you to conform to stereotypical male behavior patterns, but it does require you to accept the reality that your workplace is highly gendered with male stereotypes associated with leadership, power, and potential. Therefore, as you strive to advance in your career, you are likely to be playing a competitive game in which these stereotypes unfortunately provide many of the most important rules, and you must understand those rules to avoid or overcome their discriminatory potential.

Andie: At a gender communication workshop, I told the following story:

I was mentoring Ellen, who lived in a different city. I had dealt with her only by phone and email, so I was surprised when she told me that many of her supervisors had characterized her as disorganized and a sloppy thinker. I had always found Ellen to be sharp and focused. So the next time I was in Ellen's city, I went to visit her in person. She was dressed in what I learned was her normal work outfit, which was so casual it was hard for me to tell if she was wearing her pajamas or a sweat suit. Ellen told me she was nervous about an important meeting the next week when she would be interacting with some key company decision makers. I asked her a number of questions about the meeting and why she was nervous. I then stuck my neck out and suggested that she go to a local department store

(Continued)

and ask the personal shopper to help her "dress like a banker." Ellen was taken aback by my suggestion and, I think, a little offended. But after we talked for a while, she agreed, and she attended the meeting dressed in a professional manner.

After the meeting, she reported to me that she had received very positive reactions to her participation and had even been complimented by one of her supervisors. I don't know how much of the change was the result of Ellen's clothing, her increased self-confidence because of her new "look," or an alignment of the stars. What I do know is that Ellen started dressing "like a banker" every day, and I never again heard that she was being criticized as sloppy or disorganized.

Ellen's story is interesting in itself, but the most telling thing to come out of that workshop is what I learned afterward. Several female participants criticized my presentation to people who had not been at the workshop. These women said that I had advised Ellen to be inauthentic and to buy into traditional stereotypes. After hearing this, I had two distinct reactions. First, I realized I had not done a good job of communicating my message during that workshop. Although I have spent much of my professional life working with women to develop effective ways to overcome biases resulting from gender stereotypes, I must have come across as insensitive to issues of personal integrity and insufficiently forceful in my condemnation of gender biases. (This was a strong hint that I needed to work on my own impression management.) But my second and more important reaction was one of extraordinary sadness. I realized that the women who had criticized me were unlikely to get as far as they wanted in their own careers if they really thought that a woman would lose her authenticity if she didn't go to important meetings dressed in pajamas. We sell ourselves, our abilities, and our potential by the impressions we make. And her pajama-like attire was not making the impression Ellen needed to make.

A third reason women often resist consciously managing their impressions is because they assume they don't need to. They feel that if they just do a good job, they will be recognized as highly qualified and will therefore be advanced (as they deserve to be). Unfortunately, the workplace seldom operates in this way. Skill, competence, and hard work are certainly necessary for career advancement, but they are usually not sufficient.

Our gendered workplaces are not meritocracies. Consider the skills we identified at the beginning of this chapter as necessary for career advancement: social presence, organizational intelligence, political savvy, *and* impressive job performance. The first three of these skills depend on understanding the impressions you are making and an ability to change those impressions if they are not the ones you want to be making. Decisions about compensation and promotion generally depend on highly subjective judgments about competencies, accomplishments, and potential.[7] If you are going to move up in your organization, you need to be noticed by your supervisors and colleagues as someone with "promotability," someone clearly able to perform at the next level, and someone whose advancement will benefit your company. To be noticed in these ways requires you to manage your impressions. But—and this is the key difference between career advancement for a woman and a man in gendered workplaces—you *must not* be noticed as a woman who runs afoul of gender stereotypes because, as we address in chapter 1, these stereotypes remain powerful. And this also requires careful impression management.

Self-Monitoring

As we argued earlier in this chapter, your ability to effectively manage your impressions depends on acute self-awareness (that is, high self-monitoring).

Andie: During the summer between my second and third year of law school, I worked at a large law firm, enjoying the variety and challenge of my projects and the mix of people with whom I was working. Throughout the summer, I received high praise from many of the partners, so I was shocked when I did not get an offer to work there after graduation. When I asked why, I was told that a senior partner said I would be offered a job only "over his dead body." When I heard this, I was deeply troubled. I had met this man only once for about 15 minutes, and I had handled only one small project for him. As far as I knew, I had done a good job on the project.

I thought back to our brief meeting. When I was called to his office, his door was open, and he was sitting with his feet on his desk and his hands behind his head (one of the high-power posing positions we discuss in chapter 5). I knocked on his office door frame to catch his attention. He turned my way and looked confused. I was young and eager, and I had been told to always shake hands with someone when introducing myself. So, I walked toward his desk, extended my hand, and introduced myself. He stood up and shook my hand. It sort of looked like he motioned me toward a couch in the far corner of his office but I saw two guest chairs across from his desk, and I sat down in one of them. He gave me the assignment. I thanked him and left his office. I did the assignment, and I never gave our 15-minute meeting another thought until I was told I would not work at "his" firm. As I replayed our brief meeting in my mind, the reality of the situation finally struck me. I had totally missed the signals he had given me. By walking toward his desk and extending my hand, I had unintentionally forced him to take his feet off his desk and stand up. (I didn't know that it was considered impolite and rude for a man to shake hands without standing up.) And, by sitting down in one of his guest chairs rather than on the low couch in the far corner of his office, I had come across as

(Continued)

an assertive, pushy, uppity woman. I had been agentic when a large dose of communal behavior had been called for.

As I have recounted this story over the years, I am often asked whether I would have behaved differently if I had been a better self-monitor. Of course. I would have tried to balance my self-confidence with a softer, more deferential style. If I had been aware of the etiquette that would require him to stand up to shake my hand, I would not have extended my hand to him. But I don't think I would have sat in the far corner of his office. I would have been immediately alert to the discomfort and disapproval I was provoking in him. I might not have been able to change the eventual outcome, but I certainly would have better understood how he was reacting to my intentional and unintentional communication.

When you are a high self-monitor, you read the communication cues other people are giving you and adjust your own communication to make the impressions you want to make. You observe the situation to determine "who" you need to be and "how" you need to behave. A low self-monitor is controlled from within by her individual opinions and attitudes, and she is determined to remain "herself" no matter what the situation. It is hardly surprising, therefore, that study after study finds that high self-monitors consistently and decisively beat out low self-monitors for career promotions. High self-monitors advance further, and more often, than low self-monitors, whether they stay at one company or move from company to company.[8]

Al: For many years, I had a partner in my law firm who was an exceptionally talented lawyer. His practice was primarily mergers and acquisitions that involved lengthy and intense negotiating sessions. His negotiating ability was superb: he could ingratiate himself when this was called for, cajole and prod as needed, and storm

(Continued)

out of the room if a threat to crater the deal might win an important concession. Whatever his tactic, however, it was always purposeful and calculated. He was never really angry—or pleased—he
was just working to get the job done.

This partner disagreed with several fundamental firm policies, however. And here—where he should have been at his best as
a negotiator—he was terrible. He would get angry, sarcastic, and
petulant. It got so bad that the other partners didn't want to deal
with him. He eventually felt so isolated, he left the firm. This brilliant lawyer was a very high self-monitor when it came to negotiating on behalf of a client, but when it came to negotiating on his own
behalf, his self-monitoring ability was zero. He simply could not
step back from himself, evaluate what he needed to do to achieve
his personal objective, and control his communications to the
extent needed to do that. It was a very sad situation.

As you move up the career ladder, your job responsibilities shift from
specific tasks to leadership, motivation, and coordination.[9] To be successful
in these higher-level positions, you need to be able to maintain and manage the good opinions of others.[10] Not surprisingly, therefore, successful
senior managers in all businesses and professions are high self-monitors.[11]

Observing Nonverbal Communication

In the remainder of this chapter, we offer a series of observations about
the meaning of specific pieces of other people's nonverbal behavior.
Because nonverbal behavior can be difficult to control, it will often be
your most important source of information about the impressions you
are making on the people with whom you interact. We turn to how you
can manage your nonverbal behavior in chapter 6. We turn to managing
your verbal behavior and vocalizations, including voice tone and pitch
in chapter 7. Here, however, our focus is on your reading other people's

nonverbal communication and what this can tell you about the impressions you are making.

Facial Expressions

Facial expressions typically provide you with the most important clues about people's reactions to you. While there are many facial expressions, six of them are universal, so you need to be able to recognize and respond to them in other people.

- *Anger.* If the people with whom you are dealing are angry, their eyebrows will be lowered, their eyes wide and staring, their forehead wrinkled, and their lips either pressed together firmly or open and teeth clenched.
- *Disgust.* If they are disgusted, the bridge of their noses will be wrinkled, their upper lips raised, and their chins likely to be jutting up.
- *Fear.* If they are fearful, their eyes will be open wide, closed, or looking down; their eyebrows will be raised; and their mouths slightly open or with the corners turned down.
- *Happy.* If they are happy, the corners of their mouths will be raised (with their mouths either open or closed), wrinkles will form at the sides of their eyes, and their eyebrows will be slightly raised.
- *Sad.* If they are sad, the corners of their mouths will turn down, the inner portion of their eyebrows will raise up, and their eyes will be cast downward and might be damp from tears.
- *Surprised.* If they are surprised, their eyes will open wide so you can see the whites, their eyebrows will be raised, their mouths will be open with their jaws dropped slightly, and their heads will be held back or tilted to the side.

The better you know another person, the better you will be at reading their facial expressions. When you do not know a person well, you should be attentive to all aspects of their behavior so that after an interaction you can "read back" into their facial expressions the content you will want to be aware of the next time you encounter them.

Eye Contact

Eye contact is often the surest indication of a positive connection between two people. In the United States, Canada, and Western Europe, direct eye contact is generally recognized as showing attentiveness, honesty, confidence, and respect. Keep in mind, however, this is not the case in many cultures around the world. How people establish, maintain, terminate, or resist eye contact tells you a lot about what they are thinking and feeling. Subject to cultural differences, some messages you should be able to pick up from people's eyes include the following:

- If they look directly at you, they are likely to be sincere or confident in what they are saying.
- If they stare at you for an extended period of time, they are likely to be angry, combative, threatening, or trying to assert dominance.
- If they look up toward the ceiling, they might be deep in thought, trying to recall a prepared remark, or just plain bored.
- If they look down, they are likely to be embarrassed, ashamed, defensive, submissive, threatened, or feeling guilty. Culture often matters in interpreting eye contact or its omission. If people come from a country where eye contact is considered to be rude or disrespectful, looking down might actually be a way of showing respect.
- If they look off to the side rather than directly at you, they might be feeling guilty, something (or someone) has caught their attention, or they are distracted.
- If they look around the room, they are likely to be bored, nervous, or lying.
- If they don't look you in the eye—keep in mind culture is important here—and if they are from the United States, Canada, or Western Europe they are likely to be uncomfortable, insecure, or submissive. They are unlikely to want to offend you.

- If they look up at you with their heads down, they may be coy or confused. If they are also frowning, they are likely to be critical of something you have said or done.
- If they look at a clock, a watch, their phone, or over your shoulder, they may be disinterested, arrogant, or simply looking for someone else.

Smiling

People showing friendliness, happiness, or pleasure are likely to smile. But people also smile for all sorts of other reasons. They might smile to hide their discomfort, embarrassment, apprehension, dishonesty, nervousness, suspicion, anger, or misery.[12] You should be able to identify a genuine smile of pleasure, however, because it will light up their face, extend to their eyes, and wrinkle the sides of their eyes. Because most people can flash a social smile on command, you need to keep in mind that a social or phony smile is not likely to extend to their eyes.

Gender stereotypes can influence the ways in which we interpret and react to others' smiles. Because of gender stereotypes, people expect women to smile more than men, and women are often likely to accept the validity of the stereotype. Therefore, just because a woman is smiling does not mean she likes you or agrees with what you are saying. She might simply be trying to appear likable and pleasant, or she might feel awkward or uncomfortable, be interested in restoring harmony, or be seeking to appease a more powerful person. As a result, it is often much harder to read a woman's smiles than it is to read a man's smiles. You have to pay attention to all of her behavior, what her eyes and facial muscles reveal, and the appropriateness of the smile in the particular context.

Head Nodding

Women frequently nod their heads to show attentiveness, not necessarily to indicate agreement, as it almost always indicates in men. Men typically don't nod their heads unless they agree with what is being said. If a man does not nod his head while you are speaking, don't get flustered or assume he did not understand your points. Continue with confidence and wait for his reaction.

KEY TAKEAWAYS

- *Impression management involves a combination of agentic and communal communication styles.* We address those styles throughout this book.
- *Learn what type of self-monitor you are.* Answer the questions on the Self-Monitoring Scale at https://openpsychometrics.org/tests /SMS/ (accessed November 25, 2019).
- *Authenticity does not require you to stick to one communication style.* Rather, it requires you to remain true to your core values and what you believe in.
- *Improve your level of self-monitoring.* You don't need to psychoanalyze yourself, but you do need to have sufficiently robust conversations with yourself to be able to describe (to yourself) exactly how you feel at any given time. Study how other people react to you in different contexts. If their reactions are not the ones you expect or would like, try a different communication style.
- *Packaging your message is vital.* The objective of impression management is to ensure that your ideas are received as you want them to be understood and that they are considered fairly. This will not happen if you are focused solely on the content of your message. Its packaging is equally important, and that packaging will control the impression you make.
- *Keep in mind the importance of observing nonverbal communication in others as well as in yourself.*
- *Never, ever, believe it is your fault when you encounter gender bias.*

Chapter 5

Your Attitudes Matter

IN SEEKING TO ADVANCE IN a gendered workplace, you need to be prepared to overcome or avoid gender bias in two basic ways. The first is to be noticed as someone who is competent, confident, and capable of handling tasks and situations expected of someone holding a position senior to your present one. The second is to avoid being viewed as a pushy, unpleasant, and socially insensitive woman who is in open violation of traditional gender behavioral norms. There is an obvious tension between these two objectives, for it is hard to get yourself noticed as a competent, effective leader without also being noticed as a woman who is assertive, forceful, and decisive—that is, a woman who is not conforming to the traditional gender stereotypes. The difficulty to manage this tension is one of the primary reasons that so many women are frustrated in their efforts to advance in gendered workplaces. Effectively managing this tension depends on your wholehearted commitment to impression management and a well-developed capacity for self-monitoring, which are qualities we discuss in chapter 4. There are two other aspects of attuned gender communication that are essential: (1) the achievement and display of positive psychological and mental attitudes and (2) the ability to use a variety of communication techniques to shape the impressions other people have of you. We will start to discuss essential communication techniques in the next chapter. In this chapter, our concern is with the four key attitudes needed for career success: grit, a positive perspective on your abilities, a coping sense of humor, and a confident self-image.

Grit

Grit involves perseverance, self-discipline, tenacity, persistence, and fortitude. It is your ability to sustain an effort toward a long-term objective despite failure, adversity, and plateaus on your journey; it is your capacity to pursue a goal without giving up because of setbacks. Malcolm Gladwell, in his book *Outliers: The Story of Success*, writes that grit is one of the few personality traits that is shared by prominent leaders in all fields.[1] People with grit take the long view: they plan and execute, and then if things are not going right reformulate and execute again until they have achieved their objective. Because of the stereotypes and stereotype-driven biases in gendered workplaces, you will need grit to keep moving toward career success despite the inevitable frustrations and setbacks.

Andie: Anne is a very close friend of mine. Many years ago, after spending six years as a public interest attorney, she decided to pursue a new career in private practice. While Anne recognized the importance of the public interest work she was doing, she also realized she was not being intellectually challenged in the way she wanted to be. Employee pension and benefits planning seemed to offer the complex legal work she wanted, so she sent her résumé to every law firm in her city with a significant employee benefits practice. Despite Anne's stellar academic credentials and substantial experience, she did not receive a single positive response.

Anne came to me to discuss her career dilemma, and together we developed a plan to improve her employment prospects. She would read everything she could find about employee benefits law.

(Continued)

She would attend conferences on current legal developments in this area, and she would take all the relevant continuing legal education programs available. After she did this full-time for about six months, she prepared a new résumé that showcased her extensive self-taught knowledge and the seriousness of her commitment.

With her updated résumé in hand, Anne got an interview at one of the premier law firms in Chicago. Because she had no hands-on legal experience with advising clients on benefits law, she knew she would not get a job reflecting her years out of law school. Anne offered to start as a first-year lawyer—without credit or compensation for her six years of experience or her self-acquired knowledge. The law firm hired her, and over time she distinguished herself as one of the most accomplished and prominent benefits lawyers in the country. Eventually, a large multinational corporation lured Anne away from that law firm; she now supervises employee benefits for thousands of corporate employees. Anne has grit.

When we discuss grit, we think of women like Marie Sklodowska Curie, Joanne (J. K.) Rowling, Misty Copeland, Captain Kristen Griest, and 1st Lieutenant Shaye Haver. When Curie was denied a university education in Poland simply because she was a woman, she pursued her studies in secret while working as a tutor and governess to finance her and her sister's education. Curie moved to Paris, studied at the University of Paris, and lived with minimal comforts in an unheated garret. She began to work with her future husband in a cramped, poorly equipped laboratory. By the time Curie received her PhD, she had published more than 30 scientific papers and had been awarded the Nobel Prize in physics together with her husband. Less than 10 years later, she was awarded the Nobel Prize in chemistry. Despite encountering gender discrimination and xenophobia, Curie fearlessly pursued her goals. She had grit.

Rowling began to write her first novel when she was unemployed, recently divorced with a small child, and living in such poverty she received government assistance. She refused to let these difficult conditions define her. Rather than becoming discouraged, Rowling directed all of her energy into accomplishing the central goal of her life: finishing her novel about a school for wizards.[2] Four years later, *Harry Potter and the Sorcerer's Stone* was published to international acclaim, and the rest is history. Rowling has grit.

Copeland, a principal ballerina at American Ballet Theatre, is an unlikely ballerina. She did not start dancing until she was 13—and then only with free classes at the local Boys & Girls Club. At that time, she was living in a motel room with her mother and five siblings. Copeland is an athletic African American woman whose body does not conform to the stereotypical image of a classical ballerina. Nevertheless, she has become not just a ballerina, but perhaps the most famous ballerina in America today. Now in her late thirties, Copeland is the first star ballerina to also become a media celebrity, advertising powerhouse, model, and the subject of a major documentary.[3] Copeland has grit.

In August of 2015, Griest and Haver became the first female graduates of the grueling Army Ranger's training program. Ranger training requires physical strength and speed, but it also requires the passion and stamina to stick with long-term goals. Griest and Haver met the same standards as the 94 men with whom they graduated: hand-to-hand combat, swimming with heavy gear, carrying fallen comrades, and dropping from helicopters. The opportunity to train with the men allowed them to push themselves and expand their capabilities.[4] It is hard to think of anyone with more grit than the two of them.

Not surprisingly, grit was found to be the most important noncognitive predictor of success for women at the 200 largest law firms in the US. In a 2005 study of women's challenges in the legal workplace, including negative feedback from senior lawyers, self-doubts, and the sometimes overwhelming pace and volume of the work itself, researchers found that women with grit navigated these potential obstacles far better than women without grit.[5] The women lawyers who succeeded in the world of big law believed that if they stuck with it, despite frustrations and failures, they would reach their goals—and they were correct. Their success is underscored in a 2012 report by McKinsey & Company that found that resilience—the ability to persevere in the face of challenges and setbacks—is a trait common to successful women no matter what their career path.[6]

But if grit is essential for career success, how do you get it? Not everyone starts out as gritty as Curie and Copeland. To begin, set a clear, long-term goal for yourself and keep track of how you perform in relation to it. Make a plan that you think will get you there and revise that plan whenever necessary. Zealously follow up on what you need to do next to get to your goal. When you don't perform up to your own—or your supervisor's—satisfaction, evaluate why. Don't let anything discourage you. Find out what motivates you, makes you excited, gets you going in the morning. In other words, force yourself to become attentive to the behavior patterns that allow you to keep moving toward your career objective despite adversity and setbacks.

In this regard you may find the Grit Project, an initiative of the American Bar Association's Commission on Women, to be a valuable resource. The Grit Project offers advice and insight to help women pursue their goals despite failures and frustrations.[7] Although the Grit Project was designed to assist attorneys, its exercises and advice are valuable no matter what your career path.

Another useful approach is to think of a person whose grit you admire and then imagine how that person would address a problem or difficulty you are facing. If no one comes to mind, read more about Curie, Rowling, Copeland, Griest and Haver, or another contemporary or historical figure whose persistence and tenacity you particularly admire. Attempting to emulate the actions and thoughts of people with grit can be a strong motivator. Grit is all about not giving up on yourself. To succeed, don't give up on developing your grit.

Positive Perspective

While grit requires persistence in the pursuit of your goals despite adversity, such persistence is difficult to sustain unless you believe that it will eventually pay off. To maintain that belief, you need a positive perspective on your own abilities and capabilities. Specifically, you need to embrace the idea that you will get better—smarter, more sensible, and more skilled—through hard work, challenges, difficulties, failures, and achievements. Psychologists refer to this sort of perspective as a growth mind-set.[8] When you have a growth mind-set, you think about your intelligence, skills, and common sense as personal qualities that you can develop and increase, not as fixed and static. A growth mind-set involves viewing your mistakes as learning opportunities and your frustrations as growing pains. Such a positive perspective allows you to remain focused on your career objectives. With a growth mind-set, bias-driven barriers to your career advancement can take on a more positive aspect: they are not career stoppers but signs of the need for resourcefulness, innovation, and change.

The trick, of course, is to be able to assess what you need to do to improve and what modifications you must make in your behavior for that to happen. There are remarkable people who can do this on their own, but most of us need help, support, feedback, criticism, evaluation, and advice from others. Having your performance critiqued is rarely easy, but when you have a positive perspective on your abilities, you are likely to have the courage to acknowledge your weaknesses, the confidence to avoid responding defensively, and the willingness to undertake needed changes.

Atul Gawande is a highly accomplished surgeon, staff writer for the *New Yorker,* and best-selling author. He had been a board-certified surgeon for about eight years when he realized that his skills had not significantly improved since his third year of practice. He didn't know if he was at the top of his game or just stuck in a rut, so he invited a retired surgeon he greatly admired to observe and critique his performance during a type of surgery he had performed many times.[9] The other surgeon watched and took a lot of notes: he observed that Gawande's elbows were too high, his magnifying loupe restricted his peripheral vision, he was not paying attention to things he should, and much more. When Gawande got the report, he was taken aback by how many things he was doing wrong, but he also realized the other surgeon was right. He had been unable to evaluate his own performance and would never have known how to become a better surgeon without outside help. By deliberately seeking a rigorous evaluation of his performance, Gawande acknowledged that he probably had shortcomings and (more importantly) that he could overcome them and improve. This sort of behavior is the hallmark of people with a positive perspective on their abilities.

In your career, you probably don't need to invite someone to critique your performance, because you likely receive regular evaluations in the form of performance reviews, criticisms of specific projects, and feedback from colleagues and supervisors. If you are not getting this sort of objective, detailed evaluation, seek it out. Candid, objective evaluation of your performance is the most important resource you have for improvement. With a positive perspective on your abilities, you will treasure all the fair criticism you receive.

Humor

A healthy sense of humor is as valuable in your professional life as it is in your personal life. Physiologically, when you laugh or smile, endorphins are released into your bloodstream, reducing stress, increasing your sense of happiness, and improving your ability to cope with difficult situations. Humor can also improve your ability to connect with and influence other people. A person with a cheerful, friendly, good-natured sense of humor is generally seen by others as happy, well-adjusted, and creative. More important for your career, a person with a sense of humor is typically seen as approachable, likable, and trustworthy.

Gender stereotypes foster discrimination, but they also make many career situations extremely stressful. A strong coping sense of humor is a great ally in dealing with this sort of stress. When you inject humor into a stressful situation, you become more self-confident and less hesitant to expose yourself to potentially difficult interactions, performances, and projects.

Andie: Although my name is Andrea, everyone has always called me Andie—except my mother when she was *really* angry with me. As a young lawyer, I was called into a meeting that was already in progress. As I walked into the room, our client (who had his back to the door) said, "Andie is a girl? I can't work with a girl." Rather than taking offense or getting angry, I lightly touched his shoulder, smiled, and said something like, "I think we should start our introduction over again. Don't you?" So I walked out of the room, came back in, shook hands with the client, and proceeded as though nothing had happened. Over the years, I worked with him on several projects, and occasionally we laughed about our first meeting. When I look back, I often wonder what would have happened if my first reaction had been to take offense or get angry, rather than to smile, make a joke, and move on.

Humor allows you to achieve a degree of emotional distance between yourself and the frustrating situations you often encounter in gendered workplaces. Humor provides that emotional distance by revealing the absurdities and ridiculousness of so many manifestations of gender bias. You don't have to laugh out loud or tell a joke, but an amused "Can you believe it?" or even a wry smile can be incredibly beneficial in helping you overcome unfair treatment and mistaken criticism.

Al: Laura, a senior executive at XYZ, had just received a major promotion to replace a man named Joe. She was now in charge of XYZ's nationwide transportation facilities. As she traveled from one facility to another introducing herself and getting to know her direct reports, everything seemed to be going well. When she got to XYZ's largest facility, however, she was introduced to the employees— almost all of whom were men—by a man she later learned was a

(Continued)

close friend of Joe. Laura listened in horror as Joe's friend finished his introduction by saying he didn't think she would be "able to carry Joe's jockstrap." As she took the microphone, the employees were all laughing. After a moment of panic, Laura smiled and said, "Well, I think that's a very good thing, because I certainly wouldn't want to carry Joe's jockstrap." This time there was even more laughter, and Laura proceeded with her brief remarks before a respectful group of employees. Without her humorous comeback, Laura believes she would have faced a long and difficult time trying to establish her leadership. Because of her quip, however, she established herself as someone with a sense of humor who could hold her own in the face of a potentially hostile audience.

To understand a bit more about the benefits of a coping sense of humor, let's look at the common and powerful stereotype that women are not good at math. A 2004 study sought to determine whether a strong coping sense of humor would allow women to do mathematics without being negatively affected by this stereotype. The researchers had a group of undergraduate women complete the Coping Humor Scale before taking a math test. Half of the women were given the math test under conditions that made the math stereotype prominent, and the other half were given the math test under conditions unaffected by the math stereotype. In the conditions of stereotype threat, those women who had a strong coping sense of humor scored higher than the other women. In the conditions without stereotype threat, a sense of humor made no difference in the women's performance. The researchers concluded that a coping sense of humor is of considerable help in minimizing or overcoming the effects of stereotype threat.[10]

In another study, humor was found to be a powerful tool for managing anxiety. Study participants were told that they would receive an electric shock.[11] While waiting for the anticipated shock, some participants listened to a humorous audiotape, while others listened to an unhumorous audiotape. Those participants who listened to the humorous recording were found to have experienced less anxiety while they were waiting for the electric shock than those who had listened to the unhumorous recording.[12]

Andie: I agreed to be interviewed on a live television news program to talk about leveraged buyouts (a popular type of transaction at that time). I was well prepared. The plan was for the interviewer to go over his questions with me for about five minutes before we went live. The scene was hectic and fast moving as I watched the interview immediately before mine. I then shook hands with the interviewer, and we sat down in front of the cameras. The interviewer then said, "We're going to talk about mutual funds." "No," I said, "I was invited to speak about leveraged buyouts." He said, "I don't want to talk about that." The producer yelled, "THREE." I asked if we had three minutes, and I was told, "No. Three seconds."

As a child, I had a recurring dream about getting to school, taking off my winter coat, and finding I forgot to put on my Brownie uniform that morning. When I learned I had three seconds before a live television interview about a topic I was totally unprepared to discuss, my first thought was, "Did I put my clothes on this morning?" I looked down and was so relieved to see that I was dressed, I smiled as I looked up. That was the first camera shot of me: smiling and looking comfortable. I must admit that I have no recollection of the rest of that interview, but friends said I did great. I now purposely use that technique whenever I am in a public situation and start to feel nervous: I remind myself that at least I have my clothes on, I smile, and I proceed forward.

You can use a variety of techniques to improve your ability to use humor to cope with workplace stress:

- Every day identify two or three things that are ridiculous or downright humorous— believe us, they are there.

- Start telling short, amusing stories to your colleagues about ordinary life events. The goal is not to become a stand-up comic, just someone who can turn something sour into something semisweet.
- Develop the habit of finding a humorous aspect to the difficult, stressful, and frustrating events during the workday.
- Listen to humorous skits, monologues, and stories. Identify why they are funny and try using those techniques yourself.

Approaching challenging situations with a humorous perspective allows you to not only maintain a degree of emotional distance but also to see these situations as occasions for innovation and adaptation instead of apprehension and anxiety. Humor helps you get the job done. Jokes and laughter are not necessary, but a wry perspective on yourself and what is happening around you often is. And finally, keep the following comment in mind from Peggy Noonan, former presidential speechwriter and *Wall Street Journal* columnist: "Humor is the shock absorber of life; it helps us to take the blows."[13]

Self-Image

Real career success depends on many things, including an ability to project a self-image that is confident, powerful, creative, and in control. When you are anxious, worried about your ability to perform up to your potential, or concerned you will be seen as less competent than you are, you may find it particularly difficult to project this sort of self-image. In these sorts of stressful situations, it is enormously helpful to have techniques available that will boost your positive sense of self. You can't just tell yourself to project self-confidence. That is likely to be no more effective than telling yourself not to be stressed when you are experiencing great stress.

Fortunately, there are two proven techniques that will—at least for a relatively short period of time—increase your personal, psychological sense of yourself as strong, confident, and capable: mind priming and power posing.

Mind Priming

Our minds are "primed"—that is, conditioned, programmed, prepared, and trained—in all sorts of ways. The stereotypes you hold prime you to think about particular people in particular ways. When you are exposed to rude or cooperative behavior, your mind is primed to behave more rudely or more cooperatively than you would otherwise.[14] Similarly, when you are told that women are not good at math, you are being primed to doubt your ability to do mathematics. In all of these instances, your mind is being conditioned or programmed without your conscious involvement in the process.

You can, however, consciously prime your own mind. For example, you can adopt attitudes and outlooks that are valuable for your career advancement. This sort of conscious mind priming can alter your mind-set, change your frame of reference, or purposely trigger particular psychological associations. Whatever you call it, conscious mind priming works.

One way to prime your mind is to take a short period of time to think in a focused way or write about an occasion when you felt particularly powerful, a time of great happiness, or a particularly impressive achievement you have accomplished. Take five minutes to do this before a high-stakes interview, negotiation, evaluation, speech, presentation, or group meeting. You will perform in a more confident, commanding, and self-assured manner;[15] display more powerful nonverbal behavior;[16] and increase your sense of confidence, optimism, and control.[17] Priming your mind in this way will also reduce your anxiety and stress, and will, therefore, increase the sense others have of you as a confident leader.[18]

A 2012 study showed that participants who had primed their minds by writing about a time they felt particularly powerful were far more successful in negotiating mock business deals than those who hadn't.[19] Initially, many women we coach are highly skeptical about conscious mind priming, but those who try the technique inevitably become committed mind primers.

Andie: I frequently recommend that women prime themselves for power shortly before undertaking a new or particularly stressful activity. The following comments are typical of those I have gotten back from women who have used the technique:

- "I primed before my interview by spending five minutes concentrating, really concentrating, on a time I felt especially powerful. I got the promotion and job transfer I dreamed of. My boss told me that the interviewer said I was the most confident and qualified applicant for promotion."
- "Before a recent interview, I spent 15 minutes drafting a summary of my qualifications for the position and reflecting on my prior career achievements. During the interview I noticed that I was neither nervous nor anxious; I was poised and focused. My rapport with the interviewer felt natural, and our conversation flowed freely. I have never walked out of an interview feeling more upbeat or more positive. And, I got the job."
- "I am usually very nervous going into what I know will be a difficult negotiation. This time, I took your advice and spent five minutes writing down my strengths as a negotiator and why the changes I wanted to make in the contract made sense and were fully justified. I never became nervous or lost my self-confidence. The outcome was exactly what I had hoped for. Thank you so much. It totally works."

Positive mind priming works because the way you "speak" to yourself internally affects the way you see yourself; the way you see yourself affects the way you act; and the way you act affects the impression others form of you. The behavioral changes initially triggered by mind priming are generally short-lived (from a few minutes to an hour), but this sort of intentional self-conditioning can have long-lasting effects. In a study of three-person groups, for example, the one person in each group who had mind-primed was seen as the group leader at a rate nearly twice that expected by chance.[20] Importantly, persons perceived as group leaders are generally given more information and more opportunities to speak than others. Consequently, a perceived leader has the opportunity to perform at a higher level, reinforcing their leadership position. In other words, the "I am strong, I am a leader" mind-set you use to prime yourself for a group meeting can have a lasting effect on your status and influence within that group.

Power Posing

Mind priming is about thinking your way—in a quite specific manner—to more confident and powerful behavior. You can also affect the way you feel about yourself by using your body in a quite specific manner. By assuming and holding certain poses for a short period of time, say two minutes, you can significantly boost your self-confidence, sense of strength, risk and pain tolerance, and the forcefulness of your physical presence.

The use of body posture to increase self-confidence is often referred to as power posing, and its effect is strikingly illustrated by an interesting study. Participants were told to imagine they were about to be interviewed for their dream job. For two minutes, half of the participants assumed a pose identified with high power (think Wonder Woman standing with her legs apart and her hands on her hips), while the other half assumed a pose associated with low power (think sitting with shoulders slumped, arms close to the body, and legs together). The participants were then given five minutes to prepare a presentation. After the preparation, participants made a five-minute speech about their qualifications and why they should be hired. No correlation was found between the poses the participants assumed and the quality of the content of their speeches. Nevertheless, participants who had assumed high-power poses prior to their interviews were consistently rated as more powerful, more confident, and more dominant than the other participants. Moreover, the high-power posers were consistently judged to have maintained better composure, projected more confidence, and presented more enthusiastic speeches than did the low-power posers.[21]

This is such a dramatic result that it is worth focusing carefully on the poses associated with high power and low power. There are good pictures of these poses in Amy Cuddy's 2012 TED Talk—one of the most popular TED Talks in history and one well worth watching.[22] High-power poses include the Wonder Woman pose, the "totally confident pose" (sitting with your feet on your desk, hands behind your head, and elbows spread wide); the "all business pose" (standing and leaning forward with your hands resting on a table and your shoulders square, your chin up, and your eyes straight ahead); and the "victory stance" (standing tall with your legs apart, your head raised, and your arms held in a V high above your head). Any of these poses, held for at least two minutes before a high-stakes situation, can help you feel more powerful, which also means you will feel less anxious, inhibited, or fearful—attitudes that get in the way of performing at the top of your game.

Low-power poses involve restrictive, shrinking postures: sitting hunched or slouched down in your chair, hanging your head low, hunching your shoulders, or standing with your body stooped. Low-power poses can hurt your confidence and sense of presence in high-stakes situations.

Al: I worked with Jasmine, a woman who was trying to transition back into her career. She had gone to several disappointing interviews that did not lead to any job offers. I suggested that before her next interview she try power posing. Jasmine was dubious but agreed to give it a try. She reported that the whole interview process changed for her. She felt more confident, and the interviewer seemed to pick up on this. Instead of the scheduled 30 minutes, her interview lasted close to an hour. Before she left the interview, Jasmine was introduced to several other decision makers, and a follow-up interview was scheduled. She got the job and her career has remained on an upward trajectory.

One study looked at the effect of power posing on risk taking. Half of the participants assumed high-power poses and half assumed low-power poses. All participants were then given $2 and told they could roll dice at even odds either to win $4 or to lose the initial $2. Eighty-six percent of the high-power posers rolled the dice, as opposed to only 60 percent of the low-power posers.[23]

In another study, power posing for two minutes triggered a 20 percent increase in testosterone, a hormone linked to confidence and assertiveness, and reduced cortisol, a hormone linked to stress, by 25 percent.[24] This combination of hormonal changes increases your sense of control, engagement, and capacity. With high testosterone, you behave in a more assertive way; you don't hang back, you aren't diffident, and you don't hide your contributions. With low cortisol, you experience less stress and feel less pressure.

The notion that posture is power should hardly be surprising. Think about nonhuman primates. You know immediately which great ape is the alpha male in the family by the way he carries himself compared to the other family members. Open body postures with confident, bold gestures indicate high power. Constricted, closed-in postures indicate low power. By playing the great ape (in private) before high-stakes professional interactions, you can significantly increase both your confidence and your sense of power.

Andie: Some women were following the principles of power posing long before it had a name. Barb is a friend and a very successful senior manager. She is a tiny woman, and she finds she can be ignored in mixed-gender meetings. When Barb wants to make an important point, she gets up to get a cup of coffee or a glass of water. Then, while she is standing with the drink in one hand, she puts her other hand on the top of her chair and starts talking. Standing in this pose, she is never ignored, and her comments are always given careful consideration. Getting a drink is her excuse for standing up, but once on her feet she remains standing until she has effectively made all of her points.

KEY TAKEAWAYS

- *Determine the extent of your grit by taking the grit test at* https://angeladuckworth.com/grit-scale/.[25]
- *If you want to be grittier, follow Eleanor Roosevelt's advice to "do the thing every day you think you cannot do."* This means stretching yourself and picking yourself up after failures.
- *Belief in the possibility of growth makes it easier to stick with difficult, long-term projects.* Believe in your own ability to get better—smarter, more sensible, and more task-proficient.
- *Develop a positive perspective and a growth mind-set.* Take the mindset test at http://mindsetonline.com/testyourmindset/step1.php.[26] Seek out challenging assignments that involve activities completely new to you, and push yourself.
- *Look at the training tools for the Grit Project to learn more about developing grit and a growth mind-set*: https://www.americanbar.org/groups/diversity/women/initiatives_awards/grit-project/.[27] You don't need to be a lawyer to use them.
- *Use humor to deal with tough situations.* Test your coping sense of humor at http://academic.csuohio.edu/neuendorf_ka/chs.pdf.[28] If it is low, before going into your next stressful situation, read something humorous, listen to some comedy routines, or watch a funny movie or short video on the internet.
- *Prime your mind to increase your self-confidence before high-stakes situations.* Write a few paragraphs about a time you felt particularly powerful or happy.
- *Power posing should become part of your routine before every high-stakes situation.* Even if it feels a little weird, it works. And be sure to watch Cuddy's TED Talk on power posing at http://www.ted.com/talks/amy_cuddy_your_body_language_shapes_who_you_are.[29]

PART III

Conversations
with Others

Chapter 6

Nonverbal Communication

IN CHAPTER 4 WE DISCUSSED the importance of your ability to read the impressions other people have of you as you interact with them. These impressions of you—favorable or unfavorable, attractive or unattractive, likable or unlikable, trustworthy or untrustworthy, competent and confident or sweet but ineffective—result largely from *your* nonverbal behavior, including the vocal aspects of your communication. These behaviors include your facial expressions; your eye contact; your vocal tone, volume, rhythm, and pitch; your rate of speech, articulation, and intonation of words; your posture, gestures, and physical movements; your displays of emotion and attitude. Justified or not, people form immediate and long-lasting impressions of you and your potential largely because of your nonverbal and vocal behavior. Indeed, studies show that people draw roughly 93 percent of the meaning of the message we deliver from the nonverbal signals we display, leaving only 7 percent of what people take away about us from the actual words we use and the substance of what we are attempting to convey. We can break nonverbal behavior down further, with 55 percent of it being visual—such things as body language, facial expressions, and eye contact—and 38 percent of it vocal—such things as voice pitch, speed, volume, and tone.[1] In chapter 7 we address the vocal aspects of nonverbal behavior along with verbal and written communication. In this chapter, we focus exclusively on the interpretation and meaning of nonverbal behavior that is visually perceived—and you do not have a lot of time to get your communication right. According to research from Princeton University, when meeting someone for the first time, we make initial judgments about that person within one-tenth of one second.[2] And those first impressions tend to stick, so careful future impression management is needed to attempt to improve a bad first impression. This is not to say that people's impressions don't change once they get to know you but that it is much easier to assure people have a favorable reaction to you if their first impression of you is exactly the impression you want them to have.

Your ability to use your nonverbal behavior to manage the impressions other people have of you is an essential aspect of attuned gender communication.

Nonverbal Behavior and Stereotypes

The common gender stereotypes are based on the assumption that women are—and should be—communal, that is, nurturing, kind, sympathetic, warm, understanding, and modest. It is useful, therefore, to identify the nonverbal and vocal behaviors that reinforce these stereotypes. Common communal nonverbal and vocal behaviors include speaking in a soft, often high-pitched voice; hesitating while speaking; using incomplete sentences; assuming a closed body posture with hands held close to sides; taking up little physical space; maintaining little direct eye contact; casting eyes downward; leaning forward when listening; nodding to indicate attentiveness; touching the face, hair, or jewelry; rarely interrupting others; infrequently seeking personal recognition; smiling frequently; holding the mouth open slightly; and tilting the head to the side and up.

By contrast, common gender stereotypes are based on the assumption that men are—and should be—agentic, that is assertive, forceful, and authoritative. Common agentic nonverbal and vocal behaviors include speaking in a rapid, low, and firm tone of voice with few hesitations or pitch variations; using full sentences; frequently interrupting others; maintaining an open, upright body posture with arms apart;

gesturing in a calm, controlled, but expansive manner; moving legs and feet apart; maintaining moderately high eye contact; having a relatively neutral facial expression with head held still; leaning back when listening; and nodding only to express agreement.

As long as a woman's nonverbal and vocal behaviors conform (for the most part) to prescribed communal characteristics, she will be viewed as warm, friendly, and socially sensitive—but not suited for hugely competitive assignments or decisive leadership. If her nonverbal behavior takes on significant agentic characteristics, however, the people she is communicating with may become confused, distrustful, and critical. This backlash reaction to agentic women is well illustrated by a 1995 study[3] in which men were found to think that women who exhibited a "high-task style" were less likable, more threatening, and less influential than men exhibiting exactly the same style and delivering exactly the same message. (A high-task style involves nonverbal behaviors that are associated with authority and competence: a rapid rate of speech with a firm tone and few hesitations, an upright posture, a moderately high amount of eye contact, relatively neutral facial expressions, and unobtrusive hand gestures.) There is little indication that things have changed since that 1995 study, for the backlash reaction to agentic women remains strong.[4]

The dilemma, of course, is that women are unlikely if ever to be perceived as leaders unless they use nonverbal behaviors that have strong associations with power and competence, but by exhibiting this sort of behavior, they risk being seen as cold, aggressive, and insensitive.[5] This dilemma is further sharpened because some of the attitudes discussed in the preceding chapter—grit, positive perspective, and a confident self-image—cause women to feel and behave in more powerful and confident ways, and thus display agentic behaviors. As a result, women must find ways to exhibit agentic behavior while deflecting normal backlash by pairing this behavior with communal qualities. In other words, women need to project through their nonverbal behavior competence, confidence, and power and at the same time convey warmth, inclusiveness, and social sensitivity.

In the sections of this chapter that follow, we examine expressions, gestures, and postures (negative behaviors) that can undercut your efforts to simultaneously be seen as powerful, competent, and self-confident, *and* likable, inclusive, and socially sensitive. We then examine the non-verbal behaviors (positive behaviors) that will help you effectively project both the agentic and communal impressions you want. We discuss vocalizations in <u>chapter 7</u>.

Negative Nonverbal Behaviors

Negative nonverbal behavior generally triggers reactions that detract from the impression that you are competent, confident, and capable of leadership. Of course, no single piece of your behavior is ever exhibited in isolation, and you will always be judged on your total gestalt. Nevertheless, you want to avoid the possibility that other people will take one aspect of your behavior and use it to negatively interpret the whole of it. Therefore, the following sorts of nonverbal behavior should always be avoided.

Appearing Weak

Obviously, the last thing you want is to be seen as a woman with low power, little self-confidence, and poor task competence. Nonverbal and vocal behaviors that are typically interpreted as characteristic of a weak person include a soft, hard-to-hear tone of voice; frequent repetitions and false starts; tentative pauses in a presentation; and the use of frequent filler words such as "hum," "perhaps," "uh-huh," or "don't you think." A slumped, closed-in body posture; nervous hand gestures; and averted eyes also imply weakness. Moreover, you can come across as weak if you play with your papers or notes; grip your notes tightly with both hands; rub or wring your hands together; clutch your papers or your laptop in front of your body; cross your arms tightly across your chest; bow your head; close your hands into fists; frequent giggle or laugh; bite or pick at your nails; twist, push back, toss, flip, twirl, or adjust your hair; or play with your watch, jewelry, or a button.

Andie: Charlotte asked me to coach her after she watched a recording of herself giving a speech. Before seeing the video, she had no idea she gripped her notes so tightly and hugged them to her chest, or that she held on to the podium as if she were drowning and the podium was her life preserver. After watching the video, Charlotte realized that her nonverbal behavior was making her come across as nervous, scared, and unsure of herself, and that it was undermining her effort to be seen as a leader within her organization. As we worked together, it didn't take long for Charlotte to get rid of her weak nonverbal behavior. She was quickly able to develop a more confident, powerful approach to giving presentations. She now looks—and feels—very comfortable speaking before a large group.

Like Charlotte, you may not know the sort of nonverbal behavior to avoid unless you are keenly aware of how it both looks and feels. Record yourself speaking, or better yet find a way to get videos of yourself making presentations before groups and at meetings. First watch the recording on mute to assess your movements for indications of weakness: tics, habits, gestures, postures, and expressions that could be sending negative messages about you and your abilities. Then, consider watching the presentation again to examine how your movements combine with your speech to influence how others may see you. Finally, start working to get these behaviors out of your communication repertoire.[6]

Appearing Dominant

Domineering nonverbal behavior is the opposite of weak behavior, but that doesn't mean it is seen as positive. A domineering style involves a rigid body posture; aggressive gestures, such as pointing your finger directly at another person; speaking in a loud, unfriendly voice; maintaining constant and challenging eye contact; having a stern facial expression; making abrupt movements or gestures; and maintaining an indirect body orientation. A dominant style won't convey competence or likability, and it often will make you seem ill tempered and out of control. Although women seldom use a domineering style, be on the alert for any tendencies you might have in this direction—and check them.

Appearing Untrustworthy

Your persuasiveness, influence, and likability all depend on other people trusting you. If your nonverbal behavior leads other people to doubt your trustworthiness, all of your other efforts at impression management will fail. Behaviors negatively affecting others' perceptions of your trustworthiness or sincerity include turning your body away while you are talking to someone; talking or fidgeting during meetings or negotiations; and looking around the room instead of at the people with whom you are interacting. Significantly, this sort of "Can she be trusted?" behavior is precisely the sort of behavior you are likely to exhibit if you are anxious or unsure of yourself. This is one more reason why a confident self-image is so important. When you lack confidence in what you are saying or doing, you can be viewed not just as tentative and uncertain—but also as untrustworthy.

Positive Nonverbal Behaviors

As we have emphasized several times, the successful path through the many "too hot/too cold/rarely just right" dilemmas women face involves presenting yourself as competent *and* likable, powerful *and* warm, forceful *and* inclusive. Nonverbal and vocal behaviors that can accomplish these dual objectives include the following:

- *Your voice:* moderate volume, no extreme changes in tone or pitch, and few pauses and hesitations.

- *Your body language:* relaxed and open posture with calm, inclusive hand gestures that are smooth, natural, and not exaggerated; leaning slightly forward to listen; and not fidgeting.
- *Your eyes:* moderate eye contact, not looking down or wandering. If you are in a group of people, making eye contact with each person.
- *Your head:* held with chin slightly up.
- *Your facial expression:* warm and pleasant with frequent (but genuine) smiles and obvious attention.
- *Your mirroring:* lean forward if the other person leans forward; lean back if the other person leans back; speak at the same rate and pitch as the other person. (Mirroring is discussed later in this chapter in greater detail.)

Specific Situations and Interactions

By looking closely at a variety of specific sorts of nonverbal behavior, you can get a better sense of how you can project competence and social sensitivity.

Using Space

Power, status, and confidence are all associated with the use of physical space, with the highest-status men tending to take up the most space. Women tend to take up less space than men do, and women generally are quicker than men to retreat from the space they are occupying to make room for others. Imagine a group of people sitting around a conference table. Even if no one is speaking yet, you can probably identify the important people by the way they sit, their position at the table, and the amount of space they take up. These are all nonverbal signals of importance.

Your ability to make an impression as a person of confidence and importance will be enhanced if you develop the habit of claiming space at the table. Take up as much space as the men do. Open up your laptop or tablet. Spread out your papers, and if you have only a few papers, be sure to bring more next time. Spreading out does not mean you are being sloppy, lounging across several chairs, stretching your arms out to the sides, or pushing other people away. It does mean behaving expansively, maintaining an open body posture, resting your arms on the table, and not letting anyone take space away from you. Find a comfortable place to rest your hands. If you are standing, rest them on the podium or the top of a chair or hold them loosely and calmly at your side.

Andie: As a young lawyer, I would bring into meetings every book and piece of paper I thought I might need. I rarely (if ever) referred to them, but they provided me with two things: confidence I had them if I needed them, and an excuse to take up space. I would get to meetings early so I could sit where I wanted and spread out. Even as a young lawyer I never had a problem getting recognized or listened to at a meeting—and I was never told I was taking up too much space.

You should also take up space by using expansive outward arm gestures. Women tend to gesture toward their bodies; men tend to gesture away from their bodies. This makes women seem smaller while men appear to expand in size. Develop comfortable, smooth gestures that move away from your body. When you are standing, keep your arms loosely away from your body, stand tall, and keep your legs comfortably apart. Space is your friend; use a lot of it. Just because you are claiming space—displaying power, confidence, and status—does not mean you should be stern or unsmiling. Given gender stereotypes, you almost always want to project social sensitivity. This means smiling (when appropriate), having a pleasant facial expression, inviting responses to your comments, and actively expressing agreement with other people's ideas when you do agree and when a response is appropriate. Space is power, but in gendered workplaces, you need to use it with warmth and a sense of inclusiveness.

Smiling

We discuss whether to smile or not to smile in chapter 8, "Difficult and Tricky Interactions." As you consider the gendered implications of smiling or not, you should refer to our discussion there.

Listening and Nodding

Women and men tend to listen in different ways. When listening, women tend to lean forward and nod frequently to acknowledge they are paying attention. Men, on the other hand, tend to lean back and are not likely to nod unless they are actually in agreement with what is being said.

> *Andie:* The different ways in which women and men nod their heads were made crystal clear to me many years ago. As I walked out of a meeting with Joe, a senior male colleague, he roundly criticized me for "supporting" the position advanced by the lawyers for the other side of the deal. I was flabbergasted. I had not said a word in support of the other side's positions. I had, however, been nodding during their presentations, simply to show I was listening, not in agreement with what was being said. But my nodding had confused Joe. He would never have nodded unless he agreed with what was actually being said.

Andie's story does not mean that as a woman you should never nod except when you are in agreement with the speaker. By nodding, you can positively influence other speakers—encouraging them, engendering hope of agreement, and promoting a positive regard for yourself. Using head nodding selectively, therefore, is an effective technique for managing the impressions you make. By nodding occasionally when another person is talking, you can build rapport, enhance trust, and soften nonverbal behavior projecting competence and power. The key here is to understand why you are nodding. You never want to look like a bobblehead doll.

Al: After reading Andie's story, Jenna, a senior litigator, told us that she smiles and nods her head all of the time when she takes depositions or interviews adverse witnesses. This disarms them, and she finds she can get them to say the most amazing things that are helpful to her clients.

Mirroring

Mirroring is when a person's nonverbal and vocal behavior mimics or "reflects" the nonverbal behavior of the other person she or he is interacting with, including posture, facial expressions, and vocal tone or pitch.[7] People who are comfortable together tend to automatically mirror each other. It is likely that you mirror the nonverbal and vocal behavior of close friends and partners. If you pay attention, you will find that you often sit in the same positions, walk in sync, yawn at the same time, and use the same tone of voice while talking to one another.

Mirroring is a nonverbal or vocal signal that you are willing to be social, are part of the "group," share similar attitudes, are not interested in direct competition, are open to collaboration, and are empathetic.[8] Mirroring, thus, tends to increase a person's feelings of affiliation toward the mirroring person.[9] By using mirroring appropriately, it can be an effective impression management technique.

Research about Mirroring

Researchers often call mirroring "dynamic coupling" or "brain-bonding" because it fosters closeness, collaboration, and trust.[10] It also helps promote a deeper connection with others[11] and fosters team building.[12] Service workers who mirror their patrons' nonverbal behavior tend to receive higher tips; employees who mirror their supervisors earn better evaluations.

Being mirrored stimulates the "reward zone" of the brain.[13] This means that when you mirror someone, you cognitively reward them by making them feel good, and in turn they are likely to feel comfortable with you. In fact, some researchers claim that mirroring helps people understand each other on a deeper level—"that mimicking another's gestures and postures may help one to better understand the other's emotional state, allowing one to think in the same way as the other."[14] This means that by mirroring, you can appear more persuasive. Likability, persuasiveness, and the ability to build rapport are often considered to be byproducts of mirroring.[15]

When Not to Mirror

Improper use of mirroring can have negative effects. Consider the following:

- Mirroring sends a message that you are like—or want to be like—the other person. Piotr Winkielman, an authority on mirroring and emotional cognition, notes, "Mirroring of unfriendly or dismissive models can be costly or harm your reputation."[16]
- Mindless mirroring, or mirroring someone other people view as unfriendly or unlikable, could send a signal to those people that you value those negative traits, or that you lack the social intelligence to perceive that those traits are negative.[17]
- Don't use mirroring if you don't understand the dynamics of a particular situation, or if the other person is acting in an aggressive or hostile manner.

How to Mirror

- Mirroring often happens naturally in conversations. Of course, you should apply attuned gender communication here.

- Face the other person and give her or him your undivided attention.[18] Make eye contact and actively listen to the other person. You may occasionally nod or tilt your head as you listen to indicate you are engaged. But keep in mind our earlier comments about nodding.
- Listen to the other person's voice tone and pace. You can match it if you feel it is appropriate. If not, don't.
- Some speakers have a "punctuator"[19]—such as a nod, a raised eyebrow, or a gesture they make when they are emphasizing a point. If you can identify a speaker's punctuator, you can nod or offer an indication of affirmation using the speaker's punctuator when you are in agreement. This can show that you are fully engaged with her or him.
- If you feel you are in sync with another person, try changing your body position or tone of voice to see if they do the same.[20] If so, you've just been mirrored! This tells you that the other person may be open to understanding or accepting your perspective. Now the real negotiations can begin.
- If you want to mirror another person, you will want to remain genuine. (We discuss authenticity in chapter 8.) You need to understand the other person—not just want her or him to understand you—or you run the risk of being perceived as manipulative or inauthentic.[21] Don't try so hard to mirror others that you start to feel stressed. The point of mirroring is to develop an ability to naturally connect with another person—stressing out over whether you're actually connecting won't help you connect.

If you are initially uncomfortable with mirroring, start slowly. Develop your skills of empathy and active listening. Try to understand the other people in your organization and why they hold their beliefs and perspectives. Once you achieve a level of understanding, mirroring will start to feel natural to you. With practice, others in your organization may start to better understand you, your motivations, and your goals.

Hands and Arms

You want to use your hands and arms to emphasize, clarify, and reinforce what you are saying. For the most part, if you keep your hands visible and maintain a straight, open posture, this often happens naturally. We are not fans of prescribing the sorts of hand and arm gestures a woman should use. As long as your gestures are smooth, natural, and not exaggerated, there are many styles of gesturing that can work quite well. If your attitude is one of confidence and competence, your hand and arm movements should take care of themselves.

If you are not satisfied with your normal hand and arm gestures, watch five or six TED Talks by different women you admire. Study their gestures and evaluate the effectiveness of their body movements. When you find a style that is particularly appealing and powerful, incorporate some of its elements into your own speaking style. Practice speaking before a full-length mirror (or, better yet, record yourself): watch the way you move, hold yourself, and gesture. If you are unsure of the persuasiveness of your gestures, ask a friend to critique you as you rehearse a prepared speech.

Handshakes

Assuming social distancing is not recommended, your handshake says a great deal about you. Advising women about the all-important handshake seems to be old hat, but we still find too many women getting it wrong. Your handshake needs to be firm, not viselike or wimpy. When you shake people's hands, briefly grasp their hand confidently, look into their eyes, move your hand up and down two or three times, and release the other person's hand. Your thumbs should be up toward the ceiling and your hands perpendicular with the floor. You are striving to create an immediate impression of credibility, confidence, and power.

Sometimes when you try to make a positive impression with a firm, professional handshake, the other person—almost always a man—has different ideas. Some men automatically grasp the tips of your fingers so that you are forced to give a wimpy handshake (what we call the puppy paw handshake). Other men try to show their dominance by preventing you from shaking hands with your thumb and their thumb on the top, so they flip your hand so that your palm is facing up to the ceiling. Both of these handshakes make you appear weak, powerless, and lacking confidence. When a handshake is not going the way you want, here are some tips to keep in mind:

- If you suspect or can feel that a puppy paw handshake is about to happen, try to firmly direct your full hand into the other person's hand. Sometimes you can prevent a puppy paw handshake by extending your hand firmly and guiding your palm into the other person's hand.
- If the other person tries to flip your hand from the thumbs-up handshake position so your palm is pointing up toward the ceiling, you should try to firmly turn your and his hand back to the thumbs-up position. If you are able to do this easily, great. If not, it is not the time to engage in a wrestling match.
- In either of these awkward handshake situations, a brief and gentle touch of the other person's forearm or shoulder can show that you have confidence even if the handshake itself is not going the way you want.

Forget what you might have been told about women remaining seated for handshakes. If you are seated when someone enters the room and it is time for a handshake, stand up. If you are sitting behind your desk when you want to shake someone's hand, step around your desk so that there is nothing awkward or uncomfortable about your body posture. You don't want to lean awkwardly over your desk.

If you are meeting several people at once, stand so that you face each one squarely as you shake their hands. If anyone tries to shake your hand in a way that makes you appear powerless, do your best to grasp their whole hand and shake it firmly. Follow the tips we suggest above, and remember, there is always the next time.

Based on old etiquette rules, some older men only shake hands with a woman if she extends her hand first. This is yet another reason to always be the first to extend your hand. Don't ever be confused or embarrassed when the occasion arises to shake hands: immediately extend your hand to everyone, look each person in the eye, briefly shake their hand, and smile.

Andie: In a recent workshop, I mentioned that an older man might not shake hands with a woman unless she first extends her hand to him. Several of the women immediately started to laugh with what they told me was relief. They had all been in groups where the men shook hands with each other but did not shake their hands. They had felt slighted and upset. One woman told me she had been so rattled it hurt her performance at the meeting. None of these women had thought to extend their own hands first.

Hugs and Kisses

Assuming social distancing is not recommended, social hugging and kissing are much trickier than handshakes. In a business context, greeting someone you know well might involve a gentle hug or a light kiss on the cheek. Indeed, in the appropriate circumstances, a gentle hug and social kiss can increase your perceived warmth and social standing, thereby increasing your persuasiveness. But there are serious pitfalls in this area, especially after the #MeToo revelations from many women about the scope of unwanted and inappropriate physical contact.

When you greet a business colleague you know well and whom you have hugged and kissed in the past, you might initiate a brief gesture, ending the physical contact very quickly. If you have never hugged or kissed this person before, it is up to you to decide whether the context of the situation and your relationship makes it appropriate to do so. Such an evaluation also depends on your personality, the other person's personality, the context, and the culture of your organization. When in doubt, opt for a handshake and move on. If the other person initiates a social hug or kiss in an appropriate situation, in an appropriate manner, and for an appropriate amount of time, smile and take advantage of the solid connection. If, however, another person initiates an inappropriate or unwelcome hug or kiss, step back or turn around. You can make it clear that you will not stand for inappropriate conduct without making a scene or derailing the business meeting.

Touching

If, when, and how to touch another person in a business setting may be the trickiest of all nonverbal behavior. Again, assuming social distancing is not recommended, a light touch can be one of the most valuable tools you have for exhibiting warmth, social sensitivity, and likability. As with hugs and kisses, however, the pitfalls can be serious. Everything depends on the context, your personality, the other person's personality, your relationship with the other person, the context of the situation, and the culture of your organization.

An appropriate touch in a business setting is a brief, light touch with your hand on another person's arm, shoulder, upper back, or hand. It is never a touch on the face, head, hair, chest, lower back, waist, or body below the waist. In fact, some people are fine with a light touch on their arm, but not on their hand. There are also people who prefer not to be touched at all. Be on the lookout for nonverbal cues as to the receptivity to a touch. In suitable circumstances, most people respond positively to being lightly touched in an appropriate part of their arm or shoulder and for a fleeting amount of time; the trick is to know whether a light touch is suitable and how to do it.

Let's look at some interesting examples of the effective use of touch. A classic study of the effective use of touch involved a researcher who intentionally left a coin in a phone booth (yes, before cell phones, phone booths were quite popular), waiting for the next person to visit the booth to make a call, and when that person left the booth asking if she or he had found the coin. When the researcher lightly touched the other person when asking the question, 96 percent replied honestly; when the researcher did not touch the other person, only 63 percent replied honestly.[22] Another study found that waitresses and waiters who gently touched the arm or hand of their customers received significantly larger tips than those who did not.[23]

These studies demonstrate that touch can be a powerful tool in presenting yourself as a trustworthy and likable person. Nevertheless, as we've already said, you need to be sensitive to the context of the situation and your interpersonal relationship. A pat on a colleague's shoulder as you discuss a difficult professional problem might be a welcome and reassuring gesture. The same pat on a colleague's shoulder when you have just been promoted over that person is likely to be seen as condescending and disingenuous. Keep in mind that a lingering touch can rise to the level of sexual harassment, especially when it is considered in light of other verbal and nonverbal behavior.

A valuable way to use touch is to soften forceful behavior or get more buy-in to a particularly difficult plan of action. You can, of course, use a variety of other nonverbal and vocal behaviors for the same purposes in such circumstances—pleasant facial expressions, a soft voice, inclusive gestures—but a gentle touch might be the most effective technique for increasing the acceptance of your message. A pat on the shoulder, a squeeze of an arm, and a social hug can all express your concern, warmth, and social sensitivity. Likewise, when you ask someone to do something that may be difficult or inconvenient—"I need you to get this done today"—a gentle touch on the shoulder or arm can go a long way toward showing you appreciate the extra effort that will be involved. Keep in mind that a touch can reinforce your message, but you should always avoid it if it is not in sync with your actual feelings or if you are not sure about how the other person will interpret it.

Appearance

Your appearance is probably your single most powerful nonverbal communication tool. We are well aware that the subject of a woman's appearance is a virtual minefield. From experience, we know that any suggestion we might make about clothing, hairstyle, makeup, and accessories will expose us to charges of sexism, being out of date, undercutting self-expression, destroying authenticity, and worse. Your appearance, however, just like every other aspect of your career behavior, carries positive or negative consequences because of the gender stereotypes and discriminatory biases operating in gendered workplaces. As a result, you can get your appearance right or wrong. To put it bluntly, getting it right helps your career; getting it wrong can derail it. Therefore, just as with every other aspect of your behavior, to cope effectively with the gender stereotypes associated with appearance, you need to understand these stereotypes and develop techniques for positively dealing with them.

The double bind with respect to appearance is that a woman who is too attractive risks being viewed as not serious, lacking in competence, and low in power. On the other hand, a woman whose appearance is judged to be too bland, austere, and unattractive risks being seen as unfeminine, cold, and unlikable. As a result, women once again need to play Goldilocks and get their appearance just right.

Your appearance has a number of components: age, physical characteristics, grooming, dress, and accessories. There is little we can say about the first two, but the last three offer a wide variety of possibilities. Notably, this is the area where many women feel that any advice is intrusive, inappropriate, and suggests that they should be inauthentic. When your appearance conveys a sense that you are a person with style, presence, and importance, however, the people with whom you are interacting are likely to view you as competent as well as socially adept, friendly, and likable.

It is useful to break appearance down into two parts: how your appearance affects the way you think about yourself and how it affects the way other people think about you. First, how does your appearance affect the way you think about yourself? In 2012, researchers conducted a study to determine whether behavior is affected by the symbolic meaning your appearance has for you. In the initial part of the study, half the participants wore a lab coat described to them as a doctor's coat, and the other half wore their street clothes. Those who wore the white coat made only about half as many errors on a test of selective attention as the group in their street clothes. In the second part of the experiment, all participants wore a white coat, but half were told it was a doctor's coat and the other half were told it was a painter's coat. The group in the "doctor's coat" did significantly better on a test for sustained attention than the group in the "painter's coat," even though only the descriptors were different.[24]

Not surprisingly, these experiments were designed by Adam Galinsky, the social psychologist whose work we use as the basis for much of our discussion of mind priming in chapter 5. His white coat experiments indicate that your decisions about your appearance—how you dress, groom, and accessorize—should be dictated by the characteristics of the appearance you associate with the sort of impression you want to make. You don't need to focus on specific items of dress or grooming, such as power clothes, hair styles, or types of makeup, but you do need to focus on types of style, such as elegant *or* casual, powerful *or* cheerful, composed *or* relaxed. Once you have done that, you will realize there are a lot of looks that will accomplish your objectives.

Take, for example, three well-known women who have chosen quite different looks for themselves. Sheryl Sandberg, the COO of Facebook and author of *Lean In*, generally wears form-fitting knits, open necklines, and bright colors. Christine Lagarde, the head of the World Bank, wears dark, tailored suits that she accessorizes with bright, patterned scarves and an elegant haircut. In contrast to both of these women, Samantha Power, the former U.S. ambassador to the United Nations, wears a mishmash of clothes without any apparent consistency.

All three of these women are highly successful, confident, and powerful. Yet, the appearances they have chosen for themselves are very different, which is exactly our point. In calling attention to these women, we want to emphasize that there is no right way to dress for career success. The way you dress, groom, and accessorize should be guided by the impression you want to make and your own personal comfort in doing so.

We have not found any specific rules for the look women should strive for in pursuing career success, but we offer three general observations:

1. No two women are alike in their objectives with respect to their appearances. What works for a female coworker may be entirely wrong for you.

2. The look with which you are comfortable will depend in large part on your industry, customers/clients, geographic location, and the culture of your organization. What works in Silicon Valley is unlikely to work on Wall Street.

3. Your appearance objective, similar to your objective with respect to the rest of your nonverbal behavior, is to get the job done. You need to act in ways that facilitate your ability to accomplish the tasks and meet the challenges you face in your career. The same is true with your appearance: you need to present yourself as someone capable of accomplishing what needs to be done to sell the product, close the deal, design the building, lead the project, or whatever it is you are expected to do.

Turning to the way your appearance affects how other people regard you, your objective should be to identify how you want to be perceived and then dress accordingly. This means you need to treat your physical appearance just as seriously as you treat all other aspects of your communication. Once you are clear about the message you want to send about your seriousness, ambition, self-confidence, competence, and, yes, sexuality, then you need to figure out how to dress to convey that message. The impression you want to make will differ based on settings, objectives, and interpersonal relationships. One obvious clue is to observe how others in your industry or organization dress and then decide if you want to fit in or stand out.[25]

KEY TAKEAWAYS

- *Obtain an accurate picture of your characteristic nonverbal behavior.* Approach this in three ways: self-monitoring, directly observing yourself, and enlisting people you trust to critique your nonverbal behavior. Try to use all of these approaches to come to an understanding about the type of person your nonverbal behavior reveals you to be.

- *Find role models.* Carefully observe the nonverbal behavior of women you admire who have influence, trust, and respect. Create a list of nonverbal traits you find most attractive and influential, and start incorporating them into your own nonverbal behavior.
- *Guard against nonverbal behavior that is inconsistent with the message you are seeking to deliver.* Watch a recording of yourself to see whether your behavior is in sync with your intended message.
- *Use positive nonverbal behavior that shows agentic traits: stand tall, use space, and gesture expansively.* At the same time, consciously project the communal traits of warmth, inclusivity, and likability.
- *Smile when it feels comfortable and appropriate.* Refer to our discussion of smiling in chapter 8.
- *You will be seen as a leader if your nonverbal behavior exhibits confidence, competence, power, and warmth.* Your physical size does not matter; it is all about your behavior. Consider Ruth Bader Ginsburg, an associate justice of the US Supreme Court, who is a force of nature. At five feet tall and maybe one hundred pounds, Ginsburg is a brave and principled woman who was turned down for a clerkship on the Supreme Court in 1960 because she was a woman. Ginsburg cofounded the first law journal that focused on women's rights, coauthored the first legal textbook on sex discrimination, and argued several landmark cases before the US Supreme Court, resulting in the end of legal gender discrimination in many areas of American law. In 2009, *Forbes* recognized Ginsburg as one of the 100 Most Powerful Women, in 2015 *Time* magazine named her one of the Time 100 icons, and in 2019 she received the Berggruen Prize for having profoundly shaped human understanding and advancement. Justice Ginsburg is brilliant and articulate. Watch her as she speaks; the woman is a forceful presence and always confident.
- *Dress the part.* Your appearance gives an impression of the sort of woman you are, signaling your ambition, power, competence, and energy. Treat your physical appearance as seriously as you treat all other aspects of your nonverbal communication.

Chapter 7

Verbal, Vocal, and Written Communication

W HEN YOU SPEAK, VOCALIZE, AND write in an articulate, engaging, and friendly way, other people enjoy communicating with you. By doing so, you also present yourself as a competent, confident leader. In this chapter, we present some simple techniques you can use to enhance your ability to speak, vocalize, and write with both strength and warmth. We also identify some communication patterns you should approach with caution or avoid entirely because of the negative impressions they are likely to create.

Your Voice

In speaking, your objective should be to present yourself as an effective leader; capable problem solver; strong negotiator; and pleasant, socially sensitive person. The way you speak can either make this objective difficult or easy to achieve. Consider the voices of two iconic women: Marilyn Monroe and Margaret Thatcher. Monroe's trademark whispering, pleading, singsong voice contributed to her image as sexy, unintelligent, submissive, and in need of protection. By contrast, Thatcher's steady pitch, calculated volume shifts, and use of silences for emphasis marked her as a strong, authoritative, and capable leader. Keep in mind, therefore, that regardless of what you say, your audience will form an impression of you based on how you say it.

Some techniques you can use to project both authority and warmth are a steady tempo, moments of silence, varied volume, and controlled pitch. Stronger, fluent voices stereotypically communicate confidence and are heard as more persuasive than high-pitched, discordant ones. Regardless of the brilliance of the substantive content of what you are saying, if your speech is difficult for others to hear, is halting, involves frequent slips of the tongue, has little variation in volume, or is characterized by repetitions and vocalized pauses, you will find it difficult to make an impression as someone who is competent and persuasive.

Tempo

You should strive to speak at a steady, moderate pace (neither slow nor rushed). When your audience finds your tempo pleasant and easy to listen to, they are more likely to believe you are competent and knowledgeable. Keep in mind that if you talk too fast, you will appear excited, nervous, or uncomfortable, and your audience may believe you appear less competent.[1] On the other hand, if you speak too slowly, you run the risk of boring your listeners or giving a Marilyn Monroe impression: seductive but not very bright.

We have found three techniques particularly effective in helping women speak at an appropriate speed.

1. Match your tempo to the vocal speed of the people with whom you are speaking. By putting yourself in sync with others, you will increase your persuasiveness and enhance your impression as someone who is approachable and socially sensitive. Rehearse a speech with a stopwatch in your hand. A good rule of thumb is to speak at between 140 and 165 words per minute. At this pace, you can comfortably make occasional tempo changes and pause to emphasize your points.

2. Read a book out loud as you listen to a recording of that book read by a professional reader on an audiobook. Match your tempo to that of the reader's.

3. Watch the YouTube video of a speaker you admire, such as the video of Angelina Jolie speaking at the 2009 World Refugee Day,[2] to hear a comfortable, conversational speaker.

Your pace, of course, should depend on the content and context of your topic. When you are introducing a new and complex topic, your pace should be slower than it is when you are presenting a subject familiar to your listeners.

Moments of Silence

Pauses that involve moments of complete silence are an effective way for you to emphasize key points and underscore the importance of your message. There are various ways you can create an effective pause. For instance, when you reach a break between your ideas, you can take a sip of water, look around at your listeners, or glance down at your papers. Whatever technique allows you to pause comfortably is fine. The objective is to give your listeners time to absorb an idea you have just presented before you proceed to the next idea, to allow them to appreciate fully the importance of what you have been saying, or to pique their interest in what you will say next. Imagine a speaker saying, "That project was the most…" then pausing. You would be keen to know what was coming next and, therefore, you would be paying close attention. Pauses are particularly effective between strong parallels (such as, "of the people…by the people…for the people"), after someone has asked you a question, and at the beginning and end of your presentation.

As powerful as a moment of silence can be, many women are reluctant to pause while they are speaking for fear they will be interrupted and lose the floor. In chapter 9, we discuss techniques for holding the floor, so don't let this fear stop you from using controlled silences. When you have a group's attention, you are on stage. This is an opportunity to display your competence, mastery of the material, and the importance of your message. Short silences help you do this because they convey your power and confidence without making you appear in any way aggressive or intimidating.

Tone

You convey a great deal about yourself through your tone of voice. Common vocal tones include frustration, anger, whining, sarcasm, pleading, firmness, friendliness, humor, pleasure, warmth, submissiveness, superiority, excitement, happiness, and sadness. When you have a warm, friendly tone of voice, you make an impression of being an approachable, likable person your listeners can trust and rely on. If your tone is pleading or submissive, you make an impression as someone who doesn't merit their close attention.

Although gender stereotypes allow men in certain circumstances to bark orders, issue directives, and speak in a dominant, insistent tone of voice, this tends to be a highly counterproductive communication style for women. In gendered workplaces, women need to speak in ways that show both strength and warmth. The important point is to be aware of your tone of voice, guarantee that it reinforces your substantive message, and ensure it does not convey something about your attitude or feelings you don't want conveyed.

Volume

Finding the right volume of your speech can be challenging. If you speak too loudly, you may be perceived as aggressive. If you speak too softly, you may be seen as lacking power, competence, or confidence. One technique you can use to find the right volume is to take your cue from the other people in the conversation. Another technique is to record yourself speaking at different volume levels until you find one that seems appropriate and feels comfortable: loud enough so everyone in a medium-sized conference room can hear you without straining, but not so loud that other people find it unpleasant to listen to you.

Whatever your chosen volume level, you should vary it. Without variations, you can come off as monotonous and boring. Increase your volume to emphasize a point or focus your listener's attention, and decrease your volume to draw your listeners in and increase their anticipation. Persuasive speech holds people's interest so they pay attention to what you are saying. By varying your volume, you can do this in a particularly effective way.

Pitch

Deeper, lower-pitched voices, which usually belong to men, are stereotypically thought to be more authoritative, powerful, knowledgeable, and persuasive than higher-pitched voices, which usually belong to women. It is very difficult to change the pitch of your voice, and we generally advise women to speak with their natural voices. You should, however, be conscious of your pitch. In gendered workplaces, try to stay away from your highest registers, and keep your pitch as low as comfortable. If your natural vocal pitch bothers you, contact a voice coach for professional help.

Al: Susan is an excellent architect. She is also a very small woman with a youthful face. Her natural voice is quite high-pitched, and early in her career she spoke frequently in her higher vocal registers. Susan often failed to win major projects because she was unable to present herself as forceful and capable of leading a large team. To address this, Susan knew she could not change her size or facial appearance, but she thought she could change her voice. She hired a voice coach who, over the course of more than a year, helped her learn to speak in a lower register by relaxing her vocal chords and imagining her voice coming from down deep in her throat. Over time, her voice became noticeably lower and deeper. With more confidence in the power of her speaking ability, Susan became more effective in presenting herself as a competent, capable architect. She was awarded more projects, and she is now one of the most sought-after architects in her city.

Range

Your vocal range is the full span of the high and low notes that your voice can reach when speaking or singing. Women's voices tend to start at a higher pitch than men's and to have a larger overall range, which means that women can often unconsciously play into the traditional gender stereotype that women are emotional.

Andie: Over the years, I've frequently attended meetings with male colleagues or clients who later referred to a woman at the meeting as emotional, excited, or even irrational. Even though I had been at those same meetings, in most cases I hadn't seen or heard women being in any way emotional. When I asked my clients for examples, they typically said something like, "Didn't you hear her voice? She was out of control." They assumed that a woman's variation in the pitch of her voice meant she was highly emotional.

Because of the "women are emotional" stereotype, you should be alert to your pitch variations. Don't use a singsong-type voice, and don't drift off into your highest register unless you deliberately want to speak up there.

Undesirable Speech Patterns

The substantive content of what you have to say can be overshadowed by the way you say it. As a result, you want to be alert to the way you are vocalizing your words to assure you do not convey the impression that you are pretentious, passive, or incompetent. Effective impression management depends on banishing such verbal and vocal behavior from your speech repertoire.

Vocal Fry

Vocal fry involves speaking in the lowest possible vocal range with a pronounced croaking or guttural use of the vocal cords. When people use vocal fry, they often extend the pronunciation of words by elongating particular syllables. The Kardashians use vocal fry. Both Jill Abramson, former editor-in-chief of the *New York Times*, and George W. Bush have used vocal fry during public speaking engagements.[3] Abramson's voice, but not Bush's, was labeled as "unusual" by a linguistic researcher.[4]

Our advice about vocal fry, albeit perhaps a little stuffy, is simple: don't use it. Using this speaking style risks that you will be seen as annoying, pretentious, bored, lazy, or immature.

If you are a young woman at the beginning of your career, you already face biases based on your age, experience, and gender. Don't burden yourself further by using a speaking technique that your male superiors (and some of your female ones, too) are likely to find off-putting or worse.

Uptalk

When you ask a question, your sentences typically end with a rising intonation. Uptalk (or upspeak) involves using a rising intonation when making a declaratory statement. Valley Girls popularized uptalk in the 1980s. Women can tend to use uptalk when they don't want to be seen as giving the final word or asserting power or because they want to show solidarity with a particular group of people. Whatever the reason for using uptalk, it is a speech pattern that you should generally avoid. More experienced business and professional people are likely to find uptalk a sign that you lack competence, power, and self-confidence.

There are occasions, however, on which you may want to use uptalk to show your softer, more communal characteristics. Uptalk can be an effective technique, for example, when you want to appear to be particularly inclusive or want to demonstrate that you are fully engaged with the group in a highly cooperative task. Even so, you should use uptalk carefully. In the wrong situations, it can mark you as indecisive, lacking in confidence, and timid.

Andie: Madison is a very successful surgeon who used uptalk, in her words, "to great success throughout college." When she got to medical school and started her professional career, however, she found that her use of uptalk was confusing to other people. When she would end her instructions with a rising inflection, she was not making the positive impression she wanted. When she told her patients things like, "Take two tablets in the morning," they were puzzled. If Madison asked for a scalpel in surgery, she did not want her surgical team wondering if she really wanted a scalpel or if she was seeking their opinion about whether a scalpel was the appropriate tool. So, Madison gradually broke her habit of uptalk. It took time and a lot of practice, but she has found it has greatly improved her communication with her patients and her team.

Tag Questions

Tag questions (or tail questions) turn declaratory statements into questions by tagging a superfluous question onto the end. Here are some examples of this practice:

- "That's a good idea, *don't you think?*"
- "The purchase orders need to be signed by noon, *don't they?*"
- "We should change the marketing plan, *right?*"
- "The customer needs the product tomorrow, *don't you agree?*"

Tag questions can be annoying and confusing, so they should generally be avoided. They suggest you are unsure of your conclusion or need someone to confirm it for you. Phrases such as "Isn't it?", "Don't you agree?", "You know?", "Haven't we?", "Okay?", and "Right?" reduce the force of your statements and give the impression you lack confidence. Moreover, because tag questions suggest tentativeness, they can make you come across as uncertain, poorly prepared, or lacking a take-charge attitude.

Because tag questions, like uptalk, suggest inclusiveness and a rejection of power, there are situations in which you might want to use them to show that you are approachable and that you want others to speak up and join the discussion. In other words, when your objective is to present the communal and welcoming side of your personality, tag questions can be useful. If you are fully aware of what you are doing and believe that a tag question will lead to a better overall result, by all means use it. Otherwise, you are well advised to avoid it.

Indirectness

In a familiar double bind, if a woman speaks in a decisive manner—for example, by arguing vigorously for her point of view—the people she is dealing with may find her overly agentic, lacking in warmth, and decidedly unlikable. On the other hand, if she speaks deferentially and is not proactive, she may come across as communal and likable but not a leader. Because of this dilemma, women frequently use indirectness in an attempt to state their position without coming off as bossy, strident, or aggressive. Most of the time, however, being indirect is a bad idea. You are obscuring your ideas and instructions. Take, for example, the following phrases:

- "Do you think it is too hot in here?"
- "You might want to think about the XYZ line of cases."
- "It might be easier if we lived closer to X."
- "Would you have time to work on the Y project?"

Indirect questions like these create a strong sense of ambiguity, which you should generally avoid.

In addition, being indirect doesn't get you out of the too assertive/

too weak double bind. Instead, it creates the impression you lack confidence and certainty as to what you want. You will be far more effective in navigating this double bind if you are able to project both agentic *and* communal characteristics. Speak clearly and directly, but also smile (when appropriate), maintain a pleasant expression, express warmth, and gesture in welcoming and inclusive ways. Thus, for example, in a pleasant tone of voice and with a smile on your face say, "It's too hot in here," "Be sure to look at the XYZ line of questions," or, "It would be much easier if we lived closer to X." Using indirect phrases is a losing verbal style. As the saying goes, say what you mean and mean what you say.

Undesirable Words and Phrases

There are a number of commonplace words and phrases that may seem innocuous but severely undermine the effectiveness of your communication. Here are some key examples.

"Like"

The use of "like" in grammatically superfluous ways has become ubiquitous, at least among young women and girls. All too often we hear phrases such as these: "We, like, rock." "It's, like, an awesome dress!" "Is this, like, a necessary thing to do?" "You, like, like that guy?" We are aware that some linguists think that the grammatically unnecessary "like" is used as a tool for building relationships and is a genuine linguistic innovation. Nevertheless, we have not been able to find a single example of the grammatically superfluous use of "like" by a Fortune 500 CEO, a senior academic over age 45, or a general in the US military. Consequently, if you frequently add superfluous "likes" to your sentences, you risk the chance that your verbal behavior will be regarded as distracting and even irritating. The grammatically unnecessary use of the word "like" will not advance your effort to present yourself as mature, forceful, and competent.

Self-Deprecation

Women often undermine their own credibility by depreciating the value or relevance of their own ideas. Far too frequently, women in business settings use phrases such as the following:

- "I may be off base here, but..."
- "I don't know if this is helpful, but..."
- "Maybe I'm wrong about this, but..."
- "I'm not an expert, but..."

This sort of self-deprecation likely comes from a woman's desire not to be viewed as bossy or too assertive. This linguistic habit, however, makes you look weak, tentative, and incapable of serving as a leader. Break this habit by listening to yourself—self-monitoring—and choosing what you say for maximum impact.

"You Know"

The phrase "you know" is a filler phrase or verbal tic similar to "um," "er," "ah," "basically," "I mean," "okay," "so," and "et cetera, et cetera." Most people use filler words and phrases from time to time, but there is a reason that professional speakers are trained to avoid them. Filler words and phrases undercut your ability to project an image of competence, authority, and confidence. For example, when Caroline Kennedy sought an appointment to the US Senate in 2008, a reporter from the *New York Daily News* asked her whether she felt that President George W. Bush's tax cuts for the wealthy should be repealed. Kennedy replied, "Well, you know, that's something, obviously, that, you know, in principle and in the campaign, you know, I think that, um, the tax cuts, you know, were expiring and needed to be repealed." In 30 interviews with the *Daily News*, Kennedy used the phrase "you know" more than 200 times.[5] Because of this, she came across as inexperienced, uncertain, and lacking both knowledge and confidence. Not surprisingly, she wasn't appointed to the Senate.

If your verbal communication regularly includes "you knows" or other filler words or phrases, you should work hard to eliminate them. Two techniques we have found helpful are pausing whenever you catch yourself about to use a filler word and memorizing and then reciting fairly lengthy passages. One way or another, "you know" needs to go.

"Just"

Women tend to say "just" more frequently than men. "Just" is another word that sounds weak, seems submissive, and rarely adds anything to a statement. Questions using "just" mark you as tentative and lacking in confidence. Here are two examples:

- "Do you have just a minute?"
- "Can we just stop to just think about this?"

A former Google and Apple executive criticized women's use of "just," calling it a child word, putting the other person in the position of the parent. Ultimately, it conveys a subtle message of subordination, deference, and self-effacement. When you use "just" in a grammatically superfluous way, you weaken and confuse your message.[6]

"I'm Sorry"

Women frequently say "I'm sorry" when they are not apologizing for something they have done but instead wish to express concern or sympathy, to show solidarity, or to build and retain relationships.[7] Here are some examples.

- The boss says, "It's raining"; you say, "I'm sorry."
- The boss says, "Our client is upset"; you say, "I'm sorry."
- The boss says, "We lost the customer"; you say, "I'm sorry."
- The boss says, "Our presentation didn't go well"; you say, "I'm sorry."

However valuable the phrase "I'm sorry" might be in your personal life, it is very dangerous in your career life. Saying "I'm sorry" when you have done nothing wrong suggests you are responsible in some way for whatever has happened. Did you have something to do with that lost customer or unfavorable presentation? If not, respond in a different way.

A woman might also use "I'm sorry" when making a request to avoid being seen as assertive or aggressive. For example, she might say, "I'm sorry, but would you mind answering a few questions?" Using "I'm sorry" in this way is an attempt to appear more accessible, less threatening, and more likable, but this perception does you no good in your career if you are also seen as defensive or unsure of yourself. As a strong, confident woman, you will often need to find a way to soften your image so you are not perceived as rude, abrasive, or pushy. Saying "I'm sorry" is not the way to accomplish this.

"Feel"

Using emotional language may also prevent you from making an impression as a forceful, direct, and competent leader. Think about the impression you would make with the following statements:

- "I *feel* good about the design development."
- "How do you *feel* about the company's decision to pay so much for that property?"
- "What's your *feeling* about this undertaking?"
- "I don't *feel* good about this acquisition."
- "How do you *feel* about the other side's arguments?"

All of these statements and questions are about emotions, not facts or results. No one cares about how you feel about the decision; they want to know what you *think* about it. Emotion-based language plays directly into the widely held gender stereotype that women are emotional and not decisive; they are touchy-feely, not factual.

Emotional language should have a very limited role in your

workplace vocabulary. Use precise action verbs when you express your ideas or ask questions. Stay away from vague emotional verbs such as *feel, want,* and *need.* You should talk (and think) about the issues you face in your workplace in a direct, careful, logical manner. You are after clarity not emotion, strength not neediness, conciseness not effusiveness.

"I"

Starting your sentences with "I" is similar to using emotional language. The problem should be apparent from statements such as the following:

- "*I* believe this plan is a bad one."
- "*I* think our company should move forward with this deal."
- "*I* like the way the new communication system works."
- "*I* wonder if we could talk about the budget."

When you begin a sentence with "I," the expectation is that the sentence will be about you. But these statements are not about you; they are about the idea, the company, and the communication system. Not only do "I" statements confuse your listeners, but they also can be discounted as being merely the way *you* see things.

If you think the plan is a bad one say, "This plan is bad because X." You are not the important thing here; your ideas, skills, and persuasive power are the important things. Put them on display and get the "I" off the stage. In fact, unless you are indeed talking about yourself, drop the use of "I" altogether. In most career contexts apart from self-evaluations and claiming credit for your successes, your language will be more forceful, active, credible, intelligent, and professional if you never use "I."

Written (Mostly Electronic) Communication

When you write, avoid the same words and phrases as you should when you are speaking. As organizations rely more and more on electronic communication—email, text, instant messaging, Twitter, Facebook, other messaging apps, and other social media—you need to be sensitive to the impression you are making with your written words. You can encounter double binds in written communications just as you can in spoken communications. Therefore, many of the principles of attuned gender communication are as relevant when you are writing as they are when you are speaking.

Advantages and Disadvantages of Written Communication

From the perspective of gender stereotypes, electronic communication has drawbacks and advantages for a woman. The drawbacks all concern the risk that your message will be misunderstood. Because so much of communication is nonverbal and vocal, it is difficult, if not impossible, to electronically convey humor, sarcasm, irony, exaggeration, skepticism, disapproval, or deep emotion. This is, of course, also true for traditional business communication, but written business communication generally takes the form of routinized and formal letters. Since electronic communication is much more common and informal, the risks of it being misunderstood are much greater.

On the positive side, electronic communication significantly limits the possibility of discriminatory behavior directed against a woman. Since writers of texts and emails generally take turns responding to each other, men will find it difficult to interrupt a woman or dominate the discussion. A woman, thus, has an opportunity to present her ideas at the length and in the way she wants.

Keep in mind that electronic communication is forever, so you never want to post anything online or write anything in an email that you would not want your current or future employers to see. Don't rely on privacy settings; they don't always work the way you assume they do. Anything potentially embarrassing or that reflects badly on you does not belong in an email or posted on the internet. And remember the information on your business computer and smartphone belongs to (and can be accessed at any time by) your employer.

When working with senior colleagues, don't expect them to conform to your preferred way of communicating. If the style of your senior colleagues is face-to-face meetings, carefully consider the appropriateness of asking to call in to a meeting or participate by Skype, Zoom, or another internet meeting tool. If they email but never text, don't attempt to communicate with them by text. Similarly, if they communicate with customers only by phone and formal written communication, don't send them emails. Many younger employees avoid the phone and in-office visits because they do not want to intrude on others. Unless you have been told by a senior colleague to avoid these communication methods, however, it is best to use them.

Al: Doreen asked a new designer at her marketing firm to set up a call with a client later that day. At about 2:00 p.m., Doreen realized she had not heard back from the designer about the call. Doreen walked to the designer's desk and asked if the call had been scheduled. She was told, "I don't know; I never heard back from my email." Doreen then asked, "Did you follow up with a call?" The designer's response was, "A telephone call? I never thought of that."

Communication patterns, like appropriate work attire, are changing. Since your objective is to be noticed as someone ready to move up in *your* organization, look up, and follow the communication practices used by your senior colleagues. And it is always best to write professionally, use full sentences, and as a general rule avoid abbreviations and emoticons.

Emojis

Since emojis—popular pictograms—were added to Apple computer systems in 2011, they have become a very popular way to communicate over email, text, and social media. In 2019, for example, the number of emojis in global use was estimated to be over 3,000, with more than 700 million emojis used every day in Facebook posts alone.[8] As a result of their popularity, emojis have made headway into the workplace. In July 2019, Statista reported:

- 59 percent of people responding to its survey reported using emojis at work;
- 72 percent reported they were initially hesitant about using emojis in the workplace;
- 78 percent said that emoji use has a positive effect on the likability of the user; and
- 63 percent said that using emojis boosts the user's credibility.[9]

In the proper setting and in the proper context, emojis can provide ways for users to communicate without using words, to emphasize their message, and to provide users with an easier way to express their emotions.[10] It can, however, be difficult if not impossible to determine whether the setting and context is appropriate for emoji use. Moreover, there can be a misunderstanding as to a meaning of the selected emoji, making the user's message ambiguous. The following suggestions were provided in a December 3, 2019, blog post on Hive to better gauge whether emoji use is appropriate for the setting and context of the communication:

1. *Make sure you're using a universal emoji.* There are certain emojis that can mean one thing to one person, and something totally different to another. Make sure you're not using an emoji, or string of emojis, that can mean something inappropriate.
2. *Know your audience.* Sending a crying laughing emoji to your company's CEO might not be the best move if he's serious and buttoned up. On the other hand, sending one to your work spouse (your BFF at the office) might be a better move. Before you send, think about who you're sending it to.
3. *Read the tone of other office messages.* If other people are sending emojis in group messages over Slack or Hive, it's safe to send emojis as well. But if you've never seen an emoji grace your computer at the office, it's best to leave them for text messages.[11]

KEY TAKEAWAYS

- *Use your voice to create the impression you want.* The way you speak can play a far more important role in the impressions you make on other people than the actual substance of your ideas and opinions.
- *Make your vocal communication powerful.* Use relaxed, deep breaths to project your words and speak with power; use your diaphragm, lungs, mouth, and nose when you speak; open your mouth and pronounce your words clearly; and pause at key moments, such as just before or right after an important point.
- *Keep a steady vocal pitch while shifting between louder and softer volumes.* Use inflections to emphasize your points, use strategic pauses, and avoid long speech sequences in your highest voice range.
- *If you are feeling anxious or worried, make a special effort to keep your tone of voice even and your volume moderate.* You want your listeners to focus on the content of your message without being distracted by emotional inflections.
- *Keep your speaking speed under control.* Speak at a comfortable and conversational rate.
- *Be conscious of your tone of voice.* You generally want it to be pleasant and warm, but you need to be sure your tone is forceful and confident when needed. Your tone should never be pleading or suggest submissiveness. A sarcastic tone can turn off your listeners and reveal emotions you might not want revealed to your listeners. To help you sound confident, relax your upper body and shoulders.
- *Mind priming can positively affect your voice, so do a mind-priming exercise (discussed in <u>chapter 5</u>) before an important conversation.*
- *If you don't know what vocal fry sounds like, visit YouTube and watch a video about vocal fry or "The Kardashians Talk Back to Tweets."*[12]

- *Avoid uptalk, a passive voice, hedges, and tag questions that make you sound uncertain about your ideas, positions, and beliefs.* Avoid weak spoken or written language.
- *Speak directly and avoid ambiguity.* Make your points clearly. Speaking indirectly confuses your listeners and hurts your credibility.
- *Avoid self-deprecating statements such as "I may be off base."*
- *Learn to say "I'm sorry" only when you have something to apologize for, not to connect with other people or water down your statements and requests.* Watch how comedian Amy Schumer addresses women's misuse of "I'm sorry" in a recent sketch linked to the article "Try This Experiment If You Say 'Sorry' Too Much."[13]
- *Say what you mean.* Be sure there are no contradictions between the words you use and the vocal and nonverbal messages you are sending.
- *Listen to women you respect in the news and on the internet.* Watch a few TED Talks. Try to mimic their speaking styles. Try this as you look in a mirror or record yourself.
- *If your language is strong, your pace and volume are appropriate, and your tone is confident, then even a thin, small voice can demonstrate power.*
- *Avoid emotional words and phrases such as "I feel," "My gut tells me," and "I have a good sense for this."* It is your ideas that are important, not your feelings.
- *Write professionally.* When sending a written or electronic workplace communication, use full sentences.
- *When in doubt, skip the emojis and abbreviations.*
- *Electronic communications offer you the opportunity to think through your comments and responses.* Take advantage of this opportunity. When speaking directly to someone, your vocal and nonverbal behavior help to ensure that your meaning and intent are clear. In an email, you have only the written words, so write your emails carefully, no matter how casual they are meant to be.

PART IV

Communicating in Difficult Situations

Chapter 8

Difficult and Tricky Interactions

GENDER STEREOTYPES OFTEN LEAD WOMEN and men to interpret their interactions very differently. When this happens, women often end up disadvantaged, confused, and intimidated. Situations as common as getting an assignment, presenting the results of a project, and giving or receiving feedback may each cause misunderstandings and strained workplace relations. Both one-on-one and group interactions carry the same risks. Career dangers may arise from situations ranging from straightforward cases—saying no, apologizing, and handling compliments—to decidedly ambiguous cases—unwanted sexual advances, unflattering rumors, smiling, gaslighting, and intrusive prying into your private life.

In this chapter we identify some potentially difficult and tricky interactions, discuss the problems that gender stereotypes pose in these situations, and offer techniques for using attuned gender communication to prevent or ameliorate these difficulties. We discuss ways to handle meeting dynamics in chapter 9 and to advocate for yourself in chapter 10.

Giving and Accepting Assignments

Women and men tend to give out and accept assignments in different ways. For example, a woman might give an assignment by indirectly giving directions, almost as if she were making a suggestion, making a statement like, "It might be helpful to contact the customer to learn about that," or "You might want to consider this line of cases," or asking, "Would you be available to help me with this project?" A man in a similar situation is likely to be far more direct, making a statement like, "I want you to call the customer tomorrow," "You should carefully review this line of cases," or "I want you on this project next week."

We suspect that when a woman indirectly gives out an assignment, she wants to appear communal and avoid being seen as giving a direct order, or she wants the person accepting the assignment to feel a sense of joint project ownership. These are understandable objectives, but as we've discussed in previous chapters, a person providing indirect instructions runs the risk of appearing weak and uncertain. At the same time, the person receiving the assignment is likely to become confused by the directions or misunderstand the directions. A person (often a man) might misinterpret the woman's instructions as suggestions and fail to follow her instructions. He may decide *not* to call the customer or *not* to include an analysis of that line of cases. When this happens, she is likely to get angry and criticize him because she "told" him to call the customer or analyze those cases. He, in turn, will feel unfairly treated—after all, he thinks she only made a suggestion—and he may complain about her to others, suggesting, "She doesn't know what she wants." Meanwhile, she is likely to criticize him as being inattentive to detail and not very bright. In this example, what started as a straightforward assignment turned into a disaster that could have been easily avoided if the woman had been less concerned about appearing too agentic.

Giving an assignment is not the appropriate time to build camaraderie or create a sense of shared ownership. At *this* time, you need to be explicit and leave no ambiguity about what you want and when you want it. You can build a sense of inclusion as the project moves forward.

Women and men can also communicate differently when they receive an assignment. A woman is much more likely than a man to ask questions when she gets the project: "Should I call the customer directly?"; "Do you want more or less?"; "Are you interested in this or that?"; "When do you need my answers?" In contrast, a man is much more likely to accept an assignment, immediately saying something like, "I've got it. I'll get right on it." He typically wants to appear independent and in control; she wants to be sure she gets it right.[1]

When you receive an assignment, you have two opportunities to make favorable impressions. Your first opportunity is when you accept the assignment. When you get the assignment, portray yourself as a confident and proactive problem solver. Don't ask questions simply because you are nervous, want to make a connection, or want to appear interested. Instead, ask questions that are essential for understanding the assignment. Hold the rest of your questions until you can ask them in a concise, focused, knowledgeable, and organized way. (Some women make a short list of defined questions to ask once they have thought more about the project.) Remember, you want to be seen as competent, efficient, and highly skilled. If you fail to make the right impression when accepting an assignment, it will be very difficult to effectively make a positive impression when you complete it. Your second opportunity to make a favorable impression is when you complete the assignment.

Feedback and Criticism

Women often encounter similar issues in giving and getting feedback and criticism as they do in giving and getting assignments. In giving feedback, for example, many women bury their criticism in positive comments because they don't want to damage their relationship with the other person. A female supervisor might say to a male subordinate something like, "You really handled X great, and you should be very proud of that. But you need to work on Y." She may think that he will understand the important part of her feedback was about his poor performance with respect to Y. The man, however, may hear how great he did with X and discount her problem with Y. Or, he might just think she doesn't know what she wants and simply dismiss her criticism outright. If you find yourself tempted to sugarcoat criticism, ask yourself whether there is any possibility you might be misunderstood. If there is, drop the sugar and give the vinegar straight.

Feedback and criticism are meant to change behavior. Give them directly, firmly, and unambiguously. Focus on the problem or inadequacy— not on the person. Three key objectives in giving feedback or criticism are clarity, neutrality, and temperance.

Clarity requires you to make direct statements that are free of ambiguity and euphemisms. Neutrality requires you to use verbal and non-verbal behaviors that are free of emotion. Finally, temperance requires you to remain calm, even if you are challenged.[2]

Be sure to provide specific suggestions for improvement going forward, offer an opportunity for questions and discussion, and then move on. Use attuned gender communication to avoid coming off as harsh, stern, cold, or unsympathetic.

When you receive feedback or criticism, keep a few important points in mind:

- *Don't get emotional.* No crying, no anger, no wringing of hands, no expressions of despair. These reactions play directly into negative gender stereotypes of women as being emotional, weak, and vulnerable. If you feel that you might not be able to remain calm, excuse yourself, and only return to the discussion when you are certain you can remain calm. You want all the constructive feedback and criticism you can get, but if you react emotionally, your supervisors are likely to go soft on you in face-to-face discussions but raise their concerns later when you don't have an opportunity to directly respond to their comments.
- *Don't get defensive.* Research shows that women are far more likely than men to take criticism of their work as a personal attack. Criticism isn't (or, at least, shouldn't be) a personal attack. If you react as if negative feedback defines you as a person, you will appear insecure and weak. Treat criticism as a learning opportunity, not as an exposure of your weaknesses as a person.

- *Don't grovel and apologize excessively.* Acknowledge what you did or failed to do, say you're sorry when appropriate, ask whatever questions you need to ask, and leave it at that. Don't wallow in regret and self-reproach. What's done is done. You want to make an impression that you are taking the criticism to heart and improving as a result, not that you are remaining stuck on the past.
- *Don't make excuses.* You may feel you have a perfectly reasonable explanation for why the project didn't meet your supervisor's expectations: you were working on another deal; your mother got sick; you misunderstood the assignment; you accidentally deleted your first draft and had to start all over at the eleventh hour, or whatever. It is usually best to not go there, because it could escalate the situation into an even more unfavorable situation for you. Simply accept the feedback and make a mental note of how you might better navigate those circumstances in the future.
- *Don't leave the discussion without fully understanding what you need to do so you don't make the same mistakes again.* Ask enough questions to know what was expected of you and what you failed to deliver.

Disagreements

Workplace disagreements are of various sorts, all of which put you in difficult and tricky double-bind situations. One type of disagreement with a particularly high risk to your career involves arguing with a coworker. Such a disagreement can disrupt or destroy important personal relationships, and along with those personal relationships you can lose valuable career advancement opportunities. You can substantially reduce this danger by following a few basic ground rules.

First, when two men disagree, almost anything goes—short of bodily harm. Neither man runs a substantial risk of negative career consequences. As a woman, however, you are placed in a very different situation in gendered workplaces. You are expected because of pervasive gender stereotypes to be accommodating, nice, and warm—not assertive, forceful, and confrontational. A workplace disagreement, however, forces you to openly violate gender stereotypes. Unless you handle these disagreements carefully, you risk backlash—social or economic reprisal.

Therefore, you need to remain calm and in control of yourself. Do not raise your voice, cry, show anger, or get emotional. Do not become intimidated. Because of gender bias, your objective is for your antagonist (if possible) and all observers to come away with the impression that you are a pleasant, socially sensitive person, open to reason and primarily concerned about the best interest of your organization.

Second, in many ways, a disagreement with a coworker is often similar to dealing with an uncooperative child. Certain sorts of statements only make matters worse. For example, it is simply self-defeating to say, "I am right because I am older (smarter, more experienced, etc.)"; "You're going to do what I say because I am your mother"; or "You can't do that because it is not good for you." You will never reach a constructive resolution by asserting that you see the whole picture and your coworker doesn't; you have more experience with this type of problem than they do; or you are right because you hold a more important position in the organization. If it won't work with a child, it probably won't work with a business colleague.

Third, a disagreement with a coworker with whom you have had frequent disagreements is likely to be less about the substance of your disagreement and more about a clash of your management styles, ambitions, or personalities. Recurring disagreements are particularly dangerous for a woman because they can result in severe punishment and backlash. If you find yourself frequently disagreeing with the same person—female or male—identify the source of the conflict and determine why you dislike her or him (because you almost certainly do). Then look for ways to make your workplace styles, ambitions, or personalities complementary rather than antagonistic. With this additional insight, you might be surprised to find that after you have identified the other person's value and contributions to your team you can work together.

Fourth, whatever the nature of or reason for a disagreement, there are a few things you should never do: call names, disparage the other person's character, use sarcasm or profanity, or point your finger. Try not to let the disagreement get heated, but if it does heat up, don't storm out of the room, bang a book or your fist on the table, or raise your voice. Because of the common stereotype that women are emotional, calm is good; emotion is bad. If you are angry, it's hard to listen, and if you're emotional, it's hard for the other person to hear what you are saying.

Fifth, when a disagreement becomes personal—a test of wills, an attack on someone's competence, or a petty squabble—the risk of a professional backlash is very high. One way to keep your workplace disagreements from becoming personal is by using a coping sense of humor. As we discuss in chapter 5, when you can interact with wry amusement, don't take yourself too seriously, and smile (if not laugh outright) at the maddening, bizarre, and unfair things that happen around you, your disagreements are less likely to become personal. By bringing humor to bear on difficult and stressful situations, you can reduce your negative reactions and increase your capacity to see your adversary's point of view. As we discuss in chapter 5, humor allows you to put emotional distance between you, your coworker, and the disagreement. It can also increase your self-confidence and thus your ability to compromise, offer alternatives, and back down if that is called for. Maintain a strong coping sense of humor; it can be your career's best friend—and a valuable tool in addressing difficult and tricky workplace disagreements.

When dealing with workplace disagreements, you should approach them as occasions for new perspectives and insights—not as occasions for hostility and resentment.

Saying No

Some things should be easy for you to say no to: unwelcome sexual requests, criminal and unethical proposals, and activities that pose a high degree of risk to yourself or others. There are other situations that will come up in the course of your career, however, in which it may not be easy to refuse or it is unclear to you whether you should (or wisely can) say yes or no. We have found three specific situations that pose the greatest difficulties for women in this regard:

1. Requests to perform a task or take on a project that will not contribute in a meaningful way to advancing your career.
2. Requests to perform a task or take on a project that will advance your career but that come at a time when you are already very busy and concerned you cannot take it on responsibly.
3. Requests to change your job position within your organization when the career implications of this change are unclear.

You might not see these situations as having much to do with gender stereotypes or with communicating in ways to avoid gender bias, but your willingness to say no in these situations has everything to do with gender stereotypes. Women are expected to say yes to requests because saying yes is the communal and friendly thing to do, and women are socialized to want to be liked. Indeed, studies show that women say no far less often than men do.[3] For this reason, we believe women are overwhelmingly asked more often than men to staff the administrative and social committees, to take on more responsibilities than they should, and to perform the bulk of the nonessential, not career-enhancing, functions of the business. In our experience, women say yes to these requests far too often. As a result, women can become stuck in dead-end jobs and become frustrated by their inability to attain the key positions they desire.

Andie: Helen, a Hispanic woman, is a principal at a major consulting firm. She came to me for advice when she realized her compensation was substantially lower than that of her male counterparts. She believed she was doing everything right, and she could not

(Continued)

understand how or why this compensation disparity existed. It turned out that she was frequently being asked by her firm to speak before various Hispanic groups and audiences with high Hispanic attendance. Her senior colleagues asked her to accompany them on client pitches where her Spanish-language skills were a valuable selling point. Helen recruited employees for the firm at a dozen business schools in an effort to attract more Hispanics; she served on her firm's diversity committee; and she was responsible for developing and presenting cultural diversity awareness programs for her colleagues. When I reviewed a record of her hours spent on client projects and fees collected from clients she was responsible for, I saw that both these numbers were well below where they should have been for someone at her seniority level.

The problem was clear to me, so I started talking to her about saying no. She cut back on going on client pitches with other consultants unless she would get a share of the billing credit, she stopped participating in most recruiting events, and she ended her active involvement on the diversity committee. She actively sought more internally generated work, and she started making client pitches on her own, making use of her extensive network of important and influential Hispanic businesspeople.

Helen encountered a great deal of pushback at first: "We need to continue to do this," "The firm depends on you," and "You are the only one who can do this." But once her new pattern was established and she was behaving the same way as all of the other consultants at her level, her colleagues stopped asking her to do these "special things" that they valued without compensation. When I last spoke with Helen, she said, "I thought I was expected to say yes. When I did, people always said 'thank you' and told me how great I was. But it was only when I started saying no that my career took off and I began to be recognized as a valuable member of the team." It took a full year, but Helen's compensation went up markedly, and it has continued to increase. She is now a managing director.

When you receive a request to do something that "doesn't count" toward advancing your career, you need to think about several things before saying yes or no. First, where are you in your career? Whether you are just starting out or you are well established makes a difference in your ability to say no. If you have been with your company for less than a year or two and your boss asks you to take on a noncore project, then the request is not likely to be a request but actually an assignment. On the other hand, if you are a fully functioning member of a team with solid accomplishments behind you, you will have considerably more flexibility as to whether to say no. In either situation, however, ask yourself whether saying yes will help you to be successful in your organization. Consider whether saying yes will be useful for your career advancement, provide you with experiences to develop essential job skills, or be personally fulfilling. Unless you answer yes to at least one of these questions, you need to think seriously about saying no.

Second, consider the time commitment involved in accepting the project. Will it take you away from or disrupt your other responsibilities? Will it reduce the time you spend on things for yourself or time with your friends and family? Depending on who asks, your position in the organization, and the strategic importance for your career of accepting the request, you may conclude that you need to take on the project even if it means significantly longer hours on the job and less time while you're working on the project for yourself and your family.

Third, how many other noncore projects are you already handling? If these noncore projects are fairly distributed around your organization, you need to handle your appropriate share. But if these projects are going disproportionately to women or to you in particular "because you are so good at them," then it is time to start saying no.

But what about requests to handle essential or core projects, such as handling a new client project, supervising more customer accounts, participating on a key governance committee, or serving on a product development team? The issues here are far more straightforward than with noncore projects, but you must still consider your position in the organization and who is asking. Beyond that, consider the following two issues:

First, can you accept this assignment without your other work suffering? If your answer is no, then you would be ill-advised to accept the assignment. When the quality of your work declines or you start missing deadlines, your reputation within your organization can quickly deteriorate, and it may be very hard to recover it. If you are not in a position to say no to a request, consider ways you can respond that will allow you to appear anxious to help but unavailable. For example, you might say something like, "I cannot deliver that project next week, but I can get to it the week after." Or you might offer to take a piece of the project but not all of it. At a minimum you can discuss your other projects with your supervisor and ask how you should prioritize your workload.

Second, will accepting the assignment mean you cannot spend the time you want on yourself or with your family? You may need to consider how long this period of shortened personal time will last and weigh the benefit to your career of accepting the assignment against the cost of decreased personal time while you're working on the project. The point here is that a loss of personal time should never be an automatic reason to say no to an assignment request (assuming you are serious about career advancement).

Let's turn now to the last of the three difficult yes-or-no situations: deciding whether to accept an entirely new job or assignment in your organization. This may present the hardest of all yes-or-no decisions. Some of these requests clearly involve moving in a direction that will not advance your career. For instance, if you are an investment banker or a consultant and you are asked to give up direct client contact to fill a staff position, you are being asked to get off the fast track and basically freeze your career. If you are at an investment management firm and are asked to stop making investment decisions and supervise the back office, it is also likely where you will end your career advancement opportunities. In your own organization, you are likely to know the important but dead-end positions. If you are asked to take one of these, you basically have three choices: accept the position and start taking life a lot easier, try to persuade the requester that you are more valuable where you are, or start looking for a new job.

Sometimes, however, it is not at all clear whether a position change will enhance or kill your career. If it is not clear, ask a lot of questions, solicit the opinions of people you respect, search the internet for information, examine the gender of the people in comparable or more senior positions, and take your time deciding.

Al: Caye is a friend at a large accounting firm. She had recently been promoted to manager when she was asked to accept a transfer out of auditing into the office of the firm's CFO. The move would mean giving up the chance to become a partner, but it would also mean more predictable hours and greater job security. When we talked, I tried to probe the depth of Caye's career ambitions. How important was partnership to her? Did she ultimately want to move from public accounting to industry? Did she think about careers outside the financial area, or maybe even running a business herself? Caye was not sure of the answers to any of these questions, but she realized that if she said yes to the job in the firm's CFO's office, she would be cutting off all these other options. She was not willing to do that, so she said no. The firm was surprised but accepted her decision. As far as Caye knows, she is now on track to become a partner in another year or two.

One final word about deciding whether to say yes or no to a request that could affect your career: Give yourself the time you need to consider the answer carefully. Say something like, "Let me sleep on that, and I'll get back to you." Clarify your focus by thinking about the advice you would give to a friend in the same situation.[4] Ask yourself whether the request is being made of you because you are a woman. How would a man in your situation respond? Exactly why were you asked to do this? What is the motivation of the person making the request? Do you think that person has your best interest in mind? Has anyone already turned down the request? What's likely to come next if you say yes? What will be next if you say no?

Saying no to career-affecting requests is never easy, but sometimes saying no is the only way to keep your career on track. If you say no, try not to deliver the message by email or through another person. Find a way to say no in person or over the phone to show respect for the person making the request.

Apologies

What should you say or do when you have missed a deadline, screwed up a project, or upset an important customer or client? Men are likely to resist apologizing because they are likely to view it as a diminution of their power and an increase in the power of the person to whom they apologize. Given this power-shifting perspective, men typically view women who apologize profusely and dwell on their mistakes as weak and powerless.

Most women don't view apologies in this way. They typically view apologies as a way to repair damaged personal relationships due to serious mistakes or lapses, to show respect and empathy, to appear less agentic, or to soften their language when there is a disagreement.

There is nothing wrong with giving an appropriate apology. It can strengthen personal and professional connections, ease conflicts and tensions, and make you more likable. The key here, however, is that when you apologize, it needs to be for something that deserves an apology. In addition, an apology must be done in an appropriate way. Never apologize if you have done nothing that warrants one.

Here are some tips for deciding whether and what type of an apology are appropriate:

1. Not every mistake calls for an apology. Consider whether an apology is expected, whether it will reduce anger or disappointment,

and whether it will promote a more harmonious business relationship going forward. Unless you can answer yes to at least one of those questions, move on and put the mistake behind you.

2. Don't apologize when you disagree with another person's views or ideas. It hurts your credibility and it makes you look weak and insincere. After all, you have nothing to apologize for when you simply disagree.

3. If an apology is called for, you should make it promptly, forthrightly, and sincerely. Look the other person in the eyes, speak firmly, articulate your words without hesitating or mumbling, and be direct and brief. Wait calmly for the other person's response, and as soon as the subject of your mistake has been addressed, move on to another topic without embarrassment or discomfort.

4. An apology is not an excuse. An apology is an acknowledgment of some failure on your part. It should not be an explanation of all the reasons why you made the mistake in the first place.

5. Only apologize to the right person. You don't need to tell your colleagues, "I am so sorry I bungled John's project." Apologize to John and then put your head down, go back to work, and don't make the same mistake again. Emphasizing your mistakes by placing your regret on display makes you appear vulnerable, weak, incompetent, and lacking in confidence. A mistake is not a crime, and shame is not an appropriate emotional response.

6. Consider the position, gender, and personality of the person to whom you are apologizing. If you need to apologize to a senior person (often a man) who has been unsupportive of your career aspirations, then you need to think far more carefully about when, how, and where you apologize than when you apologize to a coworker with whom you have a close personal relationship. Your apology in the first situation is likely to be far more important to your future career than your apology in the second. Even so, just because the situation is difficult, don't put off the apology or give it in an offhand or halfhearted way.

7. Sometimes saying nothing is better than trying to smooth another person's ruffled feathers.

Emotion

A woman enters a minefield when she displays emotion in the workplace. Women are stereotypically assumed to be emotional, while men are assumed to be unemotional. As a result, when a woman shows emotion, she runs the risk of confirming the "women are emotional" and can be seen as an irrational, high-maintenance, and out-of-control female.

A man arguing his position with passion and intensity is likely to be seen as deeply committed to what he believes in. A woman doing the same thing can be seen as overwrought and excessively emotional. A man displaying anger is likely to be seen as justifiably outraged or indignant; a woman displaying the same emotion can be seen as unprofessional or as having "lost it." A man displaying pride at a recent accomplishment is likely to be seen as competent and accomplished; a woman showing the same emotion is likely to be seen as a self-centered braggart. None of this is fair, but the stereotype-driven different perception of emotional displays by men and women is a workplace reality that women must contend with.

To compete for career success you need to use attuned gender communication to show your feelings in ways that allow you to be seen as competent, intentional, and in control, not as irrational, excitable, or unstable. This is easier said than done, but it can be done and simply requires attentiveness and a high degree of self-monitoring.

Smiling

To smile or not to smile can be a double bind. When a woman smiles in a difficult or challenging situation, she can be seen as lacking toughness, courage, competitiveness, or an appreciation of the significance of the situation. For example, in their first presidential debate, while Trump attacked, Clinton smiled. David From, a political commentator for the *Atlantic*, commented by tweeting, "Who told Hillary Clinton to keep smiling like she's at her granddaughter's birthday party?" On the other hand, when a woman does not smile in what others might view as normal circumstances, she is often seen as angry, unpleasant, and difficult to deal with. Again, using Clinton as an example, when she was sweeping the Democratic primaries in mid-2016, Joe Scarborough, an MSNBC commentator, tweeted, "Smile. You just had a big night. #PrimaryDay."

When a woman does not smile *most of the time*, the double bind is made more acute because people—women and men—feel free to tell her she needs to smile. Indeed, an unsmiling woman is often asked such a question as, "Why aren't you smiling?," "What's the matter?," or "What's eating you?"

The topic of women and smiles has recently received a lot of press attention. The following are some examples of articles about women and smiling: "Tyranny of the Smile: Why Does Everyone Expect Women to Smile All the Time,"[5] "Why Do People Expect Women to Smile?,"[6] "Why Do Men Need Women to Smile?,"[7] "When Rude Customers Tell You to Smile,"[8] "What Happens When Women Don't Smile?,"[9] and "How Do You Feel about Being Told to Smile?"[10]

It has become quite popular in recent years for some people to refer to an unsmiling woman's face as a "resting bitch face" or "RBF." An RBF refers to the face of a woman when she is "perceived as angry, irritated, or simply...expressionless. It's the kind [of expression or lack of expression] a person may make when thinking hard about something—or perhaps when they're not thinking at all."[11] Indeed, because of the stereotype of the RBF, a woman often cannot display a neutral—that is, an unsmiling—face without someone (often, but not always, a man) taking offense and telling her she needs to smile.

The smile/don't smile double bind can be difficult to navigate at work. On the one hand, you want to be seen as serious and competent but you also want to appear approachable and likable. Yet when you don't smile, you can easily be seen as unpleasant and disagreeable. When you do smile, on the other hand, you may be seen as likable but not serious or competent. Thus, a woman who does not smile can be viewed as a bitch while a woman who does smile can be seen as a bimbo. So what can you do? How can you use your smile to manage the impression you want to make on the people with whom you communicate?

First of all, go to YouTube and watch several TED Talks or other videos by dynamic and popular women speakers. Pay attention to how they smile to connect with their audience, and how they can become quite direct and serious when they want to emphasize an important point. They manage the impressions they make in many ways, but one of the most important ways is through their use of smiling or not—turning on the warmth and friendliness as appropriate and turning on the seriousness as that becomes appropriate.

Keep in mind that women are most effective in gender-biased situations when they are using a combination of communal and agentic behaviors. Smiling is clearly a communal behavior that can effectively be used to emphasize your welcoming, inclusive style—when this is called for. But when decisiveness and firm action is called for, smiling is out of place and should be avoided. Unfortunately, this dichotomy puts a burden on women that men do not have to bear. Further, because decisive, forceful action is not required *most of the time*, people expect women to be smiling—or at least have a pleasant expression on their faces—*most of the time*. This is certainly unfair but it is a fact of life that women need to recognize. Women might choose *not* to smile except when they are happy, pleased, or proud of what they have accomplished. This is perfectly fine as long as they are aware of the expectations of others and are adept at managing the impressions they give to other people. Our point is only that there are stereotype-driven expectations about women and smiling that you need to be conscious of. Thus, in addition to the stereotypes that women are caring, modest, and diffident, there is a stereotype that women *should* smile.

What should you do when a person tells you that you should "smile more"? Indignation or anger is counterproductive; so is haughtily ignoring her or him. Better is a humorous comeback, such as, "I was not aware you were telling a joke," or, "Perhaps if you were funnier, I would smile more." If humor is not your preferred response, however, you might say something like, "Smile? Why? I'm thinking," also would make your point. If a man has told you to smile more than once, you might consider a direct rejoinder such as, "Telling me to smile is no different from telling me to dress more provocatively, and I consider both a form of sexual harassment." This is a bold move but can be clearly called for if a man's "advice" to smile has become unsettling, annoying, and distressing.

Crying

In our experience, six emotions are particularly problematic for women in the workplace: anger, frustration, resentment, distress, sadness, and contempt. The first five of these—anger, frustration, resentment, distress, and sadness—are fraught with problems in their own right, but they are particularly dangerous emotions for a woman because they can trigger crying, and crying at work is almost always a bad idea. With that said, researchers have found that more than 40 percent of women (compared to less than 10 percent of men) report that they have cried at work.[12]

There are biological reasons why women cry more than men: women have a higher level of the stress hormone prolactin, which is associated with increased tears, while men have a higher level of testosterone, which reduces their tendency to cry. There are also social reasons: when a woman cries, it is seen as a reflection of her tender, caring nature, but when a man cries, he is likely to be seen as weak and lacking masculinity. This socializes women to cry more than men.

Whatever reasons you might have to cry in any given work situation, we suggest you try to avoid doing so. Crying in response to work-related events—a lost customer, or client, extraordinary pressure or stress, a poor performance review, a low bonus, or frustration with the way you are being treated—is likely to reflect poorly on your competence and leadership ability. Such a display of emotion implies that you are weak, unprofessional, and lacking in control and confidence.

Crying is also likely to embarrass other people, making them leery of criticizing you to your face and inviting benevolent sexism: "She needs care and should be handled with kid gloves." Crying over work-related events at work sends the wrong message about who you are, what you are capable of, and what you want to achieve.

Telling you not to cry is not particularly helpful. We have found four techniques that can be effective if you think you are going to cry and don't want to cry:

1. *Rely on your sense of humor.* If something brings you to the brink of tears, it might have a humorous side: a quality of absurdity, incongruity, bizarreness, or just plain silliness. Focus on this humorous side; as they say, it is always better to laugh than cry.
2. *Change your location.* Try not to cry in front of your colleagues; walk around the block, get some exercise, shut your office door, or go to the washroom.
3. *Distract yourself.* Try pinching yourself really hard, concentrating on a time when you were particularly happy, or focusing on an entirely unrelated topic. In other words, shift your attention away from your current distress.
4. *Imagine someone else in your situation.* Think about the advice you would give another woman about how she should behave in this situation. This creates an emotional distance from the problem, allowing you an opportunity to regroup, collect your thoughts, and find a positive way to deal with the situation.

Almost all work-related crying has a common core: a feeling of helplessness. Whether reacting to anger, frustration, disappointment, or resentment, women often cry because they feel they have no control over what is happening in the situation. It can be devastating to feel helpless in the face of hurtful, unfair, or unfortunate circumstances, and crying is an obvious reaction. But if helplessness causes you to cry, you need to gain control of your situation so you don't feel helpless. In other words, change the dynamics of your work relationships through more effective impression management.

One final comment about crying: crying at work is not the end of the world, but you should take steps to ensure you don't get a reputation as a frequent crier. To begin with, figure out why you cried. Do everything you can to make sure it doesn't happen again. Find a way to gain a greater sense of control, and don't worry about people's reactions to your tears. Instead, concentrate on being seen going forward as competent, confident, and warm.

Anger

Anger is not an equal opportunity workplace emotion. Although women and men experience anger with the same frequency and intensity, apart from crying anger is probably the most dangerous emotion for women to display at work. In many situations, a man can express anger without negative consequences ("He was provoked"), while anger can seriously hurt a woman's credibility ("She's out of control"). This difference was well illustrated by a 2008 study in which 110 women and 70 men randomly viewed videos of female and male job applicants. The applicants were actually professional actors who performed one of two scripts: applying for a job and showing anger, or applying for a job and showing no emotion. Participants then rated the applicants as to their suitability for the job.

Angry female applicants received the lowest ratings, were offered the lowest salaries, and scored lowest in terms of competence (knowledge of their fields). Angry women were also viewed as more out of control than angry men. Notably, women who viewed the videos were just as critical of angry women as men were.[13]

Of course, a woman's status within her organization is highly relevant in determining the consequences she will face if she gets angry. An angry outburst by a female CEO is likely to be judged far differently than a similar outburst by an entry-level woman. Nevertheless, female leaders consistently report they must control their anger so as not to hurt their interpersonal relationships, a concern men don't seem to have.[14]

As unfair as this situation is, you should avoid showing anger in the office. If you are angry and don't think you can control yourself, get away: walk around the block, have a cup of coffee, or call a friend. We are not saying that you cannot let others know you are angry, just that you should do so in a controlled, unemotional way: no yelling, screaming, ranting, or cursing. If you want to express your anger, do it deliberately in a calm, forceful tone of voice. Strive to demonstrate your power, confidence, and seriousness. Look directly at the person with whom you are angry, explain why you are angry, and say what you expect to happen in the future. When you are justifiably angry and can control your anger without emotion,[15] you are in a position to make a very positive impression.

Gaslighting

Women who challenge or call out gender bias—whether it is in the form of discriminatory treatment, microaggression, or unwelcome sexual language or behavior—often experience gaslighting.[16] The term gaslighting comes from the classic 1944 movie *Gaslight*, starring Ingrid Bergman, Charles Boyer, and Joseph Cotten. In the movie, Boyer tries to drive his wife, Bergman, insane by turning the gaslights in their home off and on, up and down, and denying that there was any change to the lighting.

When women complain about language or behavior that reflects gender bias, gaslighting is common and is likely to involve being told something like the following:

- "You're too sensitive."
- "You're irrational."
- "Can't you take a joke?"
- "Calm down, you're losing it."
- "I/he/they were only joking."
- "Boys will be boys."
- "You're a man-hater."

- "We're a meritocracy here; no one is judged in a biased way."
- "I don't know what you are talking about."
- "I am not biased; some of my most valuable team members are women."

Let's look at two examples of gaslighting, brought to our attention by women we mentor. In the first example, Ellen told us that she was in a company meeting about the promotion of several candidates. When the discussion turned to a woman that Ellen knew well and thought to be highly qualified, a senior man suggested that the group did not need to consider this woman because she was pregnant and "might not stay at the company." After the meeting, Ellen approached the man in private, telling him his comment was inappropriate and possibly illegal. He replied by telling her she had obviously misinterpreted him and that if she thought he was biased she was imagining things.

In another example, Margret told us that she had been responsible for conducting a workshop for a sizable group of professionals. In welcoming the participants she asked them about their familiarity with the subject matter and explained how the presentation would proceed. Mike, a senior male colleague, spoke to the group next, saying that Margret would have made "a great kindergarten teacher" given the care with which she explained simple matters. After the workshop, Margret took Mike aside, telling him his comments were insulting and demeaning to not just her but also to their audience. Mike told her she "was too sensitive and that kindergarten teachers are the backbone of America."

Gaslighting is a (conscious or unconscious) technique used to make women who complain about gender bias doubt their assessment of ambiguous situations and to question themselves as to whether they are overreacting. As a result, gaslighting can cause women to distrust their own judgment, making them less willing to challenge behavior they believe is offensive or discriminatory.

Because gaslighting is often a response to a woman who is calling out a gaslighter's behavior, women often find it difficult or uncomfortable to double-down and press further about the gaslighter's response to her original comments. Therefore, it can be easy for women to second-guess themselves and doubt the value of continuing the conversation. One way to overcome this reaction is to have a firm grasp of the facts about gender bias in your organization: the number of women in senior management; the disparity by gender in who is getting career-enhancing assignments; the comparative salary levels, promotion rates, and longevity of women and men.

With these facts in hand when you are being gaslit, you can reply by saying something like, "You may have been unaware that your remark/ conduct reflected gender bias, so let's talk about gender bias generally in this company." In other words, one effective strategy for women subject to gaslighting is to shift the focus of the conversation off of the gaslighter's biased behavior and onto the difficulties women in general are having in the organization because of gender bias.

It can be difficult, but don't allow gaslighting to wear you down. Keep raising your hand, asking for leadership opportunities, and pointing out instances of gender discrimination. This may be difficult because gaslighting often occurs repeatedly, but remember to trust yourself and your perception of the events in question. Stay alert for gaslighting, and use every occurrence of it to challenge biased behavior.

KEY TAKEAWAYS

- *A coping sense of humor is very helpful in many of the difficult and tricky situations you face in your career.* Revisit chapter 5.
- *Speak with authority.* When you give out assignments, speak in a clear, direct, and unambiguous way. Explain what you expect to see when the results come back to you.
- *Know when to ask questions.* When accepting an assignment, balance your need to ask questions with your need to appear competent, efficient, and a proactive problem solver.

- *Giving feedback and criticism is an art.* Follow these important guidelines.
  - The other person might not hear criticism buried in positive comments; drop the sugarcoating.
  - Focus on the event or problem, not on the other person.
  - Don't sacrifice your authority by helping a subordinate save face.
  - If your feedback is met with aggression or belligerence, remain focused on making your points with clarity, neutrality, and temperance.
- *It's not personal.* When you are getting feedback or criticism, remember these essential points:
  - Don't take it personally, get emotional, or overreact.
  - Don't get defensive or make excuses.
  - Don't grovel.
  - Don't leave the conversation without understanding what you need to do differently going forward.
- *When disagreeing with a coworker*:
  - Remain calm and in control.
  - Try to find ways to work together and overcome antagonisms.
  - Try to find areas of common ground that will allow you to focus on common objectives.
  - Avoid comments that are likely to make matters worse, such as by saying you have more experience with these matters than your coworker.
  - Turn to your coping sense of humor.
- *Learn to say no.* Try a simple, "No, I can't help with that," or perhaps suggest a later deadline that you will be able to meet.
- *When you need to say no, remember these tips*:
  - Say no as infrequently as you can, so long as refusal is consistent with your career aspirations and the rest of your life. You want to have the reputation as a team player who is available to help out and accept new challenges. Once you have earned the right to say no, say it when necessary to keep your career on track.

- Say no graciously. Practice attuned gender communication and use a pleasant yet firm tone of voice. Don't get cornered into giving an excuse for your unavailability other than that your schedule (or that of your team) will not accommodate another project. Express a sincere, "I'm sorry I am not available to help out with that," but don't turn it into a lengthy apology. Focus on your desire to maintain the quality of your work while meeting other commitments.
- Take time to consider the other person's request so they know you have seriously considered it. Telling the requester you will think about whether you can accept the project can be a good approach, as long as you do not create the false expectation that you will actually accept the assignment.
- Let the requester know that you're involved in many other projects so it does not look like you cannot handle multiple projects.
- Put your boss's and your supervisor's requests ahead of requests from other colleagues who want your help to meet their own responsibilities.
- Carefully evaluate when you say no so you don't appear to be avoiding or shirking your responsibilities.
- Saying no is often a give-and-take process; be prepared for the requester to push you to change your mind. Be prepared to hold your ground.
- When appropriate, explain that by saying no you are protecting your team or meeting a deadline set by others. This allows you to show you are communal and likable.
- Offer to take responsibility for a piece of a project if you want to participate but don't have time to take on the entire project.
- Ask your supervisor to help you prioritize your projects.
- Suggest other colleagues who might be better suited or have more time to handle the project.
- Be alert for compliments with a hidden agenda. If your boss tells you, "I can't imagine what we would do without your help,"

"You're the best," or "I can't thank you enough," beware. Is your boss softening you up to accept another noncore project?

- When saying no, follow this advice.
  - Don't say yes to projects that are irrelevant to your career unless you believe you don't have a choice.
  - Don't be a doormat, good sport, or wimp who always pitches in even if it compromises your ability to deliver required projects on a timely basis.
  - Don't deliver a no, if at all possible, by email or through another person. Say no in person (or on the phone if you can't do it in person).
  - Don't say "maybe" or use uncertain words like "perhaps." Be direct and clear about your answer.
  - Don't act as if you did something wrong by saying no, but be prepared for the requester to play on your guilt.
  - Don't ignore the request or pretend the other person never asked for your help. Where appropriate, check in later to see if the project was successfully assigned. Show you actually care about the project and would have liked to help.
  - Don't be evasive in your answers. You want the requester to respect your decision, not question your justifications.
  - Don't say no because the assignment will be difficult or you don't want to work that hard. Revisit our grit discussion in chapter 5.
- *Use apologies appropriately.* An apology should be given when you have made a mistake or are at fault for something. Don't forget that apologies at work are often part of the power dynamic between yourself and your colleagues.
- *Once you apologize, move on and give it up.* Don't obsess about your mistake, don't keep bringing it up, and don't beat yourself up over it.
- *Don't get bullied or coerced into smiling when you don't want to but keep in mind the smile/don't smile double bind.*

- *Indignation and anger are typically counterproductive.* Sometimes a humorous comeback is far better than offensive behavior. If it is an ongoing situation, a firm response is often required.
- *Don't second-guess your reaction when someone gaslights you.* It can be difficult to make your point again after you are gaslit, but you should give it a try.
- *Turn a gaslighting experience into an opportunity to look at ways to correct gender bias in your organization.*

Chapter 9

Mixed-Gender Meetings

Meetings offer some of your best opportunities to demonstrate your competence and leadership abilities. Although this sounds positive, many women find meetings to be highly stressful and problematic. In a 2014 *Harvard Business Review* survey of 270 female managers in Fortune 500 companies, more than half of the women reported that mixed-gender meetings posed significant problems for them or were a "work in progress."[1] Women tell us they find these meetings uncomfortable because they generally can't break into the discussions. When women do break in, they find they are ignored, interrupted, or challenged; they get little airtime; and their ideas are not acknowledged until they are repeated by a man. Many women find that if they speak with real conviction, they are criticized for being emotional; when challenged, they feel pushed out of their comfort zone. Women often share that they become disconcerted or ill at ease if there is a conflict. They believe that men talk, interrupt, and challenge too much, and that men pay more attention to what other men say than to what women say.

Unfortunately, men typically see what happens in mixed-gender meetings very differently. In the same survey, more than a third of male managers said their female colleagues fail to state a strong point of view, and fully half said that "women allow themselves to be interrupted, apologize repeatedly, and fail to back up opinions with evidence." The men frequently described women as defensive when challenged and prone "to panic or freeze if they [lose] the attention of the room."[2]

In the course of your career, you will be in many mixed-gender meetings with many people who have control over your compensation and advancement. It is essential, therefore, that you be at the top of your game in meetings so you are able to effectively network, display your unique perspectives, and showcase your abilities. You can put a spotlight on your competence, accomplishments, potential, and warmth through attuned gender communication. In this chapter, we discuss practical techniques you can use to do just that.

When to Arrive and Leave

In many organizations, women tend to arrive on time but men tend to arrive early, using the time before the meeting to catch up on business developments, test the waters about issues likely to come up at the meeting, joke with one another, or just to discuss sports or news events. If this is the pattern where you work, make sure you arrive in time for the "premeeting meeting." Be relaxed, conversational, and interested in whatever topics are discussed—whether you are or aren't. You don't need to become a sports expert (if you're not already one) but you want to be seen as one of the team.

Use this premeeting time to get comfortable with your surroundings, to gather information about what people are thinking, and to gain a sense of the interpersonal dynamics of the people who will be at the meeting: the leaders, the followers, the idea originators, and those with whom you are most likely to have difficulties. This time before the meeting can give you an opportunity to discuss your thoughts, show your sense of humor, and engage in vigorous give-and-take. Don't worry if you don't have a chance to participate in this way. Your primary purposes in being at the premeeting are to be seen as a member of the team and to gather information that will help you perform better once the meeting starts.

Just as there is likely to be a premeeting, there is likely to be a postmeeting wrap-up. You want to be a part of this wrap-up. Don't rush off when the meeting ends. If others stick around, you should too. This is a time to deal with conflicts and differences that may have come up during the meeting. It is also a time to foster alliances, learn how others feel about the decisions that were made, and strengthen your professional connections with the leaders and rising stars. Participating in such a wrap-up session is an opportunity to build your network, show your interest in the organization, and make it clear that regardless of what happened at the meeting you have no hard feelings.

Andie: Juliet sought my advice about her stalled career progress at a large pharmaceutical company. She had joined the company on the same day as Dustin. After only a few months, however, Dustin had a lot more contacts than she did and was involved in more high-profile projects. I suggested that she keep an eye on Dustin to get a sense of how he spent his day. Juliet and Dustin were in many of the same meetings, and Juliet realized that while she came on time and left promptly (so she could "get back to business"), Dustin arrived early and was one of the last people to leave. Juliet was puzzled. She didn't understand why her "greater efficiency" was not being recognized, or why Dustin was getting better projects than she was when he was "wasting" all that time. At my suggestion, she started to arrive and leave meetings at about the same time Dustin did. Juliet was amazed at how much "business" was actually conducted pre- and postmeeting. Within a few months, Juliet was working on many of the same projects as Dustin. She told me she would never have believed that pre- and postmeeting times were more important than her original concern for efficiency.

Choose Your Seat Carefully

Leaders tend to sit at the end of the table or in a place where they can see all (or most) of the other attendees. Even if there isn't a premeeting, you should always arrive early enough to pick the seat you want. Don't sit closest to the phone, the doors, the food, or the coffee—let someone else answer the phone, get the copies made, deal with the food, and make sure there is hot coffee. Wherever you sit, be sure you take up as much space as the men do, and resist the temptation to yield the space you have initially claimed. As you sit, hold your upper body erect and your lower body quiet. Use body language that is powerful and expansive.

Interruptions

Having a seat at the table is not the same as having a voice at the meeting and being heard. The number one complaint that women have about meetings is the frequency with which they are interrupted by men, and in most cases their complaint is entirely justified. Researchers at George Washington University, for example, asked pairs of women and men to discuss preselected topics for three minutes. On average, in each of these conversations, the woman interrupted the man just once, but the man interrupted the woman more than 2.5 times.[3] Moreover, researchers from the University of California at Santa Cruz found in a meta-analysis of 43 published studies that the primary reason men interrupt women is to assert dominance and take the floor away from them.[4]

The issue you face at mixed-gender meetings, therefore, is not whether you will be interrupted but how you will deal with the interruptions. You need to hold on to the floor, and it will be difficult to do this if you become intimidated, feel confused, or lose your confidence. For if you lose the floor, you not only lose the opportunity to present your ideas, but you also come off looking weak and lacking in leadership potential.

Stand your ground. Don't let an interruption distract you or make you look uncertain or clueless. Don't let the interrupter bully you. You need to remain polite, calm, and pleasant but firm and direct. By doing so, you are emphasizing that your idea is one that you consider to be important. You are also setting a precedent that you will hold on to the floor. Here are some attuned gender communication techniques for dealing with interruptions:

- Remain confident.
- Look your interrupter directly in the eyes. Without raising your voice, in an even tone you should say something like, "Excuse me, John, I am not finished. The point I was about to make is...."
- If this is not the first occasion this person has interrupted you, you might say something stronger, such as, "Bob, I would appreciate it if you didn't interrupt me. You can speak when I am finished."
- If the interruption is a senior person you don't want to offend or embarrass, you might try something like, "Rick, would you mind if I finished my point; it will only take a minute."

Whatever approach you use, you need to respond to an interruption immediately and then continue with what you were saying. We fully appreciate how difficult this sort of direct, assertive response can be. The person interrupting you may have stood up to speak and may be considerably larger than you are, and if it's a man, his voice is probably louder and deeper than yours. Nevertheless, when you are interrupted by someone intent on taking the floor away from you—and not seeking a clarification or asking you a question—your confidence, determination, and leadership capacity are being tested in front of the other participants. With the right perspective on your abilities—the sort of perspective we discuss in chapter 5—you can develop the strength and determination, mixed with a good deal of pleasantness, to hold the floor when someone tries to take it away from you.

Dealing with a male interrupter may be particularly difficult because of gender stereotypes, especially in gendered workplaces. When you assert yourself in an effort to hold the floor, you risk being seen as aggressive and unpleasant. If you give up the floor, however, you are likely to be seen as pleasant and likable but not qualified for the competitive world of senior leadership. So here again is the familiar Goldilocks Dilemma: a woman is seen as too tough or too soft, rarely just right. As in other double-bind situations, the only way you can make the impression of being strong *and* likable is through a mix of agentic and communal verbal and nonverbal behaviors. In other words, you need to use attuned gender communication. When you tell John, Bob, or Rick that you are not giving up the floor, use a pleasant tone of voice and maintain an unemotional and nonconfrontational manner. But remember, if pleasant is not working, then it is better to be seen as competent and assertive rather than likable and irrelevant.

There are a number of other ways to prevent interruptions from forcing you to give up the floor:

- Don't pause in a way that provides other people with the opportunity to interrupt you.
- Don't use nonverbal behavior that appears to invite interruptions.
- Keep your volume up.
- Ignore signals that someone wants to interrupt you.
- Don't look directly at people who are trying to interrupt you.
- Use nonverbal behavior to show your power (think power posing).

There is some value in all of these techniques, but in our experience, when someone interrupts a woman to take the floor away from her, the only way she can effectively keep it is to deal with them directly, firmly, explicitly, and calmly.

Of course, in the best of all possible worlds you would not have to deal with interrupters all by yourself. We have known and worked with several very senior leaders who, when chairing meetings, would not stand for floor-grabbing interruptions. In the absence of this sort of leader, however, think about doing the following:

1. Talk with key meeting participants before the meeting starts; share your ideas, develop a strategy to get your points out, and discuss how to deal with interruptions.
2. If you are friendly with someone who will be at the meeting, agree to "protect" each other at the meeting. If either of you is interrupted in an attempt by someone trying to grab the floor, the other person should say something like, "Let her finish," "I want to hear her idea," or "Wait your turn." Finding the right ally can make your meetings much more comfortable and successful.
3. When another woman is interrupted at a meeting, speak up for her. It is much harder for an interrupter to take control of a discussion if they have two people to contend with rather than just one.

These are just a few of the many techniques available to deal with interruptions, but ultimately there are only two rules to remember: don't let the floor be taken away from you; and hold on to it with strength, grace, and humor.

Idea Theft

The classic Riana Duncan cartoon from *Punch* sums up a common problem women often have with their ideas being stolen.[5] Although it's wrong and unfair, men (and often women) tend to pay more attention to what men say than to what women say. A woman can make a valid, interesting, or strategy-challenging point at a meeting and watch the conversation proceed as if she had not said a word. But, as the Duncan cartoon suggests, if her point is later restated by a man, the conversation is likely to take on a new focus, with the man praised for his insight and ingenuity. Once again, in the best of all possible worlds, when this happens, the meeting leader or another powerful person at the meeting would step in to be sure the woman gets credit for her contributions.

"That's an excellent suggestion, Miss Triggs. Perhaps one of the men here would like to make it."

Reproduced with permission of Punch Cartoon Library / TopFoto.

> *Al:* Over the years I have worked closely with Jason, the chair of a professional service firm, who is a stickler for recognizing idea origination. During one meeting I attended, a young associate named Wilma made a good point that was completely ignored until one of her colleagues, Rick, made the same point a few minutes later. Jason looked directly at Rick and said, "Thanks, Rick, for restating Wilma's point. I thought it was a good one too. Now, Wilma, do you have anything more to add?"

Unfortunately, such third-party intervention doesn't happen often. You cannot depend on others to protect your ideas from theft. It is *your* responsibility to ensure *you* receive credit for *your* ideas. When some-one attempts to steal your idea, you have a choice: you can claim owner-ship or remain silent. Either way has risks. Staying silent is safe in the short term, but it is the first step down a slippery slope away from career advancement. Claiming ownership of your contributions, on the other hand, risks backlash through hostility and criticism. But it also displays confidence and competence, two key traits necessary for career advance-ment. Once again, you need to use both your agentic and communal characteristics to successfully achieve the "just right" approach.

Another method of claiming ownership of your idea involves using a coping sense of humor. Laugh and say in a light but even tone, "I am flattered you thought my idea was so good that it deserved to be repeated." Humor of this sort highlights your confidence without expos-ing you to criticism for not conforming to the traditional communal stereotype.

Piling On

Once an idea has been accepted by key meeting participants, others are likely to rush to restate and reinforce the idea. This is commonly referred to as piling on. Unfortunately, it is rare for meeting participants to pile on a woman's idea until it has been restated by a man. Therefore, you should not expect that your ideas will be taken up, repeated over and over, and praised by your male colleagues. As a result, we encourage you to show as much support as possible for the good ideas presented by other women and suggest that they do the same for you. When women openly support one another in mixed-gender meetings, it encourages all of the meeting participants to recognize the value of the woman's initial idea.

The second gendered aspect of piling on is that because women are likely to be uncomfortable or see no point in piling on an idea that has already been endorsed, they run the risk of not being seen as on the team or worse, as contrarians, troublemakers, or pessimists. Be alert to when piling on begins. If you think the idea is sound but a distinction or clarification needs to be made, speak up and make it. If you agree with the idea, say you agree. And if you disagree, be sure to make that known as well. If a consensus is being reached, you should let everyone know that you are firmly on board—or very much off the ship. Do this pleasantly and in a nonconfrontational manner, but make sure to leave no ambiguity as to where you stand on the ideas, actions, and plans that emerge from the meetings in which you participate.

Although it's wise for organizations to encourage and protect dissenting views, if you dissent from the majority view, you may be seen as uncooperative, unlikable, and responsible for disrupting the harmony of the group.[6] You are also likely to face a backlash in the form of criticism, exclusion, and social and career penalties. To avoid or minimize this backlash, be sure to dissent in an articulate, thoughtful, and powerful way that avoids emotional words and projects your social sensitivity and concern for the good of the organization. Use inclusive speech techniques. Ask questions, assent to others' points where appropriate, use first-person-plural pronouns such as "we" and "our," and maintain a friendly and understanding demeanor.

Verbal Challenges

People challenge women during meetings for one of two reasons: to assert power or to test the validity of their ideas and proposals. If you are challenged to justify a point you have made—and the challenge is about the substance of your point rather than about asserting power—you should respond forcefully and articulately to defend your point. Don't back down; don't say, "I'm not sure, but I think…"; and don't give up the floor by saying something like, "It wasn't very important." You have made a point that you thought was important enough to make, so you need to get into the rough-and-tumble to defend it.

Al: I have known Kristen, a forensic accountant, for many years. One day, she told me that she had finished supervising a huge project that involved working with a man, Trevor, she found extremely difficult to deal with. She said that he frequently challenged her proposals and seemed to seek out occasions for confrontation. She doubted Trevor respected her, much less liked her.

A month or so after the project was completed, Kristen attended a cocktail reception with her husband. Trevor was also there and he walked right up to them, shook their hands, and told Kristen's husband, "Your wife is the most accomplished and impressive project team leader I have ever worked with." When Kristen described this incident to me, she said she now realized that their continuous verbal wrestling matches were Trevor's way of testing ideas, exploring possibilities, and verifying conclusions. Kristen told me that she would never be comfortable using such a challenging, confrontational style herself, but she had gained a new understanding and respect for those who do use it, and she is now more prepared to effectively deal with those colleagues. Such verbal challenges allow her to showcase what she knows.

If your ideas are being challenged, collect your thoughts and explain in a firm, calm voice why your proposal makes sense: "The company is not ready for X because…"; "Our division needs a new strategic direction because…"; "That argument won't fly because…" You will never have a better opportunity to play a starring role at a meeting than in response to a verbal challenge. All eyes will be on you, and there is no danger that you won't be heard—unless, that is, you become confused, tentative, or uncertain. This sort of challenge gives you the opportunity to display your talents, confidence, and competitive spirit. While you should not be hostile or nasty, you don't need to try to be seen as pleasant and warm. After all, someone has just attacked your idea or proposal.

Verbal challenges that are not about the substance of your proposal, but rather represent an assertion of power, are not as easy to handle. There are two basic responses to avoid:

1. Don't become emotional. Passion is not your friend. Anger, sarcasm, and contempt undermine your credibility and alienate others.
2. Don't wilt or retreat. This challenge is about taking the floor away from you and nothing else. Any sign of weakness on your part—any sign you are soft, compromising, or defensive—will only encourage your challenger.

Power grabs in meetings are common and are almost always directed against women and low-status men. Your most important ally in fending off such a challenge is your confidence. Before you go into a meeting, assume a power pose and practice mind priming as we discuss in chapter 5. Even though you are dealing with a hostile challenger who doesn't have your best interests at heart, remember that they have given you an opportunity to demonstrate how tough, pleasant, and *prepared* you can be.

Airtime

Despite the stereotype that women talk too much, men tend to dominate mixed-gender discussions. A 2012 study found that men spoke 75 percent of the time at professional meetings even when women and men were present in equal numbers.[7] At meetings women often find they cannot get a word in edgewise, no matter how hard they try. But even in the most gender-biased organizations, you can speak and be heard if you use the right communication techniques.

If you are not getting the airtime you want, figure out what *you* can do differently. If you cannot get your points out, stand up, put one hand on the top of your chair or lean forward with both of your hands on the table, and say in a loud, firm voice, "I have an important point to make."

If you are being interrupted, hold on to the floor. If you are being blatantly ignored, interrupt the dialogue and repeat your point. Airtime is about establishing who the meeting participants believe is worth listening to. You need to find a way to make the other meeting participants *want* to listen to you.

Reaching Consensus

The objective of a typical meeting is to formulate a recommendation or plan of action. Very often, however, women and men want to reach consensus in decidedly different ways. Women are more likely to want to "think out loud" and explore the possibilities from all sides. Men, on the other hand, are more likely to want to formulate a recommendation immediately, wanting to show strength and often believing they have had sufficient opportunity to think through the problem.

Andie: Zineb is one of only three senior women in her department at a major multinational corporation. (There are more than 20 senior men.) When she gets a new project, typically involving a technology innovation, she likes to think out loud with her team about different approaches to the project, exploring the relative costs and benefits of each approach and considering their different time frames and resource utilizations. Zineb recently came to me because she found that this approach made many of her male colleagues (both supervisors and peers) uncomfortable and impatient. After talking about the problem for a while, I suggested that before Zineb thinks out loud about a project or assignment, she should directly ask her colleagues if they would like to brainstorm with her or would rather reconvene after she formulates her plans. Zineb reported back to me that about 25 percent of the time her colleagues (almost all men) say they'd like to brainstorm with her; the rest of the time, they would

(Continued)

rather pick up the discussion when she is ready to proceed forward. Although Zineb is no longer brainstorming with her team as frequently, she has much smoother interactions with them and finds it much easier to get buy-in for her ideas. They know they will have a chance for real input if they want it, but they don't have to "waste" their time if they don't want to.

Although we strongly suspect that the deliberative brainstorming approach produces the best result in most situations, the question is not which is the better approach. Rather, the question is how *you* should behave if this sort of gender tug-of-war is going on. A book based on the 2012 study we mentioned in the section about "airtime" addressed the possibility of an organization or team leader requiring unanimous consent and explicit buy-in from all participants. The authors reported that unanimous consent makes groups more inclusive, allowing more people to speak up. "Women, whose voices tend to be drowned out, got a larger share of speaking time and with it more influence on decision making.... creat[ing] more egalitarian conversational norms and...'dramatic democratic effects.'"[8]

In trying to participate in reaching a consensus, there are some obvious pitfalls you should avoid. Because unanimous consent is not typically required in business meetings, if you try to keep the discussion open after the others have reached a consensus, they may think you are slow-witted, unfocused, or an obstructionist. On the other hand, you don't want to go along to get along. If you have a point that you believe needs to be considered before a final conclusion is reached, then use the communication techniques we discuss in <u>chapters 6</u> and <u>7</u> to make sure your points get the attention they deserve. Just be certain your point is important, not a quibble. Keep in mind that a group of businesspeople who need to make a recommendation must typically compromise. Be willing to move some distance to accommodate the views of the other participants—just not so far that you would not want to be associated with the recommendation.

KEY TAKEAWAYS

- *Schedule enough time.* Attend not just the actual meeting but also the premeeting and the postmeeting wrap-up.
- *Get the attention you need.* If you find it difficult to get the attention you want, stand up. If you find that uncomfortable, use a chalkboard, whiteboard, or flip chart to have a reason to be on your feet. By claiming and holding your rightful share of physical space, you can play against, not into, common gender stereotypes and appear more powerful.
- *Keep the floor.* Consider the following ways to hold the floor:
  - Increase your volume.
  - Talk faster, but not too fast.
  - When you pause to catch your breath, keep your gestures moving to fill the pause.
  - Lightly touch the other person on the forearm if that person is close to you to acknowledge that you have more to say.
  - Lightly pat the other person's arm to suggest he or she needs to wait a little longer.
- *Listen first.* If you are challenged, always listen carefully to the question. Don't hesitate to ask the challenger to repeat the question to be sure you understand it. If you are nervous or anxious, write the question down before responding.
- *Incorporate the question into your answer to help you stay focused*: "You asked me how I got the number for the capital budget. Let me explain..."
- *Don't use weak speech.* Don't say, "I'm just thinking out loud, but..." This sounds weak and suggests that what follows has been poorly thought through, is tentative at best, and can be easily ignored. Consider our suggestions in <u>chapter 7</u>.
- *Don't take verbal opposition personally.* When you are the focus of such opposition, remind yourself that this is usually a linguistic style, not a personal attack. Don't back down; defend your ideas.

- *Jump in with both feet.* Forget the concept of airtime. Don't wait for your turn to speak; it will never come. Come prepared and speak up toward the beginning of the meeting.
- *Put the notebook down.* Don't volunteer to take meeting notes. If you are asked to do it, agree, but arrange with the meeting leader to have someone else take notes the next time.
- *Stick to an agenda.* This can prevent a contentious issue from derailing the central or important issues. Say something like, "Time to get back to the agenda," "We've spent enough time on this topic," or "Next point."
- *Consider whether to brainstorm.* Others might not be comfortable with brainstorming, and they may see this as a weakness. If others are not comfortable with brainstorming, sort your thoughts out on your own before or after the meeting.
- *Consider requiring unanimous consent.* If you are in a position to influence how decisions are made in meetings, remember the research findings that unanimous consent provides for more inclusive groups and more egalitarian conversational norms. Even if you don't adopt a unanimous consent requirement, you can apply these findings and encourage increased participation and a larger impact of women's voices.

Chapter 10

Advocating for Yourself

Many career situations require you to highlight your skills, accomplishments, and potential and to clearly communicate your ability to handle career-enhancing assignments. These situations may require you to obtain recommendation letters and demonstrate your value in strategic workplace relationships. In these and many other situations, you need to be strong, persuasive, and confident to effectively advocate for yourself. Self-advocacy, however, can be very difficult for many women. In chapter 2, "The Apple in the Room," we discuss ways in which women hold themselves back in their careers by complying with the gender stereotype that women should be modest. In that chapter we provide some suggestions about ways you can come out from behind your modesty veil without triggering a backlash from appearing over-agentic. In this chapter, we discuss additional ways to overcome your sense of a need for modesty and how you can effectively advocate for yourself.

Because of the backlash women often encounter in advocating for themselves, many women follow a "risk-adverse, conflict-avoidant strategy" in situations requiring self-promotion. That is, to avoid backlash many women often soften their self-advocacy by downplaying their accomplishments and deflecting attention away from themselves and onto others, such as their "team."[1] Although this strategy can limit backlash, women who follow it often report feeling "well-liked but underappreciated."[2] Most certainly, women who do not advocate for themselves will not advance in their careers as far and as fast as men who are typically comfortable and capable of blowing their own horns. In what follows, we present a variety of ways that women can successfully advocate for themselves—despite gender stereotypes, biases, and backlash—by applying attuned gender communication.

Another Goldilocks Dilemma

The stereotype that a woman should be modest, unpretentious, and diffident creates another all-too-familiar Goldilocks Dilemma, or double bind. If you conform to the modesty stereotype when your career advancement depends on actively promoting yourself, your career will stall from lack of recognition. If, on the other hand, you agentically advocate for yourself, you risk career and social backlash.

The following stories nicely illustrate this dilemma. The first is told by Rachel Simmons in her book *The Curse of the Good Girl: Raising Authentic Girls with Courage and Confidence*.[3] A middle school English teacher at an elite all-girls school asked her students to write an essay describing their talents and best qualities. Her students rebelled. "They felt like they were bragging. They felt like they were being snobby. They felt like they were showing off." The teacher told her students that their papers would be private; no student would need to read her story aloud. They still refused. Her students were so distraught, the teacher never did the exercise again.[4]

The second story, mentioned in chapter 2, is told in Joan C. Williams's *Harvard Business Review* article.[5] Promotion at Google requires employees to nominate themselves. When Google executives reviewed their promotion practices, they found that women nominated themselves far less frequently than men recommended themselves. It appeared that the women believed that if they engaged in self-promotion and violated the modesty stereotype, they could adversely affect their career and personal relationships with other employees. Google began a campaign to signal to its women employees that self-promotion was expected—hosting workshops on when and how to nominate oneself for promotion and including women among the workshop leaders. The gender difference in nominations at Google quickly disappeared.[6]

The third story is based on a 2019 study by Meghan I. H. Lindeman and her colleagues, "Women and Self-Promotion: A Test of Three Theories."[7] In this study, the researchers asked a group of female college students to write scholarship application essays explaining why their skills and achievements made them the most deserving scholarship recipient. Some of the participants were told the essay would be anonymous, others were told their name would be included. When the exercise was over, participants were asked to share comments on their performance. The participants who were told their names would not be disclosed did not worry about backlash. They rated their achievements higher than those participants who had been told their name would be included with their essay. The study's findings support the fact that participants who had been told they would be identified were uncomfortable about self-promoting; they feared negative social consequences. Those participants whose names were included with their essay were reluctant to openly self-advocate.

Several important points emerge from these stories. First, women generally don't like to talk or write about themselves in boastful, laudatory, or self-promoting ways. One reason for this reluctance is likely that from early childhood, many girls are told that it is not ladylike, if not downright unseemly, to explicitly call attention to themselves in boastful, prideful, or self-congratulatory ways. By age 3, girls enforce social equality on each other and avoid showing higher status by avoiding commands and boasts.[8] As a result, girls are far more likely to conceal their achievements and goals than are boys.[9] Given this early conditioning, many women find self-promotion uncomfortable. They feel that by doing so they are showing off and behaving in a conceited, immodest, and unfeminine way.

Second, women learn very early that claiming social power or superiority triggers criticism by others.[10] When a woman calls attention to her talents, accomplishments, or ambitions, she risks being stigmatized, isolated, or penalized for violating the modesty stereotype.[11]

Third, when self-promotion is not only permitted but expected, as it is at Google, women can feel safe to promote themselves and are entirely capable of doing it just as effectively as the men.

Andie: When I served on my law firm's Compensation Committee, one of my responsibilities was to read the self-evaluations written by my colleagues. I was immediately struck by how differently women and men talked about themselves. There were such fundamental differences in their content, tone, and style that I started to play a game. Without looking at my colleague's name, I would write down whether I thought the self-evaluation was written by a woman or a man. I was never wrong. These self-evaluations played directly into gender stereotypes. Men generally wrote self-laudatory self-evaluations carefully recounting their strengths and their successes. They were comfortable singing their own praises, while displaying limited (if any) modesty in describing their achievements. The men typically mentioned only positive things about themselves, omitting things that could make them look bad. In addition, the men went out of their way to make their career and compensation expectations clear. They frequently wrote sentences that begin, "I accomplished X" and "I successfully completed Y."

In contrast, the women tended to write about themselves tentatively, without recounting their successes. In fact, women often downplayed their personal contributions. Women were reluctant to use the word "I," but tended, instead, to talk exclusively about "us" and "we." Unlike the men who rarely (if ever) mentioned a negative thing about themselves, women often bent over backward to provide "full disclosure" of their weaknesses in ways that most men would think were inappropriate and self-deprecating.

The Importance of Self-Promotion

Despite this stereotype-driven difference in women's and men's "natural" inclinations, it is important that you recognize that in the competition to obtain something of value in your career—a new job, promotion, salary increase, a different work arrangement, or plum assignments—you are almost always competing against men.

This competition significantly increases the importance of and need for your ability to effectively promote yourself. To understand why, suppose a job recruiter is about to interview a woman and a man, both with MBAs from the same business school and both with comparable credentials. Let's imagine the thoughts that might be running through recruiters' minds as they are about to meet the man: "He is confident, rational, independent, and competitive; his family responsibilities won't interfere with his job performance; he will fit in with our existing team; he won't raise any concerns because of his sensitivities; his accomplishments are due to his talents; he won't be needy or prone to emotional excesses; and he probably likes sports just as we do."

You can fill in the thoughts the recruiters are likely to have as they are about to meet the woman. Have we drawn too extreme a contrast? We don't think so. Even when the recruiter is a woman, the female MBA candidate is likely to be judged as a less attractive candidate than her male competitor. In other words, to use a sports metaphor, despite their comparable credentials, the man starts out a goal or two ahead of her—goals that *she* must score simply to *even* the score.

And the only way she can score those goals is to present herself as every bit as desirable a candidate as the man, and the only way she can do that is through self-promotion.

How to Self-Promote Effectively

Before we discuss how to advocate for yourself effectively without triggering a negative backlash, we want to say a word about how you should *not* self-promote. An alpha male's style of self-promotion is to loudly and frequently blow his own horn; unhesitatingly claim personal credit for team achievements; and routinely characterize his achievements, abilities, and potential as great, exceptional, and unique. When a man does this, he is conforming to traditional male stereotypes. He can ask for what he wants in an assertive, even challenging, way. When he does so, he is likely to be recognized as hard-charging, with a good sense of his own self-worth.

In most situations you, as a woman, are unlikely to get very far with this male sort of self-complimentary behavior. Because you would be violating gender stereotypes, you would probably be seen—by both women and men—as pushy, conceited, and not a very nice person. This is an area where you simply cannot behave like a man and expect to be regarded as an effective advocate for yourself. In other words, in competing for career advancement, adopting a loud, aggressive, "in your face" style will provide you with little chance of actually winning the contest.[12]

Your most effective self-promotion involves three pieces. First, you need to make a clear, strong, supported case for yourself. Second, you need to make this case in an inviting, pleasant, "I'm on your team" way so that you come across as competent *and* likable, confident *and* warm, competitive *and* friendly. And third, you need to score enough "goals" to even the score with your male competitors—and then score another goal to win.

The hardest part of your effective self-promotion is likely to be the first step: clearly and forcefully presenting your talents and accomplishments. A recent study found that more than half of working women believe they are overlooked for promotions because they are too modest, too reluctant to be clear and direct about their qualifications, and too concerned about being seen as arrogant, big-headed, or pushy.[13] As we mentioned earlier, Google eliminated this fear by giving its women executives "permission" to self-promote. Find a way to give yourself permission to stop worrying about appearing modest and, instead, persuasively present your talents and accomplishments. One way to do this is by not thinking you are self-promoting when you talk about yourself, but rather you are providing people who need or want information about your accomplishments and capabilities with that information.

Andie: I worked with Jean several years ago when she was up for a major promotion. She had been asked to prepare a memorandum detailing her qualifications for the new position. Jean was a dynamo when it came to promoting other women, but when it came to advocating for herself, she felt uncomfortable; as she put it, she wanted no part of "shamelessly talking about how good I am." Nevertheless, she really wanted this promotion. She knew several men were angling for it, and she realized that only one person was going to get it. She came to me to help her prepare her memorandum.

We worked on her memorandum for more than a week, gathering information and crafting an accurate but punchy recitation of her recent achievements. The memo discussed the new customers she had attracted, the success she had achieved in building and strengthening her team, and an important policy initiative to which she had been a major contributor.

When the memorandum was finished, Jean showed it to her office head before sending it to the committee that would make the final decision. She had not worked directly with this man and thought he would provide a good reality check. When Jean met with him, the first thing he said to her was, "Don't you think you should be more modest?" Jean told me this made her angry but she stayed calm, smiled, and said, "I can support every word I have written. Let's start on page one." After they talked about a few specific points in her memorandum, he said, "I think you should go with this as is." She did, and she got the promotion.

I often think about Jean when I work with women who are trying to reconcile their modesty with their ambition. Women, in my

(Continued)

experience, tend to be modest because other people tell them they should be. I tell them that modesty is overrated. Warmth and a pleasant, open, and welcoming conversational style are important. But unless women clearly and effectively present the facts about their abilities, accomplishments, and potential, they are dooming their own career advancement opportunities.

So let's focus on how to effectively get across the fact that you are fully qualified for the opportunity you are seeking. First, whether your presentation is in writing or face-to-face, it needs to be clear, direct, and attention holding. At the same time, you also need to be nonconfrontational and pleasant and appear comfortable. In face-to-face situations, you need to maintain an interested and engaged facial expression, an even tone of voice, and a relaxed but erect body position inclined slightly toward the people you are addressing. Smile at appropriate times. When you claim credit for accomplishments, don't be afraid of using the word "I," but otherwise use inclusive language, including many instances of the pronoun "we" and references to the company and its objectives. Try to avoid your higher voice registers and don't appear angry, aggressive, or emotional. If you are advocating for yourself entirely in writing, as Jean was, have a good friend review it. Make sure it strikes the right balance between advocating for yourself and being a team player. And remember, regardless of the form, your objective is to persuasively convey facts about you. Unless you do that, it really doesn't matter what else you do—because you will not have successfully advocated for yourself.

If your normal style of interacting with people is interested, caring, and engaged, you will do just fine with the part of self-promotion that involves being likable. If this is not your normal style, study the earlier chapters on verbal and nonverbal communication, practice the exercises we suggest there, and don't give up. Every woman can learn to use both agentic and communal characteristics as she advocates for herself.

In-Group/Out-Group Dynamics

The last piece of effective self-promotion is dealing with the inherent advantage your male competitors have over you, scoring the goals you need to catch up from behind and then scoring the winning goal. If you are in a traditionally male career field, then you are likely to be in a gendered workplace: an organization controlled by high-status, powerful men (and a few senior women) who constitute an in-group. Because of affinity bias, members of this in-group are likely to be comfortable with one another and with those coming up who are like them. They are probably uncomfortable, however, with those coming up whom they view as unlike them (members of an out-group). This ingroup/out-group dynamic is well illustrated by a 2010 study of the attitudes of senior executive men, who all used quite similar language to describe themselves, their most successful male employees, and their sons. In contrast, they had trouble making sense of or empathizing with their female employees' choices, goals, needs, and priorities.[14]

A particularly stark example of this in-group/out-group dynamic is provided by the entertainment industry. In 2015, the American Civil Liberties Union (ACLU) of Southern California and the national ACLU Women's Rights Project asked state and federal agencies to investigate the "blatant and extreme gender inequality" in American feature films. Of the 250 top-grossing films in 2014, only seven were directed by women. As Jane Schoettle with the Toronto International Film Festival pointed out, filmmaking "is primarily about opportunities and if your opportunities are gated by those who don't give you the attention they might give to others *more like themselves,* you have difficulties."[15] Indeed, this situation is perfectly illustrated by Steven Spielberg's choice of a man, Colin Trevorrow, to direct the movie *Jurassic World.* Before *Jurassic World,* Trevorrow had only directed one half-million-dollar feature film, but Spielberg chose him because "he reminded me of myself when I was young."[16]

In your organization, the in-group/out-group dynamic may not be as extreme as it is in Hollywood, but in every traditionally male industry, profession, and job classification, there is a measure of suspicion and hostility toward those trying to break in to the top ranks who are not like those already there. Agentic women are most likely to be subject to that suspicion, because they do not reflect the stereotypical model of women most familiar to these senior male executives: the non-career women who tend to be their wives and mothers.

When you are advocating for yourself and asking for career advancement, you are challenging the status quo by asking members of the in-group to let a member of the out-group move up. To do this successfully, you need to pay careful attention to how you present yourself. Recall the eight-year study of business school graduates we discuss in chapter 4. The study found that women who used both communal and agentic communication techniques were far more successful than other women who were solely communal or solely agentic, and more successful than all of the men in terms of both compensation and promotion.[17] Your ability to use both communal and agentic behavior is the key to effectively advocating for yourself—and convincing in-group members that they can be comfortable with you moving close to joining their ranks. By using both agentic and communal communication styles, you can neutralize your male competitors' advantage, and further, you can pull ahead of them and score the winning goal in the career advancement game.

One word of caution: You may be concerned that effectively self-promoting will risk alienating or at least distancing yourself from the people with whom you work. This is admirable and can be highly beneficial, particularly if you work on team projects. It is important, however, that you do not allow your desire for social harmony to lead you to settle for a less favorable outcome than you would have achieved if you had been more focused on getting what you want. A further word of caution: While you need to persuasively present your value and qualifications in a warm and pleasant way, you should not let the negotiations end before they are really over. Being communal does not mean you cannot be agentic when that is called for. In situations that require you to self-promote, you need to be both; your objective is to advance your career, and that may very well require you to refuse to take no for an answer—at least the first time.

Al: Jennifer is a friend who is one of the few senior women at a major financial institution. She encourages the women she mentors to speak up for themselves and to forcefully advocate for themselves when it comes time for a raise or promotion. She tells me she often gets responses like, "I know I should get the promotion rather than Bill (or Mike or Joe), but I hate his phony, self-serving behavior, and I'll be damned if I'll do the same thing." Jennifer always responds to this sort of comment by saying, "So, are you telling me that when it comes time to put your kids through college and Bill has got the money from the promotion you deserved, you will be able to send him the tuition bills and he will pay them?"

When to Self-Promote

Self-promotion is appropriate in many situations in which you are not formally asked to present your qualifications. Linda Babcock, a prominent economics professor at Carnegie Mellon University, tells the story of a group of female graduate students who came to her to complain that all of the plum teaching assistant assignments had been given to men. Babcock thought this was unfair and went to the dean for an explanation. His answer was immediate and straightforward: "The men asked for the positions; none of the women did."[18] The female graduate students expected to be invited to apply. They assumed there would be a process for allocating teaching assistant positions, that all graduate students would be considered, and that assignments would be awarded based on the candidates' individual merits. The men didn't wait for such an invitation; they knew there were opportunities and went after them.[19]

The moral of Babcock's story should be obvious: career opportunities often become available without a formal invitation or selection process. You need to be on the lookout for these opportunities and quickly seize them. But even in situations in which there is a process, don't assume you can sit back and wait for the candidates to be evaluated on their merits. You need to step up and ask for it.

Andie: A number of years ago I had lunch with Monique, a managing director at a major investment bank. I shared with her an early draft of my "Self-Evaluation Dos and Don'ts." After our lunch, Monique gave my draft to her boss, the partner in charge of the office. When he next saw Monique, he told her my observations helped him understand something that had long puzzled him. During the firm's annual promotion cycle, the men up for promotion always sought him out—some daily, others weekly, but all at least once—to tell him how great a year they had had and why they deserved to be promoted. But the female candidates never reached out to him to make a pitch about why they should be promoted.

Hearing this, Monique mobilized those of her female colleagues who were up for promotion. She told them to each seek out the partner in charge of the office and tell him why they were qualified for promotion. Those women wanted to be promoted just as much as the men did, but they didn't think it was appropriate to lobby on their own behalf. They assumed that candidates for promotion would be selected based strictly on their accomplishments and that the people making the promotion decisions would have all of the information they needed or wanted. Monique's encouragement gave these women permission to self-promote—and they did just that. Once the women understood that self-promotion was a necessary part of the promotion process, they did it as effectively as the men. Monique later told me it was a record year for women's promotions.

Self-Promotion Preparation

The preparation for a situation that requires advocating for yourself has two parts: content preparation and style preparation. Keep in mind that we are not suggesting that you act in an inauthentic way, in a way that a man might act, or in an uncomfortable or phony way. Quite the contrary, we are simply suggesting that you use those aspects of *your* personality to come across as having what it takes to be terrific at that job, on that team, or with that new responsibility. Our suggestions that follow will not be relevant in all situations requiring self-promotion, but they are all worth keeping in mind.

Content Preparation

- Keep a record of your achievements, compliments, recognitions, and awards, and use them effectively.
- Advocate for yourself with the same seriousness you would use to advocate for a client, customer, or your organization. Take the time to prepare fully and give yourself the thoughtful consideration you would give to an important project.
- Collect the information you need, develop a strategy, set your priorities, and prepare an outline that will allow you to present your qualifications in a compelling way.
- Own your own contributions. You want to be sure that your accomplishments are on full display. Don't hide behind them by saying "we" when "I" is more accurate. Avoid ambiguity about your accomplishments.
- Present your request as a "win" for your organization as well as for you. Address how you can show ways you add more value to your team.
- Make sure your request is aligned with your organization's business plan or direction, marketing materials, and stated objectives.
- Make sure the justification for your request is accurate and complete and lines up with what your evaluators will be looking for.
- Demonstrate how your performance has met or exceeded your current responsibilities. If you faced professional or personal setbacks during the evaluation period, you need to discuss them yourself, and explain any decreases in production or performance.
- Make your career objectives clear to your evaluators. They won't know what you want unless you tell them.

- Be prepared to respond effectively if you get pushback to your request.
- Anticipate likely questions and reactions to your request; be prepared with detailed responses.
- If your evaluators don't know you well, make sure the content of your presentation is more detailed than it would be for a presentation to people who are familiar with you and your background.
- Remember that managing the impressions others have of you is never more important than when you advocate for yourself.
- If possible, write out your presentation beforehand. Practice it with a friend and ask for a critique. You should not read from it, but pulling it together in writing in advance will keep you focused and assure you cover all relevant points.

Style Preparation

- Watch how successful and unsuccessful people in your organization interact with senior people. You can learn from both sorts of colleagues.
- Identify a presentation style that allows you to make your points forcefully but does not make you uncomfortable or feel "out of character." You need to come across as confident and accomplished. You can't do this if you are anxious, apprehensive, or ill at ease. There are many effective styles of self-promotion; make sure the one you choose allows you to come off as sure of yourself and your value, not as reluctant, shy, or frightened.
- Your presentation style needs to be appropriate for your objectives. What sort of impression do you need to make to demonstrate that you are fully qualified for what you are asking for? If you want a new job or promotion, you need to act in a way that fits with that new role. If you want a raise, you need to present your achievements and their value to your organization. You also need to display the confidence and sense of accomplishment that comes from those achievements. If you want a challenging assignment, demonstrate the confidence, ambition, and skills to justify why you are qualified to receive what you are asking for.

- Don't forget to mind prime and power pose.
- If things don't go your way, rely on your coping sense of humor.
- When you make your presentation, think about your nonverbal behavior. You need to be engaging, persuasive, and pleasant.
- Prepare your written materials early enough so you can review, edit, and rewrite if necessary. Then, practice, practice, and practice some more.
- Don't express anger or frustration, even if it is justified. Avoid vague emotional words like "disappointed," "hope," "feel," "want," or "need."
- Use action words to describe your accomplishments and identify you with positive results. Organization, leadership, interpersonal and communication skills, initiative, and creativity are likely to be traits valued by your organization, so focus on them.
- Present your value in direct and positive ways. Use statements such as these:

  - "This has been a year of phenomenal growth for me because of _____."
  - "The projects I've handled have greatly increased my ability to do the following: _____."
  - "I have expanded my team's success in the following ways: _____."

Getting Recommendations

There are times when you will need to ask other people to advocate for you. These written and verbal recommendations are often critical to your career success. Unfortunately, the references that women receive often end up hurting them rather than helping them. Therefore, you need to pay careful attention to how you ask for references and what you tell the people who are going to give them for you.

The Problem

Many studies have looked at the differences between the recommendation letters written for women and men. In a 2010 National Science Foundation study, researchers reviewed more than 600 recommendation letters for approximately 200 applicants who had applied for eight junior faculty positions at an American university. The researchers found that the reference letters for women typically used communal terms: *helpful, kind, sympathetic, nurturing, tactful, agreeable, warm,* and *willing to help others.* In contrast, men were typically described in agentic terms: *assertive, ambitious, confident, daring, forceful, outspoken, independent,* and *intellectual.* In addition, the recommendation letters for women often had ambiguous comments such as "she might make an excellent leader," while the letters for men were far more likely to have positive claims such as "he is an established leader."[20]

The researchers wanted to determine whether the differences between the recommendation letters for the women and the men affected the letters' value as advocacy pieces. To do this, the researchers removed the names of the candidates as well as all personal pronouns. They also controlled for variables such as honors, the number of years the candidates had been in postdoctoral education, the number of papers they had published, the number of publications on which they had been lead authors, and the number of courses they had taught. The researchers then asked senior professors to evaluate the candidates based on these stripped-down recommendation letters. Their findings should hardly be a surprise—at least, not for the readers of this book. When selecting junior faculty, the communal traits so often used to praise female candidates were hardly valued at all. Indeed, the more communal traits that were mentioned in a letter, the less qualified the candidate was judged to be for the position. Correspondingly, the more agentic traits that a candidate was said to have, the more qualified the candidate was judged to be for the position.[21] Interestingly, men who wrote recommendation letters for women tended to use more agentic terms than women did when they wrote recommendation letters for women.[22] It appears likely that women think they are being nice to other women when they praise them in ways that positively identify the other women with traditional female stereotypes.

The devaluation of communal characteristics when it comes time to select people for positions calling for leadership ability is hardly limited to recommendation letters for academic positions. In a 2001 study of hiring behavior, researchers found that both female and male applicants with communal characteristics received low hiring ratings. As we have pointed out several times, however, female applicants who were able to exhibit both agentic and communal characteristics did not suffer a negative rating.[23]

In another study, researchers looked at more than 1,000 letters for a position on the medical faculty at a large American medical school. Three hundred of these letters were written for women. The researchers found the letters for women were systematically different from those written for men. The women's letters were shorter, lacked basic features that the men's letters had, often raised doubts about the candidates' abilities (including negative language), and made explicit reference to their gender. The most common possessive phrases were "her teaching" and "his research," which reinforced the stereotypes that women are teachers and students, while men are researchers and professionals.[24]

What to Do

Whether you need a written or verbal recommendation from another person, it will not be effective if it describes you in communal rather than agentic terms. Therefore, when you ask someone for a recommendation, discuss the kind of reference you need, your characteristics and achievements that are most relevant for the position, and the type of person the decision makers will be looking for. You may need to gently remind the people who will provide you with the reference to tailor the recommendation to the expectations of the decision makers by including agentic language in the reference.

KEY TAKEAWAYS

- *When you advocate for yourself, be prepared to answer all of the questions.* Anticipate and prepare for negative reactions. When challenged, remain calm and confident. Respond coherently and clearly.
- *Think about your potential.* In seeking a promotion, focus not just on your strengths and successes, but also on your potential and the future advantages to your organization.
- *Don't be shy about your accomplishments.* Don't downplay your own accomplishments by using terms like "we" or "team" unless this is the only honest way to describe what happened. It is not a question of bragging but actually owning your own accomplishments.
- *Don't settle for less.* You don't want to give up too soon. Make sure the conversation or meeting is really over before you stop explaining what you are asking for and why you should get it.
- *Because favorable recommendations are important to your career, don't ask someone for a reference unless you are confident it will be positive.* Remember to have the recommender tailor the reference to the position you seek. You want a powerful recommendation that tells the reader important and relevant things about who you are and why you are suited for the position you seek.
- *Always provide your references with information about the activities and projects that qualify you for the position you seek.* Provide whatever other background information might be useful, so your references provide the best possible recommendations.

Chapter 11

Your Career and the Rest of Your Life

W OMEN'S CAREER SUCCESS CANNOT BE measured exclusively by how far up the leadership ladder they climb or how much money they make. Unless their careers fit comfortably—and satisfyingly—with the rest of their lives, women are likely to believe something is clearly and distressingly amiss. Of course, having both a challenging, stimulating, satisfying career *and* a responsible, fun, deeply fulfilling personal life at the same time can be quite tricky.

As women attempt to fit all of the elements of their lives together in a satisfying, fulfilling way, they are often given to believe that they should seek "work-life balance" and that they cannot "have it all." While both pieces of advice are presented as sensible, unchallengeable truths, they are, in fact, nothing more than gender stereotypes used to dissuade women—for they are seldom if ever said to men—from pursuing ambitious career objectives *and* a fulfilling personal life. In what follows, we examine why these two stereotypes are so counterproductive and explore some sensible ways for women to maximize their chances of finding a sane, responsible, and satisfying combination of a career and all the other pieces of a full personal life.

Work-Life Balance

The advice that women need to achieve work-life balance seems premised on the notion that there is some sort of cosmic scale. On one side of the scale women should place their careers. On the other side they should place the rest of their lives, adding or subtracting from one side or the other side until the two sides are perfectly aligned. Achieving work-life balance also seems to assume that women's careers and personal lives are static, nonintersecting categories that don't continuously blend into each other and constantly change. Moreover, the advice that women need to find balance in their lives suggests there is a single way in which the components making up the totality of women's lives should be weighed against one another. But none of the assumptions about balance make any sense. Telling women they should find work-life balance is every bit as pernicious a gender stereotype as is telling women they should be pleasant, modest, and deferential.

Having said this, we want to make it immediately clear that all people—women and men—are happier, more satisfied, and more productive if they can find a satisfying way to combine their careers and whatever else is happening in their lives. There is, however, no single way this should be done. There is no formula as to what it will look like when accomplished and no manual providing instructions on how to do it. Different women will assign different priorities to different parts of their career and personal lives; different women will allocate their time and resources differently; different women will be guided by different values as they seek to achieve a fulfilling and satisfying way to fit the many different pieces of their lives together. Women's priorities and values also shift and change as their responsibilities, opportunities, and outlooks change. This also changes as configurations within their lives—and the ways in which they choose to live their lives—change.

We know many women who find their lives unsatisfying because they believe they have not achieved what they think is an appropriate work-life balance. While less than 2 percent of all employees intend to leave the workforce to focus on family,[1] women feel far more frustrated and guilty than men as they cope with the inevitable tensions between their careers and the needs of their partners and children. Indeed, many of these women think seriously about joining the 22 percent of women with professional degrees who are out of the workforce entirely.[2]

It is often said that men don't have to struggle to balance career and family because they are likely to have wives at home to take care of their noncareer responsibilities: childcare, meal preparation, housework, and all the other routine but essential tasks needed to maintain the semblance of order and comfort. While roughly 56 percent of all men working full-time have a partner who is also employed full-time, 81 percent of women working full-time have a partner employed full-time—meaning women who work full-time are less likely to have a partner available to manage noncareer responsibilities.[3] These numbers shift dramatically in high-earning households: just 30 percent of high-earning men have partners who work.[4] Notably, while women are the major breadwinners in only 5 percent of high-earning households, their marital status is irrelevant: high-earning women are just as likely to be married or single. Further, only 22 percent of top-earning married women have stay-at-home spouses.[5] And the fact that women perform a substantially greater share of domestic responsibilities in two-spouse households only increases the tilt of the career advancement playing field against women.

We will address shortly how women can level the playing field, but searching for work-life balance—as opposed to making sensible, realizable life choices—will not help women one whit in doing this. Women can never balance their careers and the rest of their lives. They can only fit them together in more or less satisfying ways as they grow, learn, and change.

A satisfying amalgam of all of the aspects of your life depends, in large part, on the choices you make with respect to a wide variety of matters: career field; the size and culture of your organization; your location and community; the recreational, cultural, and civic opportunities you take advantage of; the people with whom you associate; and so forth.

There are, however, two fundamental, intimate issues that are paramount in this regard: whom you choose to commit to share a long-term relationship with if you decide to so commit, and whether you have children. These decisions and how you manage their consequences are the most important factors affecting your ability to find fulfillment in both your career and the rest of your life.

Committing to a Long-Term Relationship or Getting Married

If you decide to marry or commit to a long-term relationship, the qualities that your spouse or partner possesses will be key to achieving and maintaining a successful, satisfying amalgam of your career and the rest of your life. Apart from the obvious qualities of stability, affection, and compatibility, your career and life success depend on your spouse or partner sharing domestic responsibilities and sincerely supporting your career advancement. (In what follows, we focus on male spouses and partners but much of what we write is equally applicable to same-sex couples). Unfortunately, many men fail on both of these counts.

Two researchers, writing about their findings in a 2019 *Washington Post* article, throw cold water on "conventional wisdom" that suggests "when a mother lives with a husband or male partner, her load is lighter because she has someone with whom to share parenting and other responsibilities."[6] Their research found that "when it comes to housework, that turns out not to be true." After analyzing data from more than 20,000 mothers, the researchers found that "when there's a man in the house, mothers spend more time cooking, cleaning, shopping and doing laundry than their single-mom counterparts." They also found that this was true "even when the mom brings home the proverbial bacon." Some of their findings follow:

- Women's increased economic contributions to the family have not relieved them of traditional wife and mother responsibilities.
- Mothers (whether single or married) put housework ahead of their own leisure and sleep, with these patterns consistent among

working mothers on all levels of the economic spectrum, "including those with strong feelings of equality in other parts of their lives."

- After returning home from a full day at work, married sole-breadwinner mothers spent nearly one hour on housework, compared with 11 minutes spent by married sole-breadwinner fathers.
- On their days off, married sole-breadwinner mothers do three times as much cooking, cleaning, and laundry as married sole-breadwinner fathers.

A University of Michigan study concluded that for married women with three or more children, their husbands actually increased their household load an extra seven hours per week.[7] In a 2019 Pew Research Center study, 80 percent of mothers with partners reported they regularly shop for groceries, while only 20 percent of fathers with partners reported they do the same.[8] This disparity extends into childcare: a study led by an economist at the Federal Reserve Bank of New York found that the highest-earning female executives with small children spend 25 hours per week providing childcare, while comparably earning male executives with small children spend only 10 hours per week.[9]

In another recent survey conducted by the Boston College Center for Work & Family, 62 percent of fathers of newborns who were eligible to receive paternity leave took the paternity leave that had been provided to them. Ninety-seven percent of these respondents said that "one of the top reasons to take leave was to share caregiving with their partner," yet most respondents also indicated they did not share equally in caregiving during their leave.[10] But sharing caregiving did not actually play out as anticipated. Although 75 percent of study respondents said "both genders should give the same amount of care" to newborn children, "the majority of men and nearly half of women admitted that in reality the female actually did most of it." In fact, only 2 percent of men reported doing more of the childcare than their partner.

So here's the bottom line: You may be in love with a great guy, but if he thinks he can be on the golf course on weekends while you clean the house and run errands, you need to think hard about what you really want out of life before you share a household with him.

You also need to look closely at your potential spouse's or partner's willingness to support and encourage you in your career. Because of traditional gender stereotypes, many men's sense of self-worth is closely tied to their being the sole or primary breadwinner, financial decision maker, and guide and protector of the family.[11] Therefore, you need to be certain that your partner-to-be will be happy with an ambitious partner with a full-time career. Further, you should try to learn how your prospective partner might react when you earn more money than he does, work late, frequently travel out of town, and enjoy greater professional recognition and status than he does. These are not comfortable questions to consider, much less discuss, but if you are committed to your career and to a long-term relationship, you need to know the answers to these questions.

Perhaps most importantly, you need to know what your partner honestly expects will happen if there is a conflict between his and your career demands or opportunities. A 2015 survey of nearly 25,000 Harvard Business School (HBS) graduates found that 40 percent of the female MBAs reported that their husbands' careers took priority over theirs, while 70 percent of the male MBAs said that their careers were more important than their wives' careers.[12] A partner's perception that his career is decidedly more important than his partner's career is likely to align with his expectation that she will attend to the great majority of childcare and household responsibilities.

Given the disparities in women's and men's attitudes toward and actual conduct involving work, home, and childcare, it makes sense to learn in advance what being in a long-term relationship to *that* person is likely to mean for your career. Of course, if you are already married or committed and your partner does not share domestic responsibilities or is not an enthusiastic cheerleader for your career, you don't need to give up on either your career or your relationship. It is never too late to get it right, and we have watched many couples successfully resolve conflicts about careers and domestic responsibilities with patient, extended conversations (and, in some cases, professional counseling). These women are now doing great things in both their careers and their personal lives. But, if you simply accept a grossly uneven division of responsibilities within your relationship or if you struggle to stay with your career when your partner wants you at home, you are guaranteed to experience feelings of resentment, hostility, and unhappiness.

Having Children

Even if you have the most supportive partner in the world, the decision to have children will have major implications for both your career and the rest of your life. Obviously, the decision to have a child is a deeply personal one, and each woman brings different considerations to bear as she makes it. We know that for us, our lives are richer, fuller, and more enjoyable because of our daughter than they possibly could have been without her. But being a mother brings with it career costs, new stereotype biases, more domestic responsibilities, and increased expenses. It is not a decision to be made lightly.

The costs to a woman's career of having a child can be high. A 2010 survey found that female and male MBA graduates earned similar incomes immediately following graduation, but 10 and 15 years after graduation the men's incomes substantially exceeded the women's. The researchers concluded that this compensation difference was due almost entirely to career interruptions experienced by women with children. Female MBAs with children simply had less accumulated job experience, more career interruptions, shorter work hours, and substantially lower earnings than both female MBAs without children and male MBAs with and without children.[13] Additionally, a 2017 research study examining US Census Bureau data found that among different sex couples, the earning gap between the women and the men doubles within the first two years after the woman gives birth. This gap steadily increases for the child's first five years of life before tapering off, with this pattern repeating with every additional child.[14]

Perhaps because of the recognition of these career costs, Millennial women with careers are delaying having children compared with earlier generations. This can make economic sense, because research suggests that for every year that a woman delays motherhood, her career earnings increase by 9 percent, her work experience increases by 6 percent, and her average wage rates increase by 3 percent.[15]

Regardless of timing, if you decide to have a child, you need to be ready to confront the motherhood penalty. As we discussed in chapter 1, women with children are viewed in the American workplace less positively than women without children,[16] while men with children are viewed more positively. Moreover, women with children suffer a persistent wage penalty.[17] Indeed, the survey of HBS MBA graduates found that among those women who had left the workforce to care for their children, few had done so by choice. Most of these women reported that they had been pushed out of their careers by employers who stigmatized them because they were mothers. This is just one more example of women with children facing a "death by a thousand cuts in the workplace."[18]

Much of this workplace hostility toward women with children is due to the stereotype-driven assumption that mothers are—or should be—fully committed to their children, and therefore, that they cannot be fully committed to their careers. That stereotype is the reason that 76 percent of adults think it is ideal for men with children to work full-time, but only 33 percent think it is ideal for mothers to do so.[19]

Successfully dealing with the stereotype that you cannot be both a good worker and a good mother requires you to effectively manage at least three aspects of motherhood: maternity leave, childcare, and household responsibilities. Each of these aspects is discussed below.

Maternity Leave

Managing your maternity leave involves both preparing for it and conducting yourself during it. Nearly 66 percent of women work full-time during their pregnancies.[20] Eighty-two percent of women pregnant with their first child work up to within one month of their due date, and many women continue to work right up to the time they go into labor.[21] A number of factors affect how close to your due date you decide to work:

your doctor's advice, how you feel, the preparations that need to be made before your baby is born, and the help you have in getting ready for the arrival.

Apart from the obvious factors to consider before you leave your workplace, your decision about the date you leave sends a message about your commitment to your career. This varies from organization to organization, and we are not suggesting you work until you deliver your baby in the taxi or rideshare that picks you up at your office. Our point is simply that you should be aware that everything you do once you become pregnant sends a signal about your commitment to your career. Take this into account as you decide when to start your maternity leave.

Regardless of how close to your due date you work, you need to prepare for your leave in such a way that you avoid three things. First, you don't want the projects you are working on to flounder or go off course. Second, you don't want to lose continuity, responsibility, or contact with your colleagues, clients, or customers. And third, you don't want to reinforce the stereotype that mothers are not committed to their careers. Some simple steps will help you avoid these undesirable consequences:

- Develop a list of your active matters and projects, their current status, and their likely activity during your absence.[22] Go over this list with your supervisors and discuss interim staffing needs. Talk with the people who will be handling your projects. Make sure they understand the extent, if any, to which you want to remain involved, and if you want to remain involved, when and how you want to be contacted.
- Before you leave, let your colleagues know whether you want to be kept up to date with what is happening with respect to your key projects and responsibilities as well as organizational developments that could affect you; you might want to ask to be copied on important correspondence and emails; and one way or the other, make sure that the appropriate people have your contact information.

- If you deal regularly with clients, customers, or suppliers, tell them of your pending leave and your expected return date. Make sure they know who will be handling your responsibilities during your absence. Depending on your relationship with them, you might want to let them know how they can reach you if they need to.
- For key projects, you might want to periodically check on the status of your open projects and relationships.
- Consider making an occasional visit to your office and scheduling periodic lunches with colleagues and superiors. In fact, some companies offer "stay in touch days" as a standard part of leaves to help smooth transitions back to work.
- Before you are scheduled to return, start to reconnect with your delegated projects and responsibilities. Find a way to be reintroduced to projects and responsibilities that you would have handled if you had been at work.
- Let clients, customers, vendors, and colleagues know when you will be back, and schedule face-to-face meetings with them when you return to catch up on what they have been doing while you were on leave.
- Don't come back to work until you are ready, but when you do come back, be sure you are really back. Work full days if appropriate, accept and seek out challenging projects, agree to appropriate travel if necessary, and generally be available. You are now a mother, but you also want everyone you work with to know that you are still a fully committed colleague.

Childcare

Once you are back at work, you will need to be comfortable that your child is safe and receiving plenty of care and affection. This means you need an experienced nanny; a nearby, high-quality childcare facility; a stay-at-home partner; or a fully dedicated relative or friend. High-quality childcare and education are expensive. They are well worth the cost, and we don't think an ambitious, talented woman should ever end or cut back on her career simply because of that cost. Nevertheless, successfully managing a career, personal time with a child, and the increased expense is a complex, emotional, and highly personal matter that every mother must work through for herself. As you do so, however, be careful not to fall into the trap of thinking that the cost of childcare should come out of *your* earnings and that continuing *your* career is a matter of *your* being able to earn enough money to justify the expense. Childcare is a *family* expense and should be treated as such. If you or your partner think the cost of childcare is *your* responsibility, it implies that your partner's career is more important than yours and that *your* career should continue only if it alone can fully support the additional costs of your being out of the house. This view inevitably leads to an unequal division of household responsibilities and a hierarchical domestic structure.

Household Responsibilities

Apart from childcare, if you and your partner will both be working full-time—the typical pattern for most married women with a career—then as a couple you will also need to address the issue of how to handle household responsibilities such as shopping, cooking, cleaning, laundry, bill paying, and home repairs. Without a substantial support system—which requires planning and additional expense—the arrival of a child may mean you have to struggle even harder to achieve career success and a fulfilling family life. Our advice for effectively managing these roles is to budget for outside help and be prepared to pay for the support you need.

"Having It All"

The phrase "having it all" is now trotted out in virtually every debate about women, careers, and families. In contrast to the generally upbeat attitude in the 1970s and 1980s—when it was typically assumed that talented, ambitious women *could* have it all—the prevailing attitude has now turned sour and starkly negative. When speaking at the Aspen Ideas

Festival, former PepsiCo CEO Indra Nooyi said, "I don't think women can have it all. I just don't think so."[23] Christine Lagarde, head of the World Bank, said in an NBC interview, "I think you cannot have it all at the same time."[24] In a 2016 interview, actor Mila Kunis stated, "There is no such thing. . . . Simply put, the idea of balance doesn't exist. You have to be OK with one thing not getting the attention it needs at any particular time. . . . you can't balance it."[25] And in 2018, during Michelle Obama's *Becoming* book tour, she said, "I tell women that whole 'you can have it all'—mmm, nope. Not at the same time. That's a lie."[26]

But what does "having it all" mean anyway? Obviously, it is not meant to be taken literally, say having a home in the Hamptons, a penthouse overlooking Central Park, an eight-figure job on Wall Street, and children who are world-class athletes and Nobel Prize–winning scientists. But can you have a more modest aspiration of "having it all"—say, having a successful career; a loving partner; and healthy, happy, intelligent, well-adjusted children? To truly have it all, wouldn't a woman also need fulfilling personal time, personal relationships, close family and friends, a healthy lifestyle with sufficient exercise, educational travel, adventuresome reading, civic engagement, spiritual reflection, enjoyable hobbies, community participation, aesthetic enjoyment, and so on?

Our point is that the very notion of having it all is absurd. No one can have it all; everyone must pick and choose what they want to have and do. Consequently, the right question is not whether women can have it all, but whether they can have what they sensibly want to have—and whether they can sensibly want to have a highly successful career and well-adjusted, happy, and successful children within the context of a loving personal relationship. If *that* is the question, the answer is a resounding yes. Nevertheless, in one of the most read articles in the *Atlantic*'s history, Anne-Marie Slaughter tried to explain "Why Women Still Can't Have It All."[27] Slaughter defined "a woman having it all" in what on its face appears to be a quite modest way: holding a high-level job and having the time and capacity to deal with the needs of her children. She argued vigorously, however, that a woman cannot do both unless, in her words, she is a "superwoman." Slaughter does not state explicitly why a man can successfully combine a career and children (something Slaughter clearly believes is possible) while a woman can't, but she provides hints. Her basic premise seems to be that women have to make compromises when they combine a career and a family—compromises that men are far less likely to be willing or need to make. The reason for this, Slaughter tells us, is that women do not "*feel* as comfortable as men do" leaving much of the care of their children with someone else, even their partners. Men "seem more likely to choose their job at a cost to their family, while women seem more likely to choose their family at a cost to their job." This difference between women and men is the result, in Slaughter's view, of "a maternal imperative felt so deeply that the 'choice' is reflexive."[28]

We do not want to touch the notion of a "maternal imperative"—whether it exists, is felt by all women with children, or how some women successfully combine high-stakes jobs and child-rearing despite it. We do, however, have two general comments about the points Slaughter raises.

First, we believe the claim that women must choose their career at the cost of their children or their children at the cost of their career is a false choice. In Slaughter's situation, she was a very high-ranking official in the US State Department with a teenage son with problems at school who (as she reported) had hardly spoken to her for months. She was living five days a week in a city four-and-a-half hours away from her family, working extremely long hours with no time for personal matters, and able to get home only on weekends. Slaughter's judgment that she could not satisfactorily combine *her career* with child-raising responsibilities is hardly surprising but surely not a valid basis for concluding that women generally cannot hold high-pressure, high-status jobs while raising their children. Although we would never suggest that having a demanding career and raising well-adjusted children is a piece of cake, it is entirely possible, as the many women, Andie included, who have done it demonstrate.

Second, Slaughter in the *Atlantic* article and in her 2015 book,

Unfinished Business: Women Men Work Family,[29] proposes a series of workplace reforms designed to make careers and families more easily compatible: ending the demand for continual face time, changing family values, redefining the arc of a successful career, rediscovering the pursuit of happiness, and enlisting men's help. Her basic thesis is that "we are never going to get to gender equality between men and women unless we value the work of care as much as we value paid work."[30] But Slaughter tells us little about how these reforms are going to come about, other than (ironically) speculating that more women in leadership positions would make it easier for other women to stay in the workplace. But, the very notion of a revaluation of the work of care and work for pay would seem to depend on an end to capitalism and entrepreneurship. Wholly apart from the improbability of this happening, Slaughter is completely silent in both her article and her book about what women with careers and children can do *now* to make their lives more satisfying, coherent, and rewarding. Ultimately, she offers little in the way of help or hope for women attempting to have both a successful career and a successful family life.

Women can have it all, if "all" is defined as what they sensibly choose to have. But it must be recognized that women cannot sensibly choose to have "everything"—no one can. If women want a high-powered career and healthy, happy children, they can have both at the same time, if they are willing to give up a great many of their other life goals, such as non-business travel, training for a marathon, civic engagement, university extension courses, a book project, and many other things. If women want a serious career and motherhood, these two pursuits—together with a fulfilling, loving relationship with their partner—need to be treated as the most important things in their lives. That means when something else conflicts with career or family, it must be ignored or moved aside. Therefore, women need to prioritize the totality of their lives. When career, children, and a partner are the things that matter most to a woman, everything else must be relegated to a secondary—"maybe someday"—role.

Pursuing a Career as a Mother

Even with the best childcare and household help in the world, many mothers have a deep feeling of guilt or selfishness when they are working and raising children, particularly very young children. This is often the result of the stereotype that mothers should be available to their children 24 hours a day, seven days a week. Indeed, American culture is saturated with an ideology of intensive mothering,[31] the belief that children's behavioral health, emotional health, and academic achievement all depend on the amount of time their mothers spend with them. Thus, a common belief is that the more time and attention a mother gives to her children, the better adjusted and more successful they will be. Indeed, a mother's time with her children is widely believed to be unique and irreplaceable—*by anyone*. As a matter of fact, however, this is simply not true.

In an important large-scale study, researchers using the University of Michigan's 1997 and 2002 nationally representative survey of families' activities and time usage analyzed time diaries and survey data on approximately 4,400 families and close to 7,000 children.[32] The researchers looked at three key dimensions of children's developmental outcomes: behavioral problems, emotional problems, and academic achievement. They then correlated these outcomes with the amount of time mothers engaged with their children and the time mothers were accessible to but not directly engaged with their children. The researchers found that the amount of time mothers spent with children ages 3 to 11 and 13 to 18, whether this time involved being directly engaged with them or simply being available to them, had little or no correlation with behavioral problems, emotional problems, or academic achievements. The researchers concluded that there is no empirical support for the assertion that intensive parenting is beneficial for children, finding that a mother's engaged time with her adolescent children resulted in a "very small" effect on their delinquent behavior. But they also found that a mother's time at work positively affected her adolescent children's math scores. In other words, mothers' careers outside the home were positively correlated with their children's higher math scores.[33]

These findings are confirmed by a subsequent 2019 research study that examined the effect of the time mothers and fathers spend with their children on their children's mental health. The researchers found that the amount of time mothers spend with their children had no significant impact.[34]

Apart from having no positive benefit, intensive mothering may actually harm children. Studies of college students show that those students whose parents were excessively involved with their lives had less effective emotional coping mechanisms when compared with those students who had more hands-off parents. In other words, excessive parenting can damage children's sense of autonomy and competence.[35] As Julie Lythcott-Haims, a former dean of freshmen at Stanford University, points out in her 2015 book, *How to Raise an Adult: Breaking Free of the Overparenting Trap,* college students whose parents had been intensely involved in helping them cope with day-to-day issues were not as open to new ideas and actions as were those students whose parents were more hands-off. In addition, college students with intensely involved parents were more vulnerable, anxious, and self-conscious than those students whose parents took a more relaxed approach.[36] Indeed, Lythcott-Haims argues that overinvolved parenting—not giving children enough space to work through problems on their own—is taking a serious toll on the psychological well-being of college students and is depriving them of the capacity for independent decision making.[37]

If you find yourself conflicted about being at work while your children are at home, keep in mind that no study has ever found that a mother's work outside her home adversely affects her child's well-being. Quite to the contrary. Several studies have found positive long-term effects on the academic and career achievements of children whose mothers worked outside the home.[38] One study found that children of working mothers grew up to be just as happy in adulthood as children of nonworking mothers.[39] In a 2015 study, HBS professor Kathleen McGinn found that women whose mothers had worked are more likely to have jobs themselves, hold supervisory responsibility at those jobs, and earn higher wages (23 percent more) than women whose mothers had stayed home full-time.[40] Men raised by working mothers are no less likely to have successful careers than other men, and they are more likely to share household tasks and spend more time caring for other family members. McGinn, commenting on her research, writes that there is "a lot of parental guilt about having both parents working outside the home. But what this research says to us is that [by doing so] you're . . . helping your kids."[41]

KEY TAKEAWAYS

- *Throughout your lifetime, your situation, opportunities, and responsibilities all change, shift, and take on different priorities.* Your focus therefore should be on carefully choosing what you want to be doing and how you want to be doing it at each stage of your life. Structure your time and energies accordingly, and stop trying to balance your career and the rest of your life.
- *Choosing a life partner is a decision that will have a profound and long-lasting impact on your career.* This person needs to fully share domestic responsibilities as well as value your professional ambitions and continue to support you as you advance in your career.
- *Prepare for maternity leave by meeting with your supervisors and colleagues and advising them of how your work will be handled in your absence.*
- *During maternity leave, set the terms for how you want to keep up with the status of your major projects.* When your maternity leave is close to ending, schedule face-to-face meetings with colleagues and supervisors for when you return to help you get up to speed once you return to work.
- *Make sure to prepare yourself for the added stress of the "motherhood penalty," as you are now fighting against negative stereotypes about working mothers.* When you return to work, be fully engaged. Prove your value and your commitment to your career

by volunteering for challenging projects, making yourself visible when you are in the office, and accepting appropriate travel assignments.

- *Understand that you can have whatever you sensibly choose to have, but there are costs associated with every choice.* Choose wisely and with careful attention to the consequences.
- *Don't feel guilty for raising a child and working full-time.* As studies have demonstrated, children are not harmed when their mothers have challenging careers. In fact, your career may actually help your children become more self-sufficient and confident, with more egalitarian views about family responsibilities.

GLOSSARY

The following glossary contains the key terms used in this book and is designed to provide a useful reference guide.

Affinity bias: An implicit or explicit preference for people in one's own social identity group (often thought of as the ingroup) over people in different identity groups (often outgroups). A woman can be in an ingroup in dealing with other women as a group but in the outgroup in gendered workplaces. See *gendered workplaces and social identity.*

Agentic: A word derived from *agency*; a person with agentic characteristics exhibits stereotypically masculine traits, such as being aggressive, assertive, competitive, independent, self-confident, proactive, strong, forceful, loud, stable, unemotional, and risk taking. Leaders are stereotypically seen as agentic. Both women and men have agentic characteristics.

Attuned gender communication: A phrase we have coined to refer to an integrated series of steps we set out in this book to avoid or overcome career biases you face as a woman because of gender stereotypes. Elements include (1) the cultivation and active use of four key attitudes: grit, a positive perspective on your abilities, a coping sense of humor, and a confident self-image; (2) a high level of self-awareness or self-monitoring; (3) a keen awareness of the impressions you are making on the people you deal with in your career; and (4) the ability to use a variety of communication techniques to manage and change those impressions to avoid or overcome the biases arising from the gender stereotypes that are so pervasive in gendered workplaces. You can develop and strengthen your attuned gender communication skills.

Backlash: A catchall term that refers to the negative consequences women often experience when they act in agentic ways. These negative consequences include being excluded from important meetings, networks, and events; being stigmatized as hostile, cold, bossy, unpleasant, bitchy, overbearing, and difficult to work with; being criticized for lacking in social sensitivity, warmth, and likability; being discriminated against with lower pay, fewer promotions, and fewer job opportunities; and being rendered ineffective by having contributions, ideas, and leadership potential ignored. See *agentic* and *Goldilocks Dilemma*.

Benevolent bias: An attitude often expressed by senior men (but which can also be held by senior women) who believe that traditional gender stereotypes correctly characterize women's capacities and appropriate roles. As a consequence, supervisors behave in an apparently benevolent way toward the women who work for them—solicitous, kind, considerate, concerned, helpful, protective, and patronizing—but they do not provide these women with the same career opportunities and responsibilities as the men that work for them. It is a form of subtle sexism.

Bias: We use the word *bias* to refer to the predisposition to engage in discriminatory behavior as the result of stereotypes of one sort or another. Bias can manifest itself in many ways; for example, by treating people in one social identity group less favorably than people in another group. Bias can also be demonstrated by preferentially advancing, providing more opportunities for, or compensating more generously people in one stereotyped group over another. It can also be demonstrated negatively by refusing to hire, interact with, or consider for particular tasks or projects a person from a stereotyped group. Bias can also be displayed by viewing stereotyped people as having decidedly unpleasant or objectionable personal qualities.

Communal: A word derived from *community and communion*. A person with communal characteristics exhibits stereotypically feminine traits, such as being nurturing, kind, sympathetic, concerned with the needs of others, socially sensitive, warm, approachable, understanding, solicitous of others' feelings, emotional, sentimental, gentle, domestic, family-focused, good with children, modest, and friendly. A communal a person is stereotypically seen as a good assistant or helper, not as a leader. Both men and women have communal characteristics. See *social identity*.

Double bind: A psychological state in which a person receives conflicting messages and faces a negative outcome, no matter which of two available behaviors that person adopts. For an example see *Goldilocks Dilemma*. See *social identity*.

Explicit bias: A negative attitude or preconception about people in a particular social group that a person holds consciously and explicitly endorses.

Feminine stereotypes: The traditional, often unconscious, belief that women are and should be communal and should not be (very) agentic. See *communal* and *agentic*.

Gender: Socially constructed roles, behaviors, norms, attitudes, characteristics, and activities that are viewed as appropriate and expected for women and men. The term *feminine* refers to women's socially approved characteristics and *masculine* refers to men's socially approved characteristics, as opposed to females and males as differentiated by their biological sex.[1] Not all individuals and groups of people "fit established gender norms."[2] In this book, we attempt to be sensitive to individuals and groups with gender identities other than female and male, such as nonbinary, gender nonconforming, queer, and gender-fluid individuals.

Gender bias: Bias that consists of two distinct forms: sexism and misogyny. See *bias*, *sexism*, and *misogyny*.

Gendered workplaces: Workplaces that are overwhelmingly led by men and have decidedly masculine cultures, and that are perpetuated by pervasive affinity and gender bias. Gendered workplaces include businesses, the professions, academia, government organizations, and the entertainment industry. See *affinity bias* and *gender bias*.

Goldilocks Dilemma: The double bind women face because they suffer adverse career consequences for being either communal or agentic. If a woman is communal she is viewed as likable but not as a leader; if she is agentic she is viewed as competent but also as unpleasant, cold, and unlikable. We refer to this double bind as the Goldilocks Dilemma because women are frequently viewed as too soft (too communal) or too hard (too agentic) but rarely just right. See *double bind*, *agentic*, and *communal*.

Grit: An attitude of high tenacity: a dedication to pursuing, with energy and focus, a long-term goal despite failure, adversity, and plateaus of progress.

Identity threat: The psychological state in which a person fears the loss of power or competence because of belonging to a particular social identity group. See *social identity*.

Implicit bias: A person's automatic, unconscious attribution of stereotypical characteristics to members of particular social identity groups and people with intersectionality. See *social identity* and *intersectionality*.

Impression management: A person's conscious effort to behave and communicate so as to shape or change the impressions other people have of that person. See *self-monitoring*.

Incivility: Incivility is rude or discourteous behavior that can be experienced in a variety of ways, including condescending comments; having one's competence disparaged; and social and professional snubs, such as being excluded or ignored, curtly dismissed, criticized brusquely, dealt with sarcastically, interrupted or talked over, contradicted rudely, or treated with a lack of regard. Incivility is a relatively mild form of what is often referred to as counterproductive workplace behavior. More severe forms of such behavior include interpersonal aggression, bullying, and deliberate social and professional undermining. These hostile behaviors are typically undertaken with the unambiguous intent to harm another person. Workplace incivility, by contrast, is not necessarily designed to harm someone else as much as it is to express disapproval, displeasure, or distaste at another person's conduct, appearance, or intentions.[3] Incivility is common in many organizations, with between 71 percent and 79 percent of all employees reporting that they have had uncivil encounters at work.[4] Microaggressions are a form of incivility. See *microaggressions*.

Ingroup bias: See *affinity bias*.

Intersectionality: The intersection of the distinct social identities with a woman's gender. Such identities include race, age, ability level, religion, ethnicity, gender identity, religion, social class, motherhood, and sexual orientation. A woman's intersectional characteristics contribute to her unique experiences and perspectives. See *social identity*.

Male privilege: A sense of privilege that involves the (usually unconscious) assumptions that men are superior to women at valued workplace roles, tasks, and challenges; are entitled to preference over women with respect to career opportunities, resources, and sponsorships; and are immunized from criticism for anger, aggressiveness, and self-promotion—conduct that is severely criticized when it is displayed by women.

Masculine stereotypes: The traditional, often unconscious, assumption that men are and should be agentic and that they should not need to be (very) communal. See *agentic* and *communal*.

Masculine workplaces: See *gendered workplaces*.

Microaggressions: A form of incivility involving a comment or action (often unconscious or unintentional) that expresses a prejudiced attitude toward someone who is a member of a marginalized person or group (such as a woman, a racial or ethnic minority, or an LGBTQ person).[5] Microaggressions are slights that convey a derogatory or negative view or opinion about a marginalized person or group. See *incivility*.

Mind priming: A technique for conditioning or focusing your mind so that you behave in more positive, forceful, and confident ways. This basic technique involves spending five minutes writing about a time when you felt particularly powerful or happy. Mind priming is useful before a significant career event, such as a job interview, speech, important meeting, negotiation, or sales pitch.

Misogyny: Explicit hostility to, resentment of, and anger at women who refuse to conform to traditional gender stereotypes and sexist assumptions. Sexism is the assumption that women and men should play different societal roles; misogyny is the open and active disapproval and condemnation of women who flout prescribed gender roles. See *sexism*.

Modesty: Humble and self-effacing behavior. The modesty stereotype suggests that women are expected to be selfless, deferential, and focused more on the needs and development of others, not themselves. It suggests that *simply because you are a woman*, you should be unassuming, self-effacing, and reluctant to put yourself forward.

Nonverbal behavior: "Nonverbal behavior" or "nonverbal communication" encompasses everything you do with your voice and physical being, except for spoken and written words. Your nonverbal behavior intentionally or unintentionally may convey—or misrepresent—your intentions, ideas, emotions, and instructions. Thus, it includes your body movements; facial expressions; where and how you stand, sit, and use space; how you dress, groom, and accessorize; when and how you touch other people; your vocal tone, pitch, volume, and pace: and the gestures you make. There are an estimated 1,000 nonverbal factors that contribute to the messages you send in every interpersonal interaction. See *verbal behavior*.

Outgroup: See *affinity bias*.

Power posing: A technique for using your body posture to positively affect your self-image. Posing in a high-power position such as the Wonder Woman position or the runner's victory stance for two minutes increases your testosterone and reduces your cortisol, thereby improving your confidence and reducing your anxiety.

Prejudice: An unjustifiable attitude (usually negative) about members of different identity groups from one's own. Such negative attitudes are typically based on stereotypes that disparage people's distinctive differences rather than regard them as unique and valuable characteristics. See *social identity*.

Self-monitoring: A state of acute self-awareness of the impressions you are making on the people with whom you are dealing. This awareness allows you to modify your behavior and your communication to make the impression the situation calls for. Someone who is poor at self-monitoring is not influenced by the communication cues from others, choosing to remain "herself" no matter what the situation is. See *impression management*.

Sexism: (Implicit or explicit) assumption that women should be communal caregivers and assistants, not persons with ambitions, careers, or positions similar to men's. See *communal*.

Social identity: A person's sense of oneself as a member of a social group or groups—such as race, ethnicity, gender, social class, sexual orientation, gender identification, physical ability, or religion—that creates for that person both ingroups and outgroups. Social identity is how people classify themselves and others as belonging to specific social groups.

Social identity threat: A psychological state in which a person's performance is inhibited or impaired because that person is aware that particular tasks have a strong positive association with a social identity group of which a person *is not* a member, or a strong negative association with a social identity group of which that person *is* a member.

Stereotypes: Stereotype refers to a characteristic or set of characteristics that people ascribe to people (including themselves) based on their particular distinctive social identities, such as gender, sexual orientation, gender identity, race, ethnicity, age, social class, religion, ability level, and motherhood. When people believe (consciously or unconsciously) without actual credible information that a person of a particular social group has the stereotypical characteristics associated with that group, they are making a biased or prejudiced evaluation that can lead to discriminatory consequences. Stereotypes are overly broad and unsupported generalizations about characteristics supposedly shared by members of the stereotyped group. Stereotypes function as scripts for behavior—prescribing how people should be evaluated and regarded and how others tend to relate to them. Such scripts frequently result in discriminatory behavior. See *social identity* and *intersectionality*.

Stereotype threat: A psychological state in which a person's performance is inhibited or impaired because that person is aware that particular tasks have a strong positive association with a specific social group of which a person is not a member, or a strong negative association with a social group of which the person is a member.

Verbal behavior: "Verbal behavior" or "verbal communication" is the use of words to convey information, ideas, emotions, and directions. It involves the explicit presentation of linguistic material designed to convey what you want other people to understand (or misunderstand). Verbal behavior does not include ways in which you vocalize this linguistic content, only the linguistic content itself. See *nonverbal behavior*.

Unconscious bias: See *implicit bias*.

CONCLUSION

Women's roles in a wide variety of career fields, particularly in gendered workplaces, saw dramatic changes from the mid-1960s to the mid-1990s. Since then there have been few changes, however, and women's overall progress toward career parity with men has stalled. Women start out on most high-status, high-paying career paths in numbers comparable to men (with engineering and technology being conspicuous exceptions), but women simply do not advance at the same pace or to the same extent as men. Because of women's lack of progress, they are often told they need to fix themselves: become more confident, change the way they talk, act more like men, become more ambitious, ask for what they want, delay having children, and learn to be better negotiators. At the same time, they are also told that it is their *workplaces* that need to be fixed: extensive face time needs to be eliminated; more flexibility should be provided, longer maternity leaves should be mandated, leave reentry training should be offered, quality childcare should be provided at little or no cost, telecommuting should be an option, and stricter laws should be enacted to ensure equal pay for equal work. This "workplaces need to be fixed" narrative is typically accompanied by pessimistic statements that unless workplaces are fixed, women will *never* be able to have successful careers and satisfying family lives: they can't have it all or, at least, not all at the same time.

As we hope we have made clear in this second edition, women don't need to be fixed, and our workplaces (as much as they do need to be fixed) are not likely to be fixed within a time frame meaningful to women who are working today. Instead, we have been arguing that with knowledge and effective communication techniques, women can succeed today in high-pressure careers; maintain a loving, fulfilling relationship with a partner or spouse; and raise healthy, well-adjusted, and successful children.

It is not women's fault that they have achieved less career success than men. The fault lies with the gender biases operating within our businesses and professional organizations. Because of these biases, women must compete for career advancement on a playing field that is severely tilted against them. Nevertheless, we believe women have the ability—right now and just as they are—to move forward in their careers in a manner comparable to men despite the gender-biased tilt of the field.

To do this, women must recognize that the gender stereotypes held by their career gatekeepers are the primary obstacles to their career success, and they can learn to use communication techniques that will enable them to avoid or overcome these obstacles. The problem is not women's lack of ambition, confidence, competence, or willingness to ask. Rather, the problem is the pervasiveness and strength of hurtful gender stereotypes and the unavailability—until now—of a systemic program for combatting them.

This book sets out that program. We present an integrated series of steps, what we call attuned gender communication, that you can use as you pursue your career in today's gendered workplaces. With attuned gender communication, we believe you—as a talented, ambitious woman—can successfully pursue your career objectives without gender bias sapping your ambition or delaying or destroying your career opportunities. Attuned gender communication doesn't guarantee that you will attain career success, but it does guarantee that your career won't stall or derail simply because you are a woman.

The reemergence of explicit gender bias and the exposure of the truly toxic cultures for women at so many organizations appear to have made the obstacles to women's career advancement seem even more formidable than when the first edition of *Breaking Through Bias* was published. Nevertheless, the emergence of a vibrant women's activism has given us a sense of renewed optimism. These courageous women should provide us all with the inspiration not only to individually get ahead but to work together to end explicit gender bias in all its forms and to lead America away from incivility, irrationality, and gender discrimination.

Explicit gender bias, unlike its implicit cousin, is practiced by people with bad intentions, warped values, and a regressive vision of the appropriate roles of women and men in our society. Those people can display their animosity toward women only in workplaces where implicit gender bias is tolerated and pervasive. Consequently, when women break through implicit gender bias to achieve career success, they strike a powerful blow against explicit gender bias by decisively reducing the space within which explicit gender bias can operate. Individually and together—and with the support of strong, sensible, committed men— women can make our workplaces better.

Working for their individual advancement, women can bring about the organizational and cultural changes required to expose gender bias for the hateful cancer it is. Such women can ensure equal advancement opportunities among women and men.

*   *   *

This second edition has been updated to reflect new developments since the first edition was published, the workshops we have run, the coaching we have done, the research we have conducted, and the extensive comments we have received about the first edition. We expect that you will want to read parts of this second edition more than once. We have set it up to make that easy for you. If you would like more information about any of our points, please contact us at our website, www.AndieandAl .com. We would also like to hear about your experiences in using attuned gender communication. We very much hope that we have provided you with the techniques to realize your career dreams. Be sure to let us know how you think we can make our advice even more helpful.

One final word: a successful, challenging, satisfying career *and* a fulfilling rest of your life is within your reach. Go for it!

NOTES

Introduction to This Second Edition

1. LeanIn and McKinsey & Company, "Women in the Workplace 2019," accessed December 1, 2019, https://wiw- https://womenintheworkplace .com/Women_in_the_Workplace_2019.pdf.
2. Judith Warner and Danielle Corley, "The Women's Leadership Gap," *Center for American Progress*, May 21, 2017, accessed December 1, 2019, https://www.americanprogress.org/issues/women/reports/2017/05/21/432 758/womens-leadership-gap/.
3. TeamPay, "Three Keys to Closing the Leadership Gap in Finance," March 22, 2019, accessed December 1, 2019, https://www.teampay.co/insights /closing-the-finance-leadership-gap/.
4. Jeanne Sahadi, "Only 33 Women Now Lead Fortune 500 Companies. And That's a Record High," *CNN*, May 16, 2019, accessed December 1, 2019, https://www.cnn.com/2019/05/16/success/women-ceos-fortune-500/index .html; Drew DeSilver, "Few Women Lead Large U.S. Companies, despite Modest Gains Over Past Decade," *Pew Research Center*, accessed December 1, 2019, https://www.pewresearch.org/facttank/2018/09/26/few-women -lead-large-u-s-companies-despite-modest-gains-over-pastdecade/.
5. Emma Hinchliffe, "GM's Board Will Have More Women than Men. It's Not the Only One," *Fortune*, May 20, 2019, accessed December 1, 2019, https://fortune.com/2019/05/20/women-boards-fortune-500-2019/.
6. National Association of Women Lawyers, "2019 Survey on Retention and Promotion of Women in Law Firms," https://www.nawl.org/p/cm/ld/fid =1163.
7. Association of American Medical Colleges, "Women Were Majority of U.S. Medical School Applicants in 2018," December 4, 2018, accessed December 1, 2019, https://www.aamc.org/news-insights/press-releases/women -were-majority-us-medical-school-applicants-2018.

8. Amy Paturel, "Where are All the Women Deans?" *Association of American Medical Colleges*, June 11, 2019, accessed December 1, 2019, https://www.aamc.org/news-insights/where-are-all-women-deans.

9. Bridget Turner Kelly, "Though More Women Are on College Campuses, Climbing the Professor Ladder Remains a Challenge," *The Brookings Institution*, March 29, 2019, accessed December 1, 2019, https://www.brookings.edu/blog/brown-center-chalkboard/2019/03/29/though-more-women-are-on-college-campuses-climbing-the-professor-ladder-remains-a-challenge/.

10. Judith Warner, Nora Ellmann, and Diana Boesch, "The Women's Leadership Gap," *Center for American Progress*, November 20, 2018, accessed December 1, 2019, https://www.americanprogress.org/issues/women/reports/2018/11/20/461273/womens-leadership-gap-2/.

11. Warner, "The Women's Leadership Gap."

12. Martha M. Lauzen, "Celluloid Ceiling: Behind-the-Scenes Employment of Women on the Top 100, 250, and 500 Films of 2017," *Center for the Study of Women in Television and Film*, 2018, accessed December 1, 2019, https://womenintvfilm.sdsu.edu/wp-content/uploads/2018/01/2017_Celluloid_Ceiling_Report.pdf.

13. United States Census Bureau, "Women in the Workforce: 1940–2010," accessed December 1, 2019, https://www2.census.gov/programs-surveys/sis/activities/history/hh-9_teacher.pdf.

14. Elka Torpey, "Women in Management," *US Bureau of Labor Statistics*, March 2017, accessed December 1, 2019, https://www.bls.gov/careeroutlook/2017/data-on-display/women-managers.htm?view_full.

15. LeanIn and McKinsey & Company, "Women in the Workplace 2019," accessed December 1, 2019, https://womenintheworkplace.com/Women_in_the_Workplace_2019.pdf.

16. LeanIn and McKinsey & Co., "Women in the Workplace 2018," http://wiwreport.s3.amazonaws.com/Women_in_the_Workplace_2018.pdf.

17. William Scarborough, "What the Data Says about Women in Management between 1980 and 2010," *Harvard Business Review*, February 23, 2018, accessed December 1, 2019, https://hbr.org/2018/02/what-the-data-says-about-women-in-management-between-1980-and-2010.

18. Katie Abouzahr et al., "Dispelling the Myths of the Gender 'Ambition Gap,'" *Boston Consulting Group*, April 5, 2017, accessed December 1, 2019, https://www.bcg.com/en-us/publications/2017/people-organization-leadership-change-dispelling-the-myths-of-the-gender-ambition-gap.aspx.

19. American Psychological Association, "Men and Women: No Big Differ-ence," October 20, 2005, accessed December 1, 2019, https://www.apa.org/research/action/difference.

20. Hyde Janet Sibley, "Gender Similarities and Differences," *Annual Review of Psychology*, 2014, accessed December 1, 2019, https://www.annualreviews.org/doi/10.1146/annurev-psych-010213-115057.

21. Catherine H. Tinsley and Robin J. Ely, "What Most People Get Wrong about Men and Women," *Harvard Business Review*, May-June 2018, accessed December 1, 2019, https://hbr.org/2018/05/what-most-people-get-wrong-about-men-and-women.

22. Catalyst, "Report: The Myth of the Ideal Worker: Does Doing All the Right Things Really Get Women Ahead?" October 1, 2011, accessed December 1, 2019, https://www.catalyst.org/research/the-myth-of-the-ideal-worker-does-doing-all-the-right-things-really-get-women-ahead/.

23. Roberta D. Liebenberg and Stephanie A. Scharf, "Walking out the Door: The Facts, Figures and Future of Experienced Lawyers in Private Practice," (American Bar Association 2019).

24. Warner, "The Women's Leadership Gap."

25. It is useful to distinguish between two distinct forms of gender bias: sexism and misogyny. Sexism (implicit or explicit) is the assumption that women should be caregivers and assistants, not persons with ambitions, careers, or positions similar to men's. Misogyny is always explicit. It is hostility to, resentment of, and anger at women who refuse to conform to such sexist assumptions. In other words, sexism is the assumption that women and men should play different societal roles; misogyny is the open and active disapproval and condemnation of women who flout prescribed gender roles. Sexism and misogyny can be thought of as the yin and yang of gender bias.

26. Cheryl Strayed, "She Will," in *Nasty Woman: Feminism, Resistance and Revolution*, Samhita Mukhopadhyay and Kate Harding (eds.) (New York: Picador, 2017), 33.

27. Andrea S. Kramer and Alton B. Harris, "How Do Your Workers Feel about Harassment? Ask Them," *Harvard Business Review*, January 29, 2018, accessed October 4, 2019, https://hbr.org/2018/01/how-do-your-workers-feel-about-harassment-ask-them.

28. Deborah Rhode's 2014 book, *What Women Want: An Agenda for the Women's Movement*, provides an excellent discussion of needed legal and organizational changes. She lays out a persuasive case for specific legal and institutional changes that would positively affect women's career success.

With respect to legal reform, Rhode suggests enactment of the Paycheck Fairness Act; mandated equal pay for equivalent jobs; changes in the standards of proof in sexual discrimination cases; and required employer disclosure of relevant information about gender differences in promotions, compensation, and mentoring. With respect to workplace initiatives, Rhode suggests centralized organizational responsibility to develop and oversee gender equity initiatives, rewards for successful diversity initiatives, and a requirement that recruiters objectively justify their personnel decisions. And, with respect to work and family policies, Rhode suggests paid family leave, universal childcare, prekindergarten education, legal protection against pregnancy discrimination, guaranteed six-week partial pay for serious health issues or childcare, and enactment of both the Comprehensive Child Development Act and the Flexibility for Working Families Act. Deborah Rhode, *What Women Want: An Agenda for the Women's Movement* (Oxford, UK: Oxford University Press, 2014).

29. Emphasis in the original. Cecilia E. Ford, *Women Speaking Up: Getting and Using Turns in Workplace Meetings* (London: Palgrave Macmillan, 2008).

30. David Hume, "Of the Standard of Taste," *Essays Moral, Political, Literary,* ed. Eugene F. Miller, (Indianapolis: Liberty Fund, 1985, revised edition), 239.

31. Jeanine Prime and Corinne A. Moss-Racusin, "Engaging Men in Gender Initiatives: What Change Agents Need to Know," *Catalyst,* May 4, 2009, accessed December 1, 2019, http://www.catalyst.org/research/engaging-men-in-gender-initiatives-what-change-agents-need-know/.

Chapter 1

1. Katie Abouzahr, Matt Krentz, Frances Brooks Taplett, Claire Tracey, and Miki Tsusaka, "Dispelling the Myths of the Gender Ambition Gap," *Boston Consulting Group,* April 5, 2017, https://www.bcg.com/en-us/publications/2017/people-organization-leadership-change-dispelling-the-myths-of-the-gender-ambition-gap.aspx; American Psychological Association, "Men and Women: No Big Difference," October 20, 2005, https://www.apa.org/research/action/difference.

2. Sandra Lipsitz Bem, "The Measurement of Psychological Androgyny," *Journal of Consulting and Clinical Psychology* 42(2) (1974): 155–162.

3. David Schweider, *The Psychology of Stereotyping* (New York: Guilford Press, 2004).

4. We use the term *agentic* in this book because we believe it is better to refer to these traits as agentic rather than as masculine. Both women and men have these traits.

5. We use the term *communal* in this book because we believe it is better to refer to these traits as communal rather than as feminine. Both women and men have these traits.

6. Carol T. Kulik and Mara Olekalns, "Negotiating the Gender Divide: Lessons from the Negotiation and Organizational Behavior Literatures," *Journal of Management* 38(4) (2012): 1387–1415. https://doi.org/10.1177/0149206311431307.

7. Naomi Ellemers, "Gender Stereotypes," *Annual Review of Psychology*, January 2018, accessed December 1, 2019, https://www.annualreviews.org/doi/full/10.1146/annurev-psych-122216-011719.

8. Alice H. Eagly and Steven J. Karau, "Role Congruity Theory of Prejudice toward Female Leaders," *Psychological Review*, 2002, accessed December 1, 2019, https://pdfs.semanticscholar.org/b00e/3ba04fc4b0f601b4db6f03 86d54abe710569.pdf?ga=2.132994830.1012640272.157 4119365-1576133896 .1516042834.

9. Andrea S. Kramer and Alton B. Harris, *It's Not You, It's the Workplace: Women's Conflict At Work and the Bias that Built It* (Boston: Nicholas Brealy, 2019), chapter 11.

10. Mahzarin R. Banaji, Max H. Bazerman, and Dolly Chugh, "How (Un) ethical Are You?" *Harvard Business Review*, December 2003, accessed December 1, 2019, https://hbr.org/2003/12/how-unethical-are-you.

11. Ernesto Reuben, Paolo Sapienza, and Luigi Zingales, "How Stereotypes Impair Women's Careers in Science," *Proceedings of the National Academy of Sciences*, March 10, 2014, accessed December 1, 2019, https://www .pnas.org/content/early/2014/03/05/1314788111; Daniel Z. Grunspan, Sarah L. Eddy, Sara E. Brownell, Benjamin L. Wiggins, Alison J. Crowe, and Steven M. Goodreau, "Males Under-Estimate Academic Performance of Their Female Peers in Undergraduate Biology Classrooms," *Plos* 11(2) (2016): https://journals.plos.org/plosone/article?id=10.1371/journal.pone .0148405.

12. Claire Cain Miller, "Is Blind Hiring the Best Hiring?" *New York Times Magazine*, February 25, 2016, accessed December 1, 2019, https://www .nytimes.com/2016/02/28/magazine/is-blind-hiring-the-best-hiring.html.

13. Kim Parker and Cary Funk, "Gender Discrimination Comes in Many Forms for Today's Working Women," *Pew Research Center*, November 15, 2019, accessed December 1, 2019, https://www.pewresearch.org/fact-tank

/2017/12/14/gender-discrimination-comes-in-many-forms-for-todays-wor king-women/.

14. LeanIn and McKinsey & Company, "Women in the Workplace 2019," accessed December 1, 2019, https://womenintheworkplace.com/Women _in_the_Workplace_2019.pdf.

15. Corinne A. Moss-Racusin, John F. Dovidio, Victoria L. Brescoll, Mark J. Graham, and Jo Handelsman, "Science Faculty's Subtle Gender Biases Favor Male Students," *PNAS* 109(41) (2012): 16474–16479. https://doi .org/10.1073/pnas.1211286109.

16. Moss-Racusin, "Science Faculty's Subtle Gender Biases."

17. Kim O'Grady, "How I Discovered Gender Discrimination," *What Would King Leonidas Do?*, Tumblr, July 9, 2013, accessed December 27, 2019, https://whatwouldkingleonidasdo.tumblr.com/post/54989171152/how -i-discovered-gender-discrimination.

18. Mark D. Agars, "Reconsidering the Impact of Gender Stereotypes on the Advancement of Women in Organizations," *Psychology of Women Quarterly* 28(2) (2004): 103–111. https://doi.org/10.1111%2Fj.1471-6402.2004.00127.x.

19. Catalyst, "Women 'Take Care,' Men 'Take Charge': Stereotyping of U.S. Business Leaders Exposed," accessed December 19, 2019, http://www .catalyst.org/knowledge/women-take-care-men-take-charge-stereotyping -us-business-leaders-exposed.

20. Catalyst, "Women 'Take Care,' Men 'Take Charge.'"

21. Charlotte Hedenstierna-Jonson, Anna Kjellström, Torun Zachrisson, Maja Krzewińska, Veronica Sobrado, Neil Price, Torsten Günther, Mattias Jakobsson, and Jan Stora, "A Female Viking Warrior Confirmed by Genomics," *American Journal of Physical Anthropology* 164(4) (2017): 853–860. doi:10.1002/ajpa.23308.

22. Neil Price, Charlotte Hedenstierna-Jonson, Torun Zachrisson, Anna Kjellström, Jan Storå, Maja Krzewińska, Torsten Günther, Verónica Sobrado, Mattias Jakobsson, and Anders Götherström, "Viking Warrior Women? Reassessing Birka Chamber Grave Bj 581," *Antiquity* 93(367) (2019):181–198. doi:10.15184/aqy.2018.258.

23. Price, "Viking Warrior Women?"

24. Laurie A. Rudman and Peter Glick, "Feminized Management and Backlash toward Agentic Women: The Hidden Costs to Women of a Kinder, Gentler Image of Middle Managers," *Journal of Personality and Social Psychology* 77(5) (1999): 1004–1010. https://psycnet.apa.org/doi/10.1037 /0022-3514.77.5.1004.

25. Deborah A. Prentice and Erica Carranza, "What Women and Men Should Be, Shouldn't Be, Are Allowed to Be, and Don't Have to Be: The Contents of Prescriptive Gender Stereotypes," *Psychology of Women Quarterly* 26 (2002): 279–280. https://doi.org/10.1111%2F1471-6402.t01-1-00066.

26. Kulik and Olekalns, "Negotiating the Gender Divide."

27. Andrea Kupfer Schneider, Catherine H. Tinsley, Sandra Cheldelin, and Emily T. Amanatullah, "Likeability vs. Competence: The Impossible Choice Faced by Female Politicians, Attenuated by Lawyers," *Duke Journal of Gender Law and Policy* 17 (2010): 363–384. https://scholarship.law.duke .edu/djglp/vol17/iss2/4.

28. "As Academic Gender Gap Declines, There Is Still Work to be Done," *Harbus*, April 25, 2011, accessed December 20, 2019, http://www.harbus .org/2011/gender-gap/.

29. Jodi Kantor, "Harvard Business School Case Study: Gender Equity," *New York Times,* September 7, 2013, accessed December 20, 2019, http://www .nytimes.com/2013/09/08/education/harvard-case-study-gender-equity .html.

30. Stephen Benard and Shelley J. Correll, "Normative Discrimination and the Motherhood Penalty," *Gender and Society* 24(5) (2010): 616–646; Shelley J. Correll, "Minimizing the Motherhood Penalty," Research Symposium, Gender and Work: Challenging Conventional Wisdom, *Harvard Business School,* 2013, accessed December 20, 2019, http://www.hbs.edu/faculty /conferences/2013-w50-research-symposium/Documents/correll.pdf.

31. Shelley J. Correll and Stephen Benard, "Getting a Job: Is There a Mother-hood Penalty?" *American Journal of Sociology* 112(5) (2007): 1297–1339.

32. Katherine Hanson, "The Opportunity Cost of Fertility under the Rhetoric of Choice," Northern Illinois University, November 15, 2018, unpublished study, Communications 498 Independent Study. Available from the author upon request.

33. Correll, "Getting a Job: Is There a Motherhood Penalty?"

34. Correll, "Getting a Job: Is There a Motherhood Penalty?"

35. Amy S. Wharton, *Working in America: Continuity, Conflict, and Change in a New Economic Era*, 4th Ed. (Routledge 2015).

36. Stephen Benard and Shelley J. Correll, "Normative Discrimination and the Motherhood Penalty," *Gender and Society* 24(5) (2010): 617. https://www .jstor.org/stable/25741207.

37. *Time,* "Millennials: The Me Generation," May 20, 2013, accessed December 13, 2019, https://time.com/247/Millennials-the-me-me-me-generation/.

38. Morley Winograd and Michael D. Hais, "Race? No, Millennials Care More about Gender Equality," *Atlantic*, October 25, 2013, accessed December 13, 2019, https://www.theatlantic.com/politics/archive/2013/10/race-no-mille nnials-care-most-about-gender-equality/430305/.

39. Caroline Turner, "Gender and Generational Differences: The Intersection," *Huffington Post*, updated December 6, 2017, accessed January 6, 2020, https://www.huffpost.com/entry/gender-and-generational-d_b _5974624.

40. Pershing LLC, "Americans Crave a New Kind of Leader—and Women Are Ready to Deliver," February 25, 2014, accessed December 20, 2019, https://www.pershing.com/our-thinking/thought-leadership/americans -crave-a-new-kind-of-leader-and-women-are-ready-to-deliver.

41. Benoit Dardenne, Muriel Dumont, and Thierry Bonier, "Insidious Dangers of Benevolent Sexism: Consequences for Women's Performance," *Journal of Personality and Social Psychology* 93(5) (2007): 764–779.

42. Monica Biernat, M. J. Tocci, and Joan C. Williams, "The Language of Performance Evaluations: Gender-Based Shifts in Content and Consistency of Judgment," *Social Psychology and Personality Science* 3(2) (2012): 186–192, https://doi.org/10.1177%2F1948550611415693.

43. Eden B. King, Whitney Botsford, Michelle R. Hebl, Stephanie Kazama, Jeremy F. Dawson, and Andrew Perkins, "Benevolent Sexism at Work: General Differences in the Distribution of Challenging Developmental Experiences," *Journal of Management* 38(6) (2012): 1842, doi:10.1177 /0149206310365902.

44. Irene E. De Pater, Annelies E. M. Van Vianen, Agneta H. Fischer, and Wendy P. Van Ginkel, "Challenging Experiences: Gender Differences on Task Choice," *Journal of Managerial Psychology* 24(1) (2009): 4–28.

Chapter 2

1. Claude M. Steele and Joshua Aronson, "Stereotype Threat and the Intellectual Test Performance of African Americans," *Journal of Personality and Social Psychology* 69(5) 1995: 797–811, accessed December 18, 2019, 2019, doi: 10.1037//0022-3514.69.5.797.

2. Patricia M. Gonzalez, Hart Blanton, and Kevin J. Williams, "The Effects of Stereotype Threat and Double-Minority Status on the Test Performance of Latino Women," *Personality and Social Psychology Bulletin*, May 1, 2002, accessed December 6, 2019, https://journals.sagepub.com/doi /abs/10.1177/0146167202288010.

3. Anne M. Koenig and Alice H. Eagly, "Stereotype Threat in Men on a Test of Social Sensitivity," *Sex Roles* 52(7-8) (April 2005): 489–496, accessed December 6, 2019, https:link.springer.com/article/10.1007/s11199-005-3714-x.

4. Michael Inzlicht and Talia Ben-Zeev, "A Threatening Intellectual Environment: Why Females Are Susceptible to Experiencing Problem-Solving Deficits in the Presence of Males," *Psychological Science* 11(5) (2000): 365–371.

5. Toni Schmader and Alyssa Croft, "How Stereotypes Stifle Performance Potential," *Social and Personality Psychology Compass* 5(10) (2011): 792–806.

6. Schmader, "How Stereotypes Stifle Performance Potential."

7. Thomas E. Ford, Mark A. Ferguson, J. L. Brooks, K. M. Hagadone, "Coping Sense of Humor Reduces the Effect of Stereotype Threat on Women's Math Performance," *Personality and Social Psychology Bulletin* 30(5) (2004): 643–653.

8. Anne Maass, Claudio D'Ettole, and Mara Cadinu, "Checkmate? The Role of Gender Stereotypes in the Ultimate Intellectual Sport," *European Journal of Social Psychology* 38(2) (2007), accessed December 6, 2019, https:// onlinelibrary.wiley.com/doi/abs/10.1002/ejsp.440.

9. Laura J. Kray, Adam D. Galinsky, and Leigh Thompson, "Reversing the Gender Gap in Negotiations: An Exploration of Stereotype Regeneration," *Organizational Behavior and Human Decision Processes* 87(2), March 2002: 386–409, accessed December 6, 2019, https://psycnet.apa.org /doi/10.1006/obhd.2001.2979.

10. Laura J. Kray, Leigh Thompson, and Adam Galinsky, "Battle of the Sexes: Gender Stereotype Confirmation and Reactance in Negotiations," *Journal of Personal Social Psychology* 80(6), June 2001: 942–58, accessed December 6, 2019, https://www.ncbi.nlm.nih.gov/pubmed/11414376.

11. S. L. Beilock, R. J. Rydell, and A. R. McConnell, "Stereotype Threat and Working Memory: Mechanisms, Alleviation, and Spillover," *Journal of Experimental Psychology: General* 136(2) May 2007: 256–76, accessed December 6, 2019, https://www.ncbi.nlm.nih.gov/pubmed/17500650.

12. Schmader; "How Stereotypes Stifle Performance Potential."

13. Michael Johns, Michael Inzlicht, and Toni Schmader, "Stereotype Threat and Executive Resource Depletion: Examining the Influence of Emotion Regulation," *Journal of Experimental Psychology: General* 137(4) (2008): 691–705; Michael Johns, Toni Schmader, A. Martens, "Knowing Is Half the Battle: Teaching Stereotype Threat as a Means of Improving Women's Math Performance," *Psychological Science* 16(3): March 2005,

175–9, accessed December 18, 2019, https://journals.sagepub.com/doi/abs/10.1111/j.0956-7976.2005.00799.x.

14. Ford, "Coping Sense of Humor."

15. Roxana Barbulescu and Matthew Bidwell, "Do Women Choose Different Jobs from Men? Mechanisms of Application Segregation in the Market for Managerial Workers," *Organization Science* 24(3) (2012): 737–756.

16. Barbulescu, "Do Women Choose Different Jobs from Men?"

17. Georges Desvaux, Sandrine Devillard-Hoellinger, and Mary C. Meaney, "A Business Case for Women," *McKinsey Quarterly*, September 2008, accessed December 17, 2019, http://www.rctaylor.com/Images/A_Business_Case_for_Women.pdf.

18. Irene E. DePater, Annelies E. M. Van Vianen, Agneta H. Fischer, and Wendy P. Van Ginkel, "Challenging Experiences: Gender Differences in Task Choice," *Journal of Managerial Psychology* 24(1) (2009): 4–28.

19. Kathleen Connelly and Martin Heesacker, "Why Is Benevolent Sexism Appealing? Associations with System Justification and Life Satisfaction," *Psychology of Women Quarterly* 36(4) (2012): 432–443.

20. Connelly, "Why Is Benevolent Sexism Appealing?"

21. Sarah Dinolfo, Christine Silva, and Nancy M. Carter, "High Potentials in the Pipeline: Leaders Pay It Forward," *Catalyst*, 2012, accessed December 18, 2019 https://www.catalyst.org/research/high-potentials-in-the-pipeline-leaders-pay-it-forward/.

22. "2014 WBI U.S. Workplace Bullying Survey," *Workplace Bullying Institute*. 2014, accessed December 17, 2019, https://workplacebullying.org/multi/pdf/2014-Survey-Flyer-B.pdf.

23. Hope Hodge Seck, "Controversy Surrounds Firing of Marines' Female Recruit Battalion CO," *Marine Times*, July 15, 2015, accessed December 18, 2019, http://www.marinecorpstimes.com/story/military/2015/07/07/kate-germano-fired-marine-corps-female-recruit-unit-commander/29763371/.

24. "Authentic Leadership" *Harvard Business Review Podcast* (2007), accessed November 30, 2019, https://hbr.org/2007/05/harvard-business-ideacast-43-a.html; Bill George, *Discover Your True North: Becoming an Authentic Leader*, (John Wiley & Sons, Inc.: Hoboken New Jersey, 2015); Bill George, *Authentic Leadership: Rediscovering the Secrets to Creating Lasting Value* (Jossey-Bass: San Francisco, 2003).

25. Laura Vanderkam, "What Does Authenticity Really Mean? *Fast Company*, November 20, 2015, accessed November 30, 2019, https://www.fastcompany.com/3053566/what-does-authenticity-really-mean.

26. Leon Festinger, "A Theory of Social Comparison Processes," *Human Relations* 7(2) (1954): 117–140.

27. Faye J. Crosby, "The Denial of Personal Discrimination," *American Behavioral Scientist* 27(3) (1984): 371–386; Faye Crosby, "Sex Discrimination, Personal Denial, and Collateral Damage," *Social Justice Research* 30(1) (2017): 89–105, doi:10.1007/s11211-017-0279-0.

28. Mindi D. Foster and Micha Tsarfati, "The Effects of Meritocracy Beliefs on Women's Well-Being after First-Time Gender Discrimination," *Personality and Social Psychology Bulletin* 31(12) (2005): 1730–1738.

29. Jessi Smith and Meghan Huntoon, "Women's Bragging Rights: Overcoming Modesty Norms to Facilitate Women's Self-Promotion," *Psychology of Women Quarterly* 38(4) (2013): 447–459, doi: 10.1177/0361684313515840.

30. Laura Cummins, "Modesty Holding Women Back at Work," *Female First*, October 2, 2014, https://www.femalefirst.eo.uk/womens-issues/modesty-holding-women-back-at-work-543047.html.

31. Nicholas Carlson, "Google Hiring Data Reveals Two Things Women Can Do to Get Hired and Promoted More," *Business Insider*, August 22, 2012, https://www.businessinsider.com/google-hiring-data-reveals-two-things-women-can-do-to-get-hired-and-promoted-more-2012-8.

32. Christine Silva, Nancy M. Carter, and Anna Beninger, "Good Intentions, Imperfect Execution? Women Get Fewer of the 'Hot Jobs' Needed to Advance," *Catalyst*, 2012, accessed December 18, 2019, https://www.catalyst.org/research/good-intentions-imperfect-execution-women-get-fewer-of-the-hot-jobs-needed-to-advance/.

Chapter 3

1. Mary Beard, "The Public Voice of Women," *London Review of Books*, 36(6), March 20, 2014, 11–14, accessed December 5, 2019, https://www.lrb.co.uk/v36/n06/mary-beard/the-public-voice-of-women.

2. Homer, *The Odyssey*, Emily Wilson (trans.) (New York: W. W. Norton & Company, 2018), 116.

3. Susan B. Anthony, "Fifty Years of Work for Woman," Independent, 52 (February 15, 1900), 414–17, quoted in Lynn Sherr, *Failure Is Impossible: Susan B. Anthony in Her Own Words* (Crown Publishing Group, 1995), 134.

4. Adrienne LaFrance, "The 'Undesirable Militants' behind the Nineteenth Amendment," *Atlantic*, December 5, 2019, https://www.theatlantic.com

/politics/archive/2019/06/most-dangerous-women-american-politics
/590959/.

5. "Silencing Women's Public Voices, May 24, 2016, accessed December 3, 2019,
http://andieandal.com/silencing-womens-public-voices/; Rachel Thompson, "The Most Harassed Women Online Share Why They're Not Logging Off," *Mashable*, 2018, accessed December 5, 2019, https://mashable
.com/2018/06/18/online-harassment-trolling-women/; Jamie Bartlett, "The Trolling and Abuse of Women Rooted in Online Cultures," *Medium*, March 1, 2018, accessed December 3, 2019, https://medium.com/@jamie
.bartlett/the-trolling-and-abuse-of-women-rooted-in-online-cultures
-667a54d4f88d; Natalie Gil, "4 Women on Death Threats, Abuse Online & What They're Doing to Stop the Trolls," *Refinery29*, April 30, 2018, accessed December 3, 2019, https://www.refinery29.com/en-gb/2018/04
/196751/sexist-online-abuse-trolling.

6. Ancient Origins, "The Rape of the Sabine Women," February 2, 2015, accessed December 5, 2019, https://www.ancient-origins.net/news-history
/rape-sabine-women-002636.

7. Kate Millett, *Sexual Politics* (New York: Columbia University Press, 1969, 2016).

8. Shulamith Firestone, *The Dialectic of Sex: The Case for Feminist Revolution* (New York: Straus and Giroux, paperback edition, 2003).

9. Susan Brownmiller, *Against Our Will; Men, Women and Rape* (New York: Fawcett Books, 1975).

10. Andrea Dworkin, *The Complete Works of Andrea Dworkin*, from *RadFem Archive*, January 29, 2012, available in pdf, epub, and Kindle formats, http://radfem.org/dworkin/.

11. All quotations are from Andrea Dworkin, "Rape Atrocity and the Boy Next Door" in Johanna Fateman and Amy Scholder (ed.), *Last Days at Hot Slit: The Radical Feminism of Andrea Dworkin* (South Pasadena: Semiotext(e), 2019): 94.

12. Dworkin, "Rape Atrocity."

13. Michelle Goldberg, "Not the Fun Kind of Feminist: How Trump Helped Make Andrea Dworkin Relevant Again," *New York Times*, February 23, 2019, accessed December 22, 2019, 2019, https://www.nytimes.com/2019
/02/22/opinion/sunday/trump-feminismandreadworkin.html.

14. Jeremy Diamond, "Trump Escalates Attacks on Clinton's Character," *CNN*, August 5, 2016, accessed December 22, 2019, https://www.cnn
.com/2016/08/05/politics/donald-trump-hillary-clinton-unhinged-lock
-her-up/index.html.

15. Tessa Berenson, "Watch Donald Trump Call Hillary Clinton a 'Nasty Woman,'" *Time*, October 19, 2016, accessed December 22, 2019, https://time.com/4537960/donald-trump-hillary-clinton-nasty-woman-debate/.

16. "Trump Calls Clinton 'Crooked,' Says She Lies about Him," *NBC News*, May 27, 2016, accessed December 22, 2019, https://www.nbcnews.com/video/trump-calls-clinton-crooked-says-she-lies-about-him-6943344531972.

17. Howard Stern, "Howard Stern," Interview by CNN KFILE, October 2016, https://soundcloud.com/user-704098053/howard-stern, 5:32; Elizabeth Preza, "Howard Stern Says Trump's 'Misogynist, Sexist' Comments Are Exactly 'Who Trump Is,'" *Alternet*, October 27, 2016, accessed December 22, 2019, https://www.alternet.org/2016/10/howard-stern-says-trumps-misogynist-sexist-comments-are-who-trump/.

18. Jeva Lange, "61 Things Donald Trump Has Said about Women," *The Week*, October 16, 2018, https://theweek.com/articles/655770/61-things-donald-trump-said-about-women; Donald Trump (@realDonaldTrump), "@BetteMidler talks about my hair but I'm not allowed to talk about her ugly face or body—so I won't. Is this a double standard?" October 28, 2012, accessed December 22, 2019, https://twitter.com/realDonaldTrump/status/262583859709882369.

19. Donald Trump (@realDonaldTrump), "@ariannahuff is unattractive both inside and out. I fully understand why her former husband left her for a man—he made a good decision," August 28, 2012, accessed December 22, 2019, https://twitter.com/realDonaldTrump/status/240462265680289792; Janell Ross, "So Which Women Has Donald Trump Called 'Dogs' and 'Fat Pigs'?," *Washington Post*, August 8, 2015, accessed December 22, 2019, https://www.washingtonpost.com/news/the-fix/wp/2015/08/08/so-which-women-has-donald-trump-called-dogs-and-fat-pigs/; Michael D. Shear and Eileen Sullivan, "'Horseface,' 'Lowlife,' 'Fat Ugly': How the President Demeans Women," *New York Times*, October 16, 2018, accessed December 22, 2019, https://www.nytimes.com/2018/10/16/us/politics/trump-women-insults.html.

20. Jack Mirkinson, "Donald Trump Writes Blistering Letter to Gail Collins, *New York Times* Columnist," *Huffington Post*, June 9, 2011, accessed December 22, 2019, https://www.huffpost.com/entry/donald-trump-gail-collins-new-york-times_n_847015.

21. Kate Samuelson, "Who Is Alicia Machado? She Says Donald Trump Called Her 'Miss Piggy,'" *Time*, September 27, 2016, accessed December 22, 2019, https://time.com/4509243/donald-trump-miss-universe-alicia-machado-piggy-housekeeping/.

22. Michael D. Shear and Eileen Sullivan, "Trump Calls Omarosa Man-igault Newman 'That Dog' in His Latest Insult," *New York Times*, August 14, 2018, accessed December 22, 2019, https://www.nytimes.com/2018 /08/14/us/politics/trump-omarosa-dog.html; Donald Trump (@real-DonaldTrump), "When you give a crazed, crying lowlife a break, and give her a job at the White House, I guess it just didn't work out. Good work by General Kelly for quickly firing that dog!" August 14, 2018, accessed December 22, 2019, https://twitter.com/realDonaldTrump/status /1029329583672307712.

23. Harry Hurt, "Donald Trump Gets Small," *Esquire Classic*, May 1, 1991, 27.

24. Garance Burke, "AP: 'Apprentice' Cast and Crew Say Trump Was Lewd and Sexist," *AP News*, October 3, 2016, accessed December 22, 2019, https://apnews.com/2778a6ab72ea49558445337865289508; Libby Nelson, "Donald Trump's History of Misogyny, Sexism, and Harassment: A Com-prehensive Review," *Vox*, October 12, 2016, accessed August 3, 2019, https://www.vox.com/2016/10/8/13110734/Donald-Trump-Leaked-Audio -Recording-billy-bush-sexism.

25. "US Election: Full Transcript of Donald Trump's Obscene Videotape," *BBC News*, October 9, 2016, accessed December 22, 2019, https://www.bbc .com/news/election-us-2016-37595321.

26. Katie Tur, *Unbelievable: My Front-Row Seat to the Craziest Campaign in American History* (New York: HarperCollins Publishers, 2018), 240.

27. Prachi Gupta, "Trump Supporters Sell Truly Disgusting Shirts Outside a Rally for the Candidate," *Cosmopolitan*, April 19, 2016, accessed Decem-ber 22, 2019, https://www.cosmopolitan.com/politics/news/a57107/donald -trump-t-shirts-misogynistic/; Kristen Bellstrom, "Trump Supporters Are Selling 'Trump That Bitch' T-shirts Featuring Hillary Clinton," *For-tune*, April 25, 2016, accessed December 22, 2019, https://fortune.com/201 6/04/25/trump-clinton-misogynistic-merch/.

28. Peter Beinart, "Fear of a Female President," *Atlantic*, October 2016, accessed December 22, 2019, https://www.theatlantic.com/magazine /archive/2016/10/fear-of-a-female-president/497564/; Rachel Franzin, "'Lock Her Up' Chant Breaks Out at Trump Rally," *The Hill*, August 1, 2019, https://thehill.com/homenews/campaign/455874-lock-her-up-chant -breaks-out-at-trump-rally.

29. Rebecca Morin, "What We Know about the 'Send Her Back' Chants That Erupted at Trump's North Carolina Rally," *USA Today*, July 18, 2019, accessed December 22, 2019, https://www.usatoday.com/story/news

/politics/2019/07/18/what-we-know-send-her-back-chants-directed-ilhan
-omar/1769042001/.

30. Catherine Kim, "Twitter Bans Ilhan Omar's GOP Rival for Tweeting about Hanging the Congresswoman," *Vox*, November 30, 2019, accessed December 5, 2019, https://www.vox.com/policy-and-politics/2019/11/30/2 0989348/twitter-ban-danielle-stella-ilhan-tweeting-treason-hanged.

31. "The Meanie, the Lightweight, the Crazies, and the Angry, Dissembling Elitists," *The Cut*, accessed December 22, 2019, https://www.thecut .com/2019/11/lessons-from-six-women-running-for-president.html.

32. Kathleen Parker, "What a Shame Cruelty Isn't an Impeachable Offense," *Washington Post*, December 20, 2019, accessed December 22, 2019, https://www.washingtonpost.com/opinions/what-a-shame-that-cruelty -isnt-an-impeachable-offense/2019/12/20/af94af66-2373-11ea-86f3 -3b5019d451db_story.html.

33. Katie Rogers, "White Women Helped Elect Donald Trump," *New York Times*, November 9, 2016, https://www.nytimes.com/2016/12/01/us/politics /white-women-helped-elect-donald-trump.html; Moira Donegan, "Half of White Women Continue to Vote Republican. What's Wrong with Them?'" *The Guardian*, November 9, 2018, accessed December 22, 2019, https:// www.theguardian.com/commentisfree/2018/nov/09/white-women-vote -republican-why.

34. Nicholas A. Valentino, Carly Wayne, and Marzia Oceno, "Mobilizing Sexism: The Interaction of Emotion and Gender Attitudes in the 2016 US Presidential Election," *Public Opinion Quarterly* 82(51) 2018, emphasis in original.

35. Valentino, "Mobilizing Sexism."

36. Brian F. Schaffner, Matthew Macwilliams, and Tatishe Nteta, "Understanding White Polarization in the 2016 Vote for President: The Sobering Role of Racism and Sexism," *Political Science Quarterly* 133(1) (Spring 2018): 9–34, https://onlinelibrary.wiley.com/doi/abs/10.1002/polq.12737.

37. Mark Setzler and Alixandra B. Yanus, "Why Did Women Vote for Donald Trump," *PS: Political Science & Politics* 51(3) (July 2018): 523–527, https:// doi-org.proxy.lawrence.edu:2443/10.1017/S1049096518000355.

38. Rebecca Solnit, "A Nation Groomed and Battered," in *Nasty Women: Feminism, Resistance, and Revolution in Trump's America*, Samhita Mukhopadhyay and Kate Harding (eds.) (New York: Picador, 2017), 129.

39. Nancy Coleman, "Ruling in Paul Haggis Case Gives Lift to #MeToo Lawsuits," *New York Times*, December 27, 2019, accessed January 3, 2019 https:// www.nytimes.com/2019/12/27/arts/paul-haggis-appeal-ruling.html.

40. Andrea S. Kramer and Alton B. Harris, "How Do Your Workers Feel about Harassment? Ask Them." *Harvard Business Review*, January 29, 2018, accessed December 1, 2019, https://hrb.org/2018/how-do-your-workers-feel-about-harasment-ask-them.

41. Anemona Hartocollis and Yamiche Alcindor, "Women's March Highlights as Huge Crowds Protest Trump: 'We're Not Going Away,'" *New York Times*, January 21, 2017, accessed December 22, 2019, https://www.nytimes.com/2017/01/21/us/womens-march.html.

42. Emily Steel and Michael S. Schmidt, "Bill O'Reilly Thrives at Fox News, Even as Harassment Settlements Add Up," *New York Times*, April 1, 2017, accessed December 22, 2019, https://www.nytimes.com/2017/04/01/business/media/bill-oreilly-sexual-harassment-fox-news.html.

43. Brian Steinberg, "Fox News Fires Bill O'Reilly Amid Sexual Harassment Storm," *Variety*, April 19, 2017, accessed December 22, 2019, https://variety.com/2017/tv/news/bill-oreilly-fired-fox-newssexual-harassment-murdoch-1202044514/.

44. Ronan Farrow, "From Aggressive Overtures to Sexual Assault: Harvey Weinstein's Accusers Tell Their Stories," *New Yorker*, October 10, 2017, accessed December 22, 2019, https://www.newyorker.com/news/news-desk/from-aggressive-overtures-to-sexual-assault-harvey-weinsteins-accusers-tell-their-stories.

45. Mary Pflum, "A Year Ago, Alyssa Milano Started a Conversation about #MeToo," *NBC News*, October 15, 2018, accessed December 22, 2019, https://www.nbcnews.com/news/usnews/year-ago-alyssa-milano-started-conversation-about-me-too-these-women-n920246.

46. Nadja Sayej, "Alyssa Milano on the #MeToo Movement: 'We're Not Going to Stand for It Any More,'" *The Guardian*, December 1, 2017, accessed December 22, 2019, https://www.theguardian.com/culture/2017/dec/01/alyssa-milano-mee-too-sexual-harassment-abuse.

47. Aisha Harris, "She Founded MeToo. Now She Wants to Move Past the Trauma," *New York Times*, October 15, 2018, accessed December 22, 2019, https://www.nytimes.com/2018/10/15/arts/tarana-burke-metoo-anniversary.html.

48. Linda Hirshman, *Reckoning: The Epic Battle against Sexual Abuse and Harassment* (Boston: Houghton Mifflin, 2019).

49. Hirshman, *Reckoning*.

50. Ashwini Tambe, "Why #MeToo Happened in 2017," *National Public Radio*, February 7, 2018, http://www.npr.org/2018/02/07/583910310/why-metoo.

51. Amy Chozick, "Hillary Clinton Ignited a Feminist Movement. By Losing," *New York Times*, January 13, 2018.

52. Jodi Kantor and Megan Twohey, *She Said; Breaking the Sexual Harassment Story that Helped Ignite a Movement* (London: Penguin Press, 2019).

53. Megan Cerullo, "Sexual Harassment Allegations Are Down Sharply Since Harvey Weinstein First Accused," *CBS News*, June 19, 2019, accessed December 22, 2019, https://www.cbsnews.com/news/metoo-index-shows -lowest-rate-of-accusations-since-harvey-weinstein/.

54. Megan Cerullo, "Harassment Allegations Slide Since Harvey Weinstein Accused," *MSN*, June 20, 2019, accessed December 22, 2019, https://www .msn.com/en-us/money/companies/harassment-allegations-slide-since -harvey-weinstein-accused/ar-AAD7W3P?pfr=1.

55. Stop Street Harassment, "The Facts Behind the #MeToo Movement," February 2018, http://www.stopstreetharassment.org/wp-content/uploads /2018/01/Full-Report-2018-National-Study-on-Sexual-Harassment-and -Assault.pdf.

56. Catalyst, "Quick Take: Women in the Workforce—United States," June 5, 2019, accessed December 22, 2019, https://www.catalyst.org/research /women-in-the-workforce-united-states/.

57. Chai R. Feldblum and Victoria A. Lipnic, "Breaking the Silence," *Harvard Business Review*, January 26, 2018, https://hbr.org/2018/01/breaking -the-silence.

58. Feldblum, "Breaking the Silence."

59. Joan C. Williams, Jodi Short, Margot Brooks, Hilary Hardcastle, Tiffanie Ellis, and Rayna Saron, "What's Reasonable Now? Sexual Harassment Law After the Norm Cascade," *Michigan State Law Review* (2019), 139 Table, https://digitalcommons.law.msu.edu/lr/vol2019/iss1/4/.

60. Andrea Johnson, Kathryn Menefee, and Ramya Sekaran, "Progress in Advancing MeToo Workplace Reforms in #20 States by 2020," *National Women's Law Center*, July 2019, accessed December 22, 2019, https:// nwlc-ciw49tixgw5lbab.stackpathdns.com/wp-content/uploads/2019 /07/20-States-By-2020-report.pdf.

61. Ksenia Keplinger, Stephanie K. Johnson, Jessica F. Kirk, and Liza Y. Barnes, "Women at Work: Changes in Sexual Harassment between September 2016 and September 2018," *PLoS ONE* 14(7): (2019), e0218313, https://doi .org/10.1371/journal.pone.0218313.

62. Ellen Gabler, Jim Rutenberg, Michael M. Grynbaum, and Rachel Abrams, "NBC Fires Matt Lauer, the Face of 'Today.'" *New York Times*, November 9,

2017, accessed December 22, 2019, https://www.nytimes.com/2017/11/29/business/media/nbc-matt-lauer.html.

63. Jodi Kantor and Megan Twohey, "Harvey Weinstein Paid Off Sexual Harassment Accusers for Decades," *New York Times*, October 5, 2017, accessed December 22, 2019, https://www.nytimes.com/2017/10/05/us/harvey-weinstein-harassment-allegations.html.

64. Farrow, "From Aggressive Overtures to Sexual Assault."

65. Kim Barker and Ellen Gabler, "Charlie Rose Made Crude Sexual Advances, Multiple Women Say," *New York Times*, November 20, 2017, accessed December 22, 2019, https://www.nytimes.com/2017/11/20/us/charlie-rose-women.html.

66. Jenny Singer, "How Many Men at CBS Had Heard That Eliza Dushku Was Sexually Threatened on Tape?" *Forward, The Shmooze*, December 19, 2018, accessed December 22, 2019, https://forward.com/schmooze/416342/cbs-sexual-harassment-scandal-implicates-top-execs-showrunner-actors-and/; John Koblin, "The Year of Reckoning at CBS: Sexual Harassment Allegations and Attempts to Cover Them Up, *New York Times*, updated December 17, 2018, accessed December 22, 2019, https://www.nytimes.com/2018/12/14/business/media/cbs-sexual-harassment-timeline.html.

67. Emily Steel, "Fox Establishes Workplace Culture Panel After Harassment Scandal," *New York Times*, November 20, 2017, accessed December 22, 2019, https://www.nytimes.com/2017/11/20/business/media/fox-news-sexual-harassment.html.

68. Emily Steel, "How Bill O'Reilly Silenced His Accusers," *New York Times*, April 4, 2018, accessed December 22, 2019, https://www.nytimes.com/2018/04/04/business/media/how-bill-oreilly-silenced-his-accusers.html.

69. Sarah Ellison, "Inside the Final Days of Roger Ailes's Reign at Fox News," *Vanity Fair*, September 22, 2016, accessed December 22, 2019, https://www.vanityfair.com/news/2016/09/roger-ailes-fox-news-final-days.

70. Gabriel Sherman, "The Revenge of Roger's Angels," *New York Times*, September 5, 2016, accessed December 22, 2019, http://nymag.com/intelligencer/2016/09/how-fox-news-women-took-down-roger-ailes.html.

71. Stephanie K. Johnson, Ksenia Keplinger, Jessica F. Kirk, and Liza Barnes, "Has Sexual Harassment at Work Decreased Since #MeToo?" *Harvard Business Review*, July 18, 2019, accessed December 22, 2019, https://hbr.org/2019/07/has-sexual-harassment-at-work-decreased-since-metoo.

72. Johnson, "Has Sexual Harassment at Work Decreased since #MeToo?"

73. Sofia Kluch and Megan Brenan, "U.S. Women Feel Less Respected than European, Canadian Peers," *Gallup*, March 8, 2019, accessed December 22, 2019, https://news.gallup.com/poll/247205/women-feel-less-respected -european-canadian-peers.aspx.

74. Kluch, "U.S. Women Feel Less Respected than European, Canadian Peers."

75. Kramer, "How Do Your Workers Feel about Harassment?"

76. Joanna L. Grossman, "The Culture of Compliance: The Final Triumph of Form over Substance in Sexual Harassment Law," *Harvard Women's Law Journal* 26 (2003): 49–63, https://ssrn.com/abstract=2865996.

77. Kevin Stainback, Sibyl Kleiner, and Sheryl Skaggs, "Women in Power: Undoing or Redoing the Gendered Organization?" *Gender and Society* 30(1) (February 2016): 109–35.

78. Colleen Chesterman, Anne Ross-Smith, and Margaret Peters, "The Gendered Impact on Organizations of a Critical Mass of Women in Senior Management," *Policy and Society* 24(4) (2005): 69–91.

79. Chesterman, "The Gendered Impact on Organizations."

80. Chesterman, "The Gendered Impact on Organizations."

Chapter 4

1. While we discuss a woman's ability to effectively manage the impressions she makes in terms of being able to use both communal and agentic behavior, Professor Deborah Gruenfeld of Stanford Business School makes much the same point by talking about "playing low" and "playing high." While Gruenfeld is basically concerned with the projection of power by both women and men and does not concern herself explicitly with gender bias, she is very clear that when you want to exhibit power, you should "play high"—be agentic—and when you want to build personal connections, you should "play low"—be communal. Deborah Gruenfeld, "Playing High, Playing Low and Playing It Straight," YouTube, September 24, 2013, accessed November 23, 2019, https://www.youtube.com/watch?v=zbUX3B GXJlc&index=3&list=PL_I4p0xEPo8rXiClfU9vYlqwpAY0MYt3-.

2. Erving Goffman, *Presentation of Self in Everyday Life* (New York: Doubleday Anchor Books, 1959).

3. Olivia O'Neill and Charles O'Reilly III, "Reducing the Backlash Effect: Self-Monitoring and Women's Promotion," *Journal of Occupational and Organizational Psychology* 84(4) (2010): 825–832.

4. O'Neill and O'Reilly, "Reducing the Backlash Effect."

5. Sandy J. Wayne and Robert C. Liden, "Effects of Impression Management on Performance Ratings: A Longitudinal Study," *Academy of Management Journal* 38(1) (1995): 232–260, www.jstor.org/stable/256734; Val Singh, Savita Kumra, and Susan Vinnicombe, "Gender and Impression Management: Playing the Promotion Game," *Journal of Business Ethics* 37(1) (2002): 77–89, 78, www.jstor.org/stable/25074734.

6. "Authentic Leadership," *Harvard Business Review Podcast* (2007), accessed November 30, 2019, https://hbr.org/2007/05/harvard-business -ideacast-43-a.html; Bill George, *Discover Your True North: Becoming an Authentic Leader,* (John Wiley & Sons, Inc.: Hoboken, New Jersey, 2015); Bill George, *Authentic Leadership: Rediscovering the Secrets to Creating Lasting Value* (Jossey-Bass: San Francisco, 2003).

7. Francis J. Flynn and Daniel R. Ames, "What's Good for the Goose May Not Be As Good for the Gander: The Benefits of Self-Monitoring for Men and Women in Task Groups and Dyadic Conflicts," *Journal of Applied Psychology* 91(2) (2006): 272–281, https://doi.org/10.1037/0021-9010.91.2.272; O'Neill and O'Reilly III, "Reducing the Backlash Effect."

8. Andrew J. Dubrin, *Impression Management in the Workplace: Research, Theory, and Practice* (New York: Taylor & Francis, 2011).

9. Singh, "Gender and Impression Management," 87.

10. Singh, "Gender and Impression Management," 87.

11. Singh, "Gender and Impression Management," 78.

12. Amy J. Cuddy, Matthew Kohut, and John Neffinger, "Connect, Then Lead," *Harvard Business Review* 91(78) (2013): 56, accessed January 3, 2020, https://hbr.org/2013/07/connect-then-lead.

Chapter 5

1. Malcolm Gladwell, *Outliers: The Story of Success* (New York: Little, Brown and Company, 2008).

2. J. K. Rowling, "The Fringe Benefits of Failure, and the Importance of Imagination," *Harvard Gazette,* accessed December 26, 2019, http://news .harvard.edu/gazette/story/2008/06/text-of-j-k-rowling-speech/.

3. Joshua Barajas, "Misty Copeland Makes History as American Ballet Theatre's First Black Principal Ballerina," *PBS NewsHour,* June 30, 2015, accessed December 26, 2019, http://www.pbs.org/newshour/rundown/misty -copeland-makes-history-first-female-african-american-principal-dancer/.

4. Lise Eliot, "Hardwired for Combat? First Female Army Ranger Graduates Prove Grit Beats Gender in Military Training," *Huffington Post,* August

31, 2015, accessed December 26, 2019, http://www.huffingtonpost.com/lise -eliot/hardwired-for-combat-first-female-army-ranger-graduates-prove -grit-beats-gender-in-military-training_b_8057094.html.

5. Milana Hogan, "Non-Cognitive Traits That Impact Female Success in Big Law," PhD diss., University of Pennsylvania, 2013.

6. Joanna Barsh and Lareina Yee, *Unlocking the Full Potential of Women at Work,* McKinsey & Company, accessed December 26, 2019, https://www .mckinsey.com/business-functions/organization/our-insights/unlocking -the-full-potential-of-women-at-work.

7. "The Grit Project: True Grit and a Growth Mindset," *American Bar Association*, accessed December 26, 2019, https://www.americanbar.org/groups /diversity/women/initiatives_awards/grit-project.

8. Carol S. Dweck, *Mindset: The New Psychology of Success: How We Can Learn to Fulfill Our Potential,* Updated Edition (New York: Ballantine Books, 2006).

9. Atul Gawande, "Personal Best," *New Yorker,* September 26, 2011, accessed November 21, 2019, https://www.newyorker.com/magazine/2011 /10/03/personal-best.; Atul Gawande, "Want to Get Great at Something? Get a Coach," TED 2017, accessed November 23, 2019, https://www .ted.com/talks/atul_gawande_want_to_get_great_at_something_get _a_coach.

10. Thomas E. Ford, Mark A. Ferguson, Jenna L, Brooks, and Kate M. Hagadone, "Coping Sense of Humor Reduces Effects of Stereotype Threat on Women's Math Performance," *Personality and Social Psychology Bulletin* 30(5) (2004): 643–653.

11. Nancy A. Yovetich, J. Alexander Dale, and Mary A. Hudak, "Benefits of Humor in Reduction of Threat-Induced Anxiety," *Psychological Reports* 66(1) (1990): 51–58.

12. Yovetich, "Benefits of Humor."

13. Peggy Noonan, quote, accessed December 26, 2019, https://www.quotetab .com/quote/by-peggy-noonan/humor-is-the-shock-absorber-of-life-it -helps-us-take-the-blows.

14. John A. Bargh, Mark Chen, and Laura Burrows, "Automaticity of Social Behavior: Direct Effects of Trait Construct and Stereotype Activation on Action," *Journal of Personality and Social Psychology* 71(2) (1996): 230–244; John A. Bargh, Annette Lee-Chai, Kimberly Barndollar, Peter M. Gollwitzer, and Roman Trotschel, "The Automated Will: Nonconscious Activation and Pursuit of Behavioral Goals," *Journal of Personality and Social Psychology* 81(6) (2001): 1014–1017.

15. John R. Sparks, Charles S. Areni, and K. Chris Cox, "An Investigation of the Effects of Language Style and Communication Modality on Persuasion," *Communication Monographs* 65(2) (1998): 108–125.

16. Dana R. Carney, Judith A. Hall, and Lavonia Smith LeBeau, "Beliefs about the Nonverbal Expression of Social Power," *Journal of Nonverbal Behavior* 29(2) (2005): 105–123; Judith A. Hall, Erik J. Coats, and Lavonia Smith LeBeau, "Nonverbal Behavior and the Vertical Dimension of Social Relations: A Meta-Analysis," *Psychological Bulletin* 131(6) (2005): 898–924.

17. Nathanael J. Fast, Deborah H. Greenfield, Niro Sivanathan, and Adam D. Galinsky, "Illusory Control: A Generative Force behind Power's Far-Reaching Effects," *Psychological Science* 20(4) (2009): 502–508; Cameron Anderson and Adam D. Galinsky, "Power, Optimism, and Risk-Taking," *European Journal of Social Psychology* 36 (2006): 511–536.

18. Joris Lammers, David Dubois, Derek D. Rucker, and Adam D. Galinsky, "Power Gets the Job: Priming Power Improves Interview Outcomes," *Journal of Experimental Social Psychology* 49(4) (2013): 776–779.

19. Adam D. Galinsky and Gavin J. Kilduff, "Be Seen as a Leader," *Harvard Business Review,* December 2013, accessed December 26, 2019, https://hbr.org/2013/12/be-seen-as-a-leader.

20. Galinsky, "Be Seen as a Leader."

21. Amy J. Cuddy, S. Jack Schultz, and Nathan E. Fosse, "P-Curving a More Comprehensive Body of Research on Postural Feedback Reveals Clear Evidential Value for Power-Posing Effects: Reply to Simmons and Simonsohn (2017)," *Psychological Science* 29(4) (2018): 656–66. doi:10.1177/0956797617746749.

22. Amy Cuddy, "Your Body Language Shapes Who You Are," TED, accessed December 26, 2019, http://www.ted.com/talks/amy_cuddy_your_body_language_shapes_who_you_are.

23. Cuddy, "Your Body Language Shapes Who You Are"; Kim Elsesser, "Power Posing Is Back: Amy Cuddy Successfully Refutes Criticism," *Forbes,* April 3, 2018, accessed November 23, 2019, https://www.forbes.com/sites/kimelsesser/2018/04/03/power-posing-is-back-amy-cuddy-successfully-refutes-criticism/#347c016c3b8e; James Clear, "How to Be Confident and Reduce Stress in 2 Minutes per Day," accessed November 23, 2019, https://jamesclear.com/body-language-how-to-be-confident.

24. Dana R. Carney, Amy J. C. Cuddy, and Andy J. Yap, "Power Posing: Brief Nonverbal Displays Affect Neuroendocrine Levels and Risk Tolerance," *Psychological Science* 21(10): 1363–1368; Julia Hanna, "Power Posing: Fake

It until You Make It," *Working Knowledge,* accessed December 26, 2019, http://hbswk.hbs.edu/item/6461.html.

25. Accessed December 26, 2019.
26. Accessed December 26, 2019.
27. "The Grit Project: True Grit and a Growth Mindset."
28. Herbert M. Lefcourt, "Humor: The Psychology of Living Buoyantly," (New York: Klewer Publishing, 2001), accessed December 26, 2019, http://academic.csuohio.edu/neuendorf_ka/chs.pdf.
29. Cuddy, "Your Body Language Shapes Who You Are."

Chapter 6

1. Kelly Cummings, "Nonverbal Communication and First Impressions," Honors thesis, Kent State University, May 2011.
2. Tonya Reiman, *The Power of Body Language* (New York: Pocket Books, 2007) page 10.
3. Linda L. Carli, Suzanne J. LeFleur, and Christopher C. Loeber, "Nonverbal Behavior, Gender, and Influence," *Journal of Personality and Social Psychology* 68(6) (1995): 1030–1041.
4. Madeline E. Heilman, Aaron S. Wallon, Daniella Fuchs, and Melinda Mo Tamkins, "Penalties for Success: Reactions to Women Who Succeed at Male Gender-Typed Tasks," *Journal of Applied Psychology* 89(3) 2004: 416–427; Laurie A. Rudman and Julie E. Phelan, "Backlash Effects for Disconfirming Gender Stereotypes in Organizations," *Research in Organizational Behavior* (28) (2008): 61–79, accessed November 29, 2019, https://doi.org/10.1016/j.riob.2008.04.003.
5. Carli, "Nonverbal Behavior, Gender, and Influence."
6. Alison R. Fragale, "The Power of Powerless Speech: The Effects of Speech Style and Task Interdependence on Status Conferral," *Organizational Behavior and Human Decision Processes* 101 (2006): 243–261.
7. Sue Shellenbarger, "Use Mirroring to Connect with Others: Adopting the Same Gestures, Posture, or Tone Can Enhance Bonding and Help with Networking or Negotiating—But be Subtle about It," *Wall Street Journal,* September 20, 2016, accessed December 24, 2016, https://www.wsj.com/articles/use-mirroring-to-connect-with-others-1474394329.
8. Andrew J. Arnold and Piotr Winkielman, "The Mimicry among Us: Intra- and Inter-Personal Mechanisms of Spontaneous Mimicry," *Journal of Nonverbal Behaviors* (2019). https://doi.org/10.1007/s10919-019-00324-z.

9. Piotr Winkielman, Paula Niedenthal, Joseph Wielgosz, Jiska Eelen, and Liam C. Kavanagh, "Embodiment of Cognition and Emotion," *APA Handbook of Personality and Social Psychology: Vol. 1. Attitudes and Social Cognition* (2015): 151–175. http://dx.doi.org/10.1037/14341-004.

10. Shellenbarger, "Use Mirroring to Connect with Others."

11. Shellenbarger, "Use Mirroring to Connect with Others."

12. Carol Kinsey Goman, "The Art and Science of Mirroring," *Forbes*, May 31, 2011, accessed December 24, 2019, https://www.forbes.com/sites/carol kinseygoman/2011/05/31/the-art-and-science-of-mirroring/#6ac663401318.

13. Todd A. Fonseca, "Mirroring Body Language: 4 Steps to Successfully Mirror Others," *Science of People*, accessed December 26, 2019, https://www .scienceofpeople.com/mirroring/.

14. Piotr Winkielman, "Embodiment of Cognition and Emotion."

15. Jeff Thompson, "Mimicry and Mirroring Can Be Good or Bad: Mirroring and Mimicry May Increase or Decrease Rapport and Liking," *Psychology Today*, September 9, 2012, accessed December 26, 2019, https:// www.psychologytoday.com/us/blog/beyond-words/201209/mimicry -and-mirroring-can-be-good-or-bad.

16. Ernest A, Jasmin, "Don't Copycat an Unpopular Boss's Behavior, Study Reminds," *MSNBC*, August 1, 2011, accessed December 26, 2019, https:// www.nbcnews.com/health/body-odd/dont-copycat-unpopular-bosss -behavior-study-reminds-flna1C6437233.

17. Jasmin, "Don't Copycat"; Winkielman, "Embodiment of Cognition and Emotion."

18. "Mirroring Body Language"; Shellenbarger, "Use Mirroring to Connect with Others."

19. Fonseca, "Mirroring Body Language."

20. Fonseca, "Mirroring Body Language"; Shellenbarger, "Use Mirroring to Connect with Others."

21. Fonseca, "Mirroring Body Language"; Shellenbarger, "Use Mirroring to Connect with Others."

22. Chris L. Kleinke, "Compliance to Requests Made by Gazing and Touching Experimenters in Field Settings," *Journal of Experimental Social Psychology* 13(3) (1977): 218–223, https://doi.org/10.1016/0022-1031 (77)90044-0.

23. April H. Crusco and Christopher G. Wetzel, "The Midas Touch: The Effects of Interpersonal Touch on Restaurant Tipping," *Personality and Social Psychology Bulletin* 10(4) (1984): 512–517; Amy S. Ebesu Hubbard, A. Allen Tsuji, Christine Williams, and Virgilio Seatriz Jr., "Effects of Touch on

Gratuities Received in Same-Gender and Cross-Gender Dyads," *Journal of Applied Social Psychology* 33(11) (2003): 2427–2438.

24. Hajo Adam and Adam D. Galinsky, "Enclothed Cognition," *Journal of Experimental Social Psychology* 48(4) (2012): 918–925.

25. For a summary of the research on the relationships between a person's dress and how that affects the behavior of others toward that person, see Kim K. P. Johnson, Jeong-Ju Yoo, Minjeong Kim, Sharron J. Lennon, "Dress and Human Behavior: A Review and Critique," *Clothing & Textiles Research Journal* 26(1) (2008): 3–22.

Chapter 7

1. David B. Duller, Beth A. LePoire, R. Kelly Aune, and Silvie V. Ely, "Social Perceptions as Mediators of the Effect of Speech Rate," *Human Communication Research* 19(2) (1992): 286–311.

2. Angelina Jolie, "Angelina Jolie Speak[s] on World Refugee Day 2009," *United Nations High Commissioner for Refugees*, YouTube, June 20, 2009, accessed December 27, 2019, https://www.youtube.com/watch?v =q6msUKyiYic.

3. Douglas Quenqua, "They're Like, Way Ahead of the Linguistic Currrrve," *New York Times*, February 27, 2012, accessed December 27, 2019, https://www.nytimes.com/2012/02/28/science/young-women-often -trendsetters-in-vocal-patterns.html.

4. Marc Lieberman, "Jill Abramson's Voice," *Language Log*, October 18, 2011, accessed December 27, 2019, http://languagelog.ldc.upenn.edu/nll /?p=3504.

5. Michael Saul, "Caroline Kennedy No Whiz with Words," *New York Daily News*, December 29, 2008, accessed December 27, 2019, http:// www.nydailynews.com/news/politics/caroline-kennedy-no-whiz-words -article-1.355586.

6. Ellen Petry Leanse, "Google and Apple Alum Says Using This One Word Can Damage Your Credibility," *Business Insider*, June 25, 2015, accessed December 27, 2019, http://www.businessinsider.com/former-google-exec -says-this-word-can-damage-your-credibility-2015–6.

7. Rachel Simmons, *The Curse of the Good Girl: Raising Authentic Girls with Courage and Confidence* (New York: Penguin Books, 2009), 70. Simmons recognizes the excessive use of apologies among women as an attempt to appear communal, but warns that excessive apologies may cause women to adopt subordinate roles in their personal and professional lives.

8. Katharina Buchholz, "In 2019, Global Emoji Count Is Growing to More than 3000," *Statista.com*, July 17, 2019, accessed December 6, 2019, https://www.statista.com/chart/17275/number-of-emojis-from-1995-bis-2019/.

9. *Statista*, "People Like Emojis at Work, but Feel Unsure at First," July 17, 2019, accessed December 6, 2019, https://www.statista.com/chart/18717/emoji-use-at-work/.

10. Billie Brand, "Why It's Easier to Express Our Emotions in Emojis," *i-d Vice*, May 26, 2015, accessed December 6, 2019, https://i-d.vice.com/en_us/article/xwxamz/why-its-easier-to-express-our-emotions-in-emojis.

11. Michaela Rollings, "You Might Be Surprised at the Three Most-Used Emojis at Work," *Hive*, December 3, 2019, accessed December 6, 2019, https://hive.com/blog/most-used-emojis-work/.

12. "The Kardashians Talk Back to Tweets," YouTube, April 1, 2011, accessed December 27, 2019, https://www.youtube.com/watch?v=d8jL8qz7dwM.

13. Lindsey Stanberry, "Try This Experiment if You Say 'Sorry' Too Much," *Refinery29*, August 3, 2015, accessed December 27, 2019, http://www.refinery29.com/saying-sorry-at-work#.ozt2ol:Jlf7. Amy Schumer, "I'm Sorry," accessed December 27, 2019, https://vimeo.com/253499468.

Chapter 8

1. Anthony Mulac, Karen T. Erlandson, W. Jeffrey Farrar, Jennifer S. Hallet, Jennifer L. Molloy, and Margaret Prescott, "Uh-huh. What's That All About? Differing Interpretations of Conversational Backchannels and Questions as Sources of Miscommunication across Gender Boundaries," *Communication Research* 25(6) (1998): 641–668.

2. Holly Weeks, "Taking the Stress out of Stressful Conversations," *Harvard Business Review*, July-August 2001, accessed December 29, 2019, https://hbr.org/2001/07/taking-the-stress-out-of-stressful-conversations.

3. Katharine Ridgway O'Brien, "Just Saying 'No': An Examination of Gender Differences in the Ability to Decline Requests in the Workplace," PhD diss., Rice University, 2014.

4. O'Brien, "Just Saying 'No.'"

5. Katy Waldman, "The Tyranny of the Smile: Why Does Everyone Expect Women to Smile All the Time?," *Slate*, June 18, 2013, accessed December 7, 2019, https://slate.com/human-interest/2013/06/bitchy-resting-face-and-female-niceness-why-do-women-have-to-smile-more-than-men.html.

6. J. R. Thorpe, "Why Do People Expect Women to Smile?," *Bustle*, July 6, 2017, accessed December 7, 2019, https://www.bustle.com/p/why-do -people-expect-women-to-smile-67360.

7. Sarah Laing, "Why Do Men Need Women to Smile?," *Flare*, July 25, 2018, accessed December 7, 2019, https://www.flare.com/news/greg-rickford -marieke-walsh-smile-women/.

8. "When Rude Customers Tell You to Smile…," *Reddit*, accessed December 5, 2019, https://www.reddit.com/r/TalesFromRetail/comments/agdduo /when_rude_customers_tell_you_to_smile/.

9. "What Happens When Women Don't Smile," *Dame Magazine*, May 31, 2018, accessed December 5, 2019, https://www.damemagazine.com/2018 /05/31/what-happens-when-women-dont-smile/.

10. Shannon Doyne, "How Do You Feel about Being Told to Smile?," *New York Times*, April 23, 2018, accessed December 5, 2019, https://www.nytimes .com/2018/04/23/learning/how-do-you-feel-about-being-told-to-smile .html.

11. Jessica Bennett, "I'm Not Mad. That's Just My RBF," *New York Times*, August 1, 2015, accessed December 5, 2019, https://www.nytimes.com /2015/08/02/fashion/im-not-mad-thats-just-my-resting-b-face.html.

12. Anne Kreamer, *It's Always Personal: Navigating Emotion in the New Workplace* (New York: Penguin, 2013).

13. Victoria L. Brescoll and Eric Luis Uhlmann, "Can an Angry Woman Get Ahead? Status Conferral, Gender, and Expression of Emotion in the Workplace," *Psychological Science* 19(3) (2008): 268–275.

14. Donald E. Gibson and Ronda Callister, "Anger in Organizations: Review and Future Directions" (paper presented at the 22nd Annual International Association of Conflict Management Conference, Kyoto, Japan, June 15–18, 2009).

15. Anne Karpf, *The Human Voice: How This Extraordinary Instrument Reveals Essential Clues about Who We Are* (New York: Bloomsbury USA, 2006), 55.

16. Kathleen McCauliffe, "Gaslighting 101: Are You Being Manipulated at Work?," *Career Contessa*, February 21, 2019, accessed December 7, 2019, https://www.careercontessa.com/advice/gaslighting-in-the-office/; Stephanie Olsen, "How to Tell if They're Gaslighting You at Work," *Inhersight .com*, accessed December 7, 2019, https://www.inhersight.com/blog/insight -commentary/gaslighting?_n=57725927; Hollie Richardson, "What Happened When I Was Gaslit by My Boss," *Refinery29*, September 15, 2019,

accessed December 7, 2019, https://www.refinery29.com/en-gb/gaslighting
-at-work; Samantha Young, "Gaslighting at Work—When You Think You
Are Going Crazy," Accessed December 30, 2019, https://www.linkedin
.com/pulse/gaslighting-work-when-you-think-going-crazy-samantha
-young; George Simon, "Gaslighting as a Manipulation Tactic: What It Is,
Who Does It, and Why," accessed December 30, 2019, https://counselling
resource.com/features/2011/11/08/gaslighting/.

Chapter 9

1. Kathryn Heath, Jill Flynn, and Mary Davis Holt, "Women, Find Your
   Voice," *Harvard Business Review,* June 2014, accessed June 24, 2015,
   https://hbr.org/2014/06/women-find-your-voice.
2. Heath, "Women, Find Your Voice."
3. Adrienne B. Hancock and Benjamin A. Rubin, "Influence of Communication Partner's Gender on Language," *Journal of Language and Social Psychology* 34(1) (2015): 46–64.
4. Kristin J. Anderson and Campbell Leaper, "Meta-Analyses of Gender
   Effects on Conversational Interruption: Who, What, When, Where, and
   How," *Sex Roles* 39(3–4) (1998): 225–252.
5. Riana Duncan, "Excellent Suggestion, Miss Triggs," *Punch,* 1988.01.08.11.
   tif, available at http://punch.photoshelter.
6. Leslie Perlow and Stephanie Williams, "Is Silence Killing Your Company?"
   Engineering Management Review 31(4) (2003): 18–23.
7. Christopher F. Karpowitz, Tali Mendelberg, and Lee Shaker, "Gender
   Inequality in Deliberative Participation," *American Political Science
   Review* 106(3) (2012): 533–547; Christopher F. Karpowitz and Tali Mendelberg, *The Silent Sex: Gender, Deliberation and Institutions* (Princeton:
   Princeton University Press, 2014); Soraya Chemaly, "In Mixed Gender
   Groups, Can You Guess Who Talks the Most?" *Role Reboot,* October 22,
   2018, accessed December 26, 2019, http://www.rolereboot.org/culture
   -and-politics/details/2015-10-in-mixed-gender-groups-can-you-guess
   -who-talks-the-most/.
8. Chemaly, "In Mixed Gender Groups."

Chapter 10

1. Priya Fielding-Singh, Devon Magliozzi, and Swethaa Ballakrishnen, "Why
   Women Stay Out of the Spotlight at Work," *Harvard Business Review,*

August 28, 2018, accessed December 26, 2019, https://hbr.org/2018/08/sgc-8-28-why-women-stay-out-of-the-spotlight-at-work.

2. Fielding-Singh, "Why Women Stay Out."

3. Rachel Simmons, *The Curse of the Good Girl: Raising Authentic Girls with Courage and Confidence* (New York: Penguin, 2010).

4. Simmons, *The Curse of the Good Girl,* 102.

5. Joan C. Williams, "Hacking Tech's Diversity Problem," *Harvard Business Review,* October 2014, accessed December 31, 2019, https://hbr.org/2014/10/hacking-techs-diversity-problem.

6. Williams, "Hacking Tech's Diversity Problem."

7. Meghan I. H. Lindeman, Amanda M. Durik, and Maura Dooley, "Women and Self-Promotion: A Test of Three Theories," *Psychological Reports* 122(1) February 2019: 219–230, accessed December 7, 2019, https://journals.sagepub.com/doi/pdf/10.1177/0033294118755096.

8. Joyce F. Benenson, "The Development of Human Female Competition: Allies and Adversaries," *Philosophical Transactions of the Royal Society B: Biological Sciences* 368(1361) (2013): 1–11, doi: 10.1098/rstb.2013.0079.

9. Benenson, "The Development of Human Female Competition."

10. Benenson, "The Development of Human Female Competition"; Stephanie Thomson, "A Lack of Confidence Isn't What's Holding Back Working Women," *Atlantic,* September 20, 2018, accessed December 7, 2019, https://www.theatlantic.com/family/archive/2018/09/women-workplace-confidence-gap/570772/.

11. Julie E. Phelan, Corinne A. Moss-Racusin, and Laurie A. Rudman, "Competent yet Out in the Cold: Shifting Criteria for Hiring Reflect Backlash toward Agentic Women," *Psychology of Women Quarterly* 32(4) (2008): 406–413, https://doi.org/10.1111%2Fj.1471-6402.2008.00454.x.

12. Timothy A. Judge, Beth A. Livingston, and Charlice Hurst, "Do Nice Guys—and Gals—Really Finish Last? The Joint Effect of Sex and Agreeableness on Income," *Journal of Personality and Social Psychology* 102(2) (2012): 390–407; Madeline E. Heilman, "Gender Stereotypes and Workplace Bias," *Research in Organizational Behavior* 31 (2012): 113–135, https://doi.org/10.1016/j.riob.2012.11.003.

13. Over half of working women believe they are overlooked for promotions because they are too modest; too reluctant to be clear and direct about their qualifications; and too concerned about being seen as arrogant, big-headed, or pushy. Laura Cummins, "Modesty Holding Women Back at Work," *Female First,* accessed December 31, 2019, http://www.femalefirst.co.uk/womens-issues/modesty-holding-women-back-at-work-543047.html.

14. Sarah J. Tracy and Kendra Dyanne Rivera, "Endorsing Equity and Applauding Stay at Home Moms: How Male Voices on Work-Life Reveal Aversive Sexism and Flickers of Transformation," *Management Communication Quarterly* 24(1) (2010): 3–43, https://doi.org/10.1177/0893318909 352248.

15. John Anderson, "The Film Fatales Collective Trains a Lens on Gender Inequality," *New York Times,* August 21, 2015, accessed December 31, 2019, https://www.nytimes.com/2015/08/23/movies/the-film-fatales -collective-trains-a-lens-on-gender-inequality.html.

16. Anderson, "The Film Fatales Collective,"

17. Olivia O'Neil and Charles O'Reilly III, "Reducing the Backlash Effect: Self-Monitoring and Women's Promotion," *Journal of Occupational and Organizational Psychology* 84(4) (2010): 825–832.

18. Shankar Vedantam, "Salary, Gender, and the Social Cost of Haggling," *Washington Post,* July 30, 2007, accessed January 1, 2020, http://www .washingtonpost.com/wp-dyn/content/article/2007/07/29/AR20070729 00827.html.

19. Vedantam, "Salary, Gender, and the Social Cost of Haggling."

20. Juan M. Madera, Michelle R. Hebl, and Randi C. Martin, "Gender and Letters of Recommendation for Academia: Agentic and Communal Differences," *Journal of Applied Psychology,* 94(6) (2009): 1591–1599, doi: 10.1037 /a0016539.

21. Madera, "Gender and Letters of Recommendation."

22. Madera, "Gender and Letters of Recommendation."

23. Laurie A. Rudman and Peter Glick, "Prescriptive Gender Stereotypes and Backlash toward Agentic Women," *Journal of Social Issues* 57(4) (2001): 743–762, https://psycnet.apa.org/doi/10.1111/0022-4537.00239.

24. Frances Trix and Carolyn Psenka, "Exploring the Color of Glass: Letters of Recommendation for Female and Male Medical Faculty," *Discourse & Society* 14(2) (2003): 191220, https://doi.org/10.1177%2F0957926 503014002277; Corinne A. Moss-Racusin, John F. Dovidio, Victoria L. Brescoll, Mark J. Graham, and Jo Handelsman, "Science Faculty's Subtle Gender Biases Favor Male Students," *Proceedings of the National Academy of Sciences,* September 17, 2012, accessed December 7, 2019, https://www .pnas.org/content/early/2012/09/14/1211286109, (interventions addressing faculty gender bias might advance the goal of increasing the participation of women in science); A. Hoffman, W. Grant, M. McCormick, E. Jezewski, P. Matemavi, and A. Langnas, "Gendered Differences in Letters of Recommendation for Transplant Surgery Fellowship Applications," *Journal of*

Surgical Education, 76(2), March-April 2019: 427–432, accessed December 7, 2019, https://www.ncbi.nlm.nih.gov/pubmed/30266555, (finding gender differences exist in letters of recommendation for surgical fellowship applicants); J. M. Madera, M. R. Helb, H. Dial, et al., "Raising Doubts in Letters of Recommendation for Academia: Gender Differences and Their Impact," *Journal of Business and Psychology*, 34(3), June 2019: 287–303, accessed December 7, 2019, https://link.springer.com/article/10.1007 /s10869-018-9541-1 (both female and male recommenders use more doubt raisers in letters of recommendation for women compared to men; certain types of doubt raisers result in negative outcomes for both genders; and because doubt raisers are more frequent in letters about women, women are at a disadvantage relative to men); Pauline Filipou, Segal Mahajan, Allison Deal, et al., "The Presence of Gender Bias in Letters of Recommendations Written for Urology Residency Applicants," *Urology* 134, December 2019: 56–61 accessed December 7, 2019, https://www.sciencedirect .com/science/article/pii/S0090429519307903, (significant linguistic differences exist between letters of recommendation written for women and men applying into urology, suggesting that gender bias may permeate resident recruitment, negatively affecting the likelihood of women matching into urology).

Chapter 11

1. Lean In and McKinsey & Company, "Women in the Workplace, 2019," accessed December 1, 2019, https://womenintheworkplace.com/Women _in_the_Workplace_2019.pdf.
2. Sylvia Ann Hewlett, "Executive Women and the Myth of Having It All," *Harvard Business Review,* April 2002, accessed December 29, 2019, http:// hbr.org/2002/04/executive-women-and-the-myth-of-having-it-all.
3. Lean In, "Women in the Workplace, 2019."
4. Lila MacLellan, "70% of Top Male Earners in the US Have a Spouse Who Stays Home," *Quartz*, April 30, 2019, accessed January 2, 2020, https:// qz.com/work/1607995/most-men-in-the-top-1-of-us-earners-have-a-spouse -who-stays-home/.
5. MacLellan, "70% of Top Male Earners in the US Have a Spouse Who Stays Home."
6. Liana C. Sayer and Joanna R. Pepin, "Moms Spend Even More Time on Housework When a Man's in the House. Here's Why," *Washington Post,* May 8, 2019, accessed January 1, 2020, https://www.washingtonpost.com

/opinions/moms-spend-even-more-time-on-housework-when-a-mans-in
-the-house-heres-why/2019/05/08/319da006-71ba-11e9-8be0-ca575670
e91c_story.html.

7. Julie Scagell. "The Average Full-Time Working Woman Spends 21 Hours a Week on Housework," *Scary Mommy*, August 27, 2019, https://www.scary mommy.com/working-women-spend-21-hours-chores/.

8. Katherine Schaeffer, "Among U.S. Couples, Women Do More Cooking and Grocery Shopping than Men," *Pew Research Center*, September 24, 2019, accessed January 2, 2020, https://www.pewresearch.org/fact-tank /2019/09/24/among-u-s-couples-women-do-more-cooking-and-grocery -shopping-than-men/.

9. Claire Cain Miller, "Even among Harvard Graduates, Women Fall Short of Their Work Expectations," *New York Times*, November 28, 2014, accessed January 1, 2020, https://www.nytimes.com/2014/11/30/upshot/even -among-harvard-graduates-women-fall-short-of-their-work-expectations .html.

10. Miranda Bryant, "More Fathers Are Taking Paternity Leave, but Others Are Still Doing All the Work," *The Guardian*, November 18, 2019, accessed January 1, 2020, https://www.theguardian.com/money/2019/nov/17/more -fathers-are-taking-paternity-leave-but-mothers-are-still-doing-all-the -work.

11. Hannah Seligson, "Why the Sting of Layoffs Can Be Harder for Men," *New York Times*, January 31, 2009, accessed January 1, 2020, https://www .nytimes.com/2009/02/01/jobs/01layoff.html.

12. "Life & Leadership Survey After HBS," Harvard Business School, May 2015, https://www.hbs.edu/women50/docs/L_and_L_Survey_2Findings_12final .pdf; Jessica Grose, "It's Not Your Kids Holding Your Career Back. It's Your Husband," *Slate*, November 18, 2014, accessed January 1, 2020, https://slate .com/human-interest/2014/11/harvard-business-school-study-it-s-not-kids -but-husbands-that-hold-women-s-careers-back.html.

13. Marianne Bertrand, Claudia Goldin, and Lawrence F. Katz, "Dynamics of the Gender Gap for Young Professionals in the Financial and Corporate Sectors," *American Economic Journal* 2(3) (2010): 228–255, doi: 10.1257 /app.2.3.228.

14. YoonKyung Chung et al. "The Parental Gender Earnings Gap in the United States," *US Census Bureau, Center for Economic Studies,* November 2017, accessed January 1, 2020, https://www2.census.gov/ces/wp/2017 /CES-WP-17-68.pdf.

15. Victoria Stilwell, "Fewer Millennial Moms Show U.S. Birth Rate Drop Lasting," *Bloomberg Business*, September 16, 2014, accessed January 1, 2020, https://www.bloomberg.com/news/articles/2014-09-16/fewer-millennial -moms-show-u-s-birth-rate-drop-lasting.

16. Claire Cain Miller, "The Motherhood Penalty vs. the Fatherhood Bonus: A Child Helps Your Career, if You're a Man," *New York Times*, September 6, 2014, accessed January 1, 2020, https://www.nytimes.com/2014/09/07 /upshot/a-child-helps-your-career-if-youre-a-man.html; Shelley J. Correll and Stephen Benard, "Getting a Job: Is There a Motherhood Penalty?" *American Journal of Sociology* 112(5) (2007): 1297–1339, https://doi .org/10.1086/511799.

17. Chung, "The Parental Gender Earnings Gap."

18. Katharine Zaleski, "Female Company President: 'I'm Sorry to All the Mothers I Worked With,'" *Fortune*, March 3, 2015, accessed January 1, 2020, http://fortune.com/2015/03/03/female-company-president-im-sorry -to-all-the-mothers-i-used-to-work-with/.

19. Juliana Menasce Horowitz, "Despite Challenges at Home and Work, Most Working Moms and Dads Say Being Employed Is What's Best for Them," *Pew Research Center*, September 12, 2019, accessed January 1, 2020, https:// www.pewresearch.org/fact-tank/2019/09/12/despite-challenges-at-home -and-work-most-working-moms-and-dads-say-being-employed-is-whats -best-for-them/.

20. George Gao and Gretchen Livingston, "Working While Pregnant Is Much More Common than It Used to Be," *Pew Research Center*, March 31, 2015, accessed January 1, 2020, http://www.pewresearch.org/fact -tank/2015/03/31/working-while-pregnant-is-much-more-common-than -it-used-to-be/.

21. George Gao, "Working While Pregnant"; Bourree Lam, "Yes, There Really Are More Pregnant Women in the Office," *Atlantic*, April 8, 2015, accessed January 1, 2020, http://www.theatlantic.com/business/archive /2015/04/yes-there-really-are-more-pregnant-women-at-the-office /389763/.

22. Consider speaking with Human Resources to better understand company, state and federal policies regarding your maternity leave. Some policies may offer certain types of job protections; it is important for you to know your rights while you are on leave.

23. Mauro Whiteman, "PepsiCo CEO Indra Nooyi: 'I Don't Think Women Can Have It All Either,'" *Aspen Idea Blog*, July 1, 2014, accessed January 1,

2020, http://www.aspeninstitute.org/about/blog/pepsico-ceo-indra-nooyi -i-don-t-think-women-can-have-it-all-either.

24. Matthew Sparkes, "Christine Lagarde: 'Women Can't Have It All,'" *Business Insider,* September 26, 2012, accessed January 1, 2020, http://www .businessinsider.com/christine-lagarde-women-cant-have-it-all-2012–9.

25. Katie Van Syckle, "Mila Kunis Says There's No Such Thing as Having It All," *The Cut,* accessed January 2, 2020, https://www.thecut.com/2016/07 /mila-kunis-bad-moms-having-it-all.html.

26. Maya Salem, "Does 'Having It All' Mean Doing It All?" *New York Times,* December 30, 2019, https://www.nytimes.com/2018/12/07/business/miche lle-obama-women-having-it-all.html.

27. Anne-Marie Slaughter, "Why Women Still Can't Have It All," *Atlantic,* July/August 2012, accessed January 1, 2020, http://www.theatlantic.com /magazine/archive/2012/07/why-women-still-cant-have-it-all/309020/.

28. Slaughter, "Why Women Still Can't Have It All."

29. Slaughter, *Unfinished Business: Women Men Work Family* (New York:Random House, 2015).

30. Ellen McCarthy, "She Famously Said that Women Can't Have it All. Now She Realizes that No One Can," *Washington Post,* August 26, 2016, accessed January 1, 2020, https://www.washingtonpost.com/lifestyle/style /she-famously-said-that-women-cant-have-it-all-now-she-realizes-that -no-one-can/2016/08/26/889944e4-5bf3-11 e6-831d-0324760ca856_story .htm.

31. Sharon Hayes, *The Cultural Contradictions of Motherhood* (Yale U. Press, 1998); Linda Rose Ennis (ed.), *Intensive Mothering: The Cultural Contradictions of Modern Motherhood* (Demeter Press: 2014); Fiona Joy Green, "Intensive Mothering," in Andrea O'Reilly, editor, *Encyclopedia of Motherhood.*

32. Melissa A. Milkie, Kei A. Nomaguchi, and Kathleen E. Denny, "Does the Amount of Time Mothers Spend with Children or Adolescents Matter?" *Journal of Marriage and Family* 77(2) (2015): 355–372, doi: 10.1111 /jomf.12170.

33. Milkie, "Does the Amount of Time Mothers Spend with Children or Adolescents Matter?"

34. Anne Roeters and Kirsten van Houdt, "Parent-Child Activities, Paid Work Interference, and Child Mental Health," *Wiley Online Library, John Wiley & Sons, Ltd* (10.1111), March 6, 2019, https://onlinelibrary.wiley.com /doi/10.1111/fare.12355.

35. Terri LeMoyne and Tom Buchanan, "Does 'Hovering' Matter? Helicopter Parenting and Its Effect on Well-Being," *Sociological Spectrum* 31(4) (2011): 399–418, https://doi.org/10.1080/02732173.2011.574038; Chris Segrin, Alesia Woszidlo, Michelle Givertz, and Neil Montgomery, "Parent and Child Traits Associated with Overparenting," *Journal of Social and Clinical Psychology* 32(6): 569–595, doi: 10.1521/jscp.2013.32.6.569; Holly H. Schifferin, Miriam Liss, Haley Miles McLean et al., "Helping or Hovering? The Effects of Helicopter Parenting on College Students' Well-Being," *Journal of Child and Family Studies* 23(3) (2014): 548–557 doi:10.1007/s10826-013-9716-3.

36. Julie Lythcott-Haims, *How to Raise an Adult: Break Free of the Overparenting Trap and Prepare Your Kid for Success* (New York: Henry Holt and Company, 2015).

37. Julie Lythcott-Haims, "Kids of Helicopter Parents Are Sputtering Out," *Slate*, July 5, 2015, accessed January 1, 2020, http://www.slate.com/articles/double_x/doublex/2015/07/helicopter_parenting_is_increasingly_correlated_with_college_age_depression.html.

38. Denise-Marie Ordway, "What Research Says about the Kids of Working Moms." *Journalist's Resource*, 13 August. 2018, https://journalistsresource.org/studies/economics/jobs/working-mother-employment-research/.

39. Dina Gerdeman, "Kids of Working Moms Grow into Happy Adults," *HBS Working Knowledge*, July 16, 2018, accessed January 2, 2020, https://hbswk.hbs.edu/item/kids-of-working-moms-grow-into-happy-adults.

40. Carmen Nobel, "Kids Benefit from Having a Working Mom," *HBS Working Knowledge,* May 15, 2015, accessed September 13, 2015, http://hbswk.hbs.edu/item/kids-benefit-from-having-a-working-mom.

41. Nobel, "Kids Benefit from Having a Working Mom."

Glossary

1. "Gender, Equity, and Human Rights," *World Health Organization*, accessed December 30, 2019, https://www.who.int/gender-equity-rights/en/.

2. "Gender, Equity, and Human Rights: Gender," *World Health Organization*, accessed December 30, 2019, https://www.who.int/gender-equity-rights/understanding/gender-definition/en/.

3. Angeline Goh, "An Attributional Analysis of Counterproductive Work Behavior (CWB) in Response to Occupational Stress" (dissertation, University

of South Florida, November 21, 2006), http://digital.lib.usf.edu/content/SF/S0/02/62/13/00001/E14-SFE0001895.pdf.

4. Lilia M. Cortina, "Unseen Injustice: Incivility as Modern Discrimination in Organizations," *Academy of Management Review* 33(1) (January 2008): 55–75.

5. "Microaggression," *Merriam-Webster, s.v.,* accessed December 27, 2018, https://www.Merriam-Webster.com/dictionary/microaggression.

ACKNOWLEDGMENTS FOR SECOND EDITION

We want to thank the following people for their help with the research and revisions to *Breaking Through Bias* that are reflected in the substantial amount of new material added to this second edition: Cynthia K. Harris, Christina Sedall, Zoe McGrath, Les Harris, Charles Curtis, Anthony Warren, Kay Bowers, Frances Krasnow, Roseanne Rega, Ursula Laskowski, Katherine Hanson, Ann Kowalsky, Alicia Simons, Chris Haigh, Tess Wood, Marisa McGrenera, Victoria Lozano, and Jennifer Zordani.

ACKNOWLEDGMENTS FOR FIRST EDITION

The time, effort, and ideas of many people have gone into the writing of this book. Starr M. Rayford has provided us with editorial and research support that has helped us sharpen our prose, organize the manuscript, and coordinate its completion. Kay Bowers has been tirelessly good humored as she typed and retyped our many drafts and revisions. Kristine Johnson, Katie Ahern, Margaret Hanson, Olivia Clark Silver, and Dan Lambert have read and reread draft chapters, always providing insightful, constructive comments. At the risk of missing some of our reviewers, commenters, supporters, and others, we would like to thank the following: Bethany Harris, Ann Fourt, Darla Zink, Charlie and Rochelle Curtis, Mary Jo Stockman, Angela Corsa, Elizabeth Kroger, Judy and Adrian Coté, Brenda Dunn-Kinny, Wendy Manning, Jessica Cullen Smith, Wendy White-Eagle, Leslie Fenton, Rose Stubi, Steve Pflaum, Ruth Goran, Jennifer Mikulina, Krista Vink-Venegas, Angela Vasandani, Lee Richard Tschanz, Melinda Kleehamer, Mary Pat Farrell, Jen Berman, Wileen Chick, Marc S. Zaslavsky, Frances H. Krasnow, Susan J. Schmitt, Marlene Greenberg, The Dancin' Queens, Jennifer Wojan, Candace P. Davis, Cheryl S. Wilson, Jill Melnicki, Mary Wuilloud, Emily Vasiliou, Carol Frohlinger, Mary Lou Pier, Pam Simon, Robin Hadrick, Robin Cantor, Suzanne DeVries, Vickie Drendel, Ellen Turner, Kinga Staromiejska, Yang Connita Yang, Erica Harris, Catherine and Michael Zuckert, Valencia Ray, Tina Davis Milligan, and Kathleen Callahan.

We would also like to thank everyone at our publisher, Bibliomotion, for their first-rate professionalism and advice, with a special shout-out going to Alicia Simons, Erika Heilman, and Jill Friedlander. Also thanks to Lee McEnany Caraher, who suggested we work with Bibliomotion in the first place.

REFERENCES

Abouzahr, Katie, Matt Krentz, Frances Brooks Taplett, Claire Tracey, and Miki Tsusaka. "Dispelling the Myths of the Gender 'Ambition Gap.'" *Boston Consulting Group,* April 5, 2017. Accessed December 1, 2019. https://www .bcg.com/en-us/publications/2017/people-organization-leadership-change -dispelling-the-myths-of-the-gender-ambition-gap.aspx.

Adam, Hajo, and Adam D. Galinsky. "Enclothed Cognition." *Journal of Experimental Social Psychology* 48(4) (2012): 918–925.

Agars, Mark D. "Reconsidering the Impact of Gender Stereotypes on the Advancement of Women in Organizations." *Psychology of Women Quarterly* 28(2) (2004): 103–111.

American Psychological Association. "Men and Women: No Big Difference." October 20, 2005. Accessed December 1, 2019. https://www.apa.org/research /action/difference.

Ancient Origins. "The Rape of the Sabine Women." February 2, 2015. Accessed December 5, 2019. https://www.ancient-origins.net/news-history/rape-sabine -women-002636.

Anderson, Cameron, and Adam D. Galinsky. "Power, Optimism, and Risk-Taking." *European Journal of Social Psychology* 36(4) (2006): 511–536.

Anderson, John. "The Film Fatales Collective Trains a Lens on Gender Inequality." *New York Times,* August 21, 2015. Accessed December 31, 2019. https://www.nytimes.com/2015/08/23/movies/the-film-fatales-collective -trains-a-lens-on-gender-inequality.html.

Anderson, Kristin J., and Campbell Leaper. "Meta-Analyses of Gender Effects on Conversational Interruption: Who, What, When, Where, and How." *Sex Roles* 39(3–4) (1998): 225–252.

Anthony, Susan B. "Fifty Years of Work for Woman." *Independent,* 52 (February 15, 1900). Quoted in Lynn Sherr, *Failure Is Impossible: Susan B. Anthony in Her Own Words.* Crown Publishing Group, 1995.

Arnold, Andrew J., and Piotr Winkielman. "The Mimicry among Us: Intra- and Inter-Personal Mechanisms of Spontaneous Mimicry." *Journal of Nonverbal Behaviors* (2019). https://doi.org/10.1007/s10919-019-00324-z.

"As Academic Gender Gap Declines, There Is Still Work to be Done." *Harbus*, April 25, 2011. Accessed January 2, 2020. http://www.harbus.org/2011/gender-gap/.

Association of American Medical Colleges. "Women Were Majority of U.S. Medical School Applicants in 2018." December 4, 2018. Accessed December 1, 2019. https://www.aamc.org/news-insights/press-releases/women-were-majority-us-medical-school-applicants-2018.

"Authentic Leadership." *Harvard Business Review Podcast* (2007). Accessed November 30, 2019. https://hbr.org/2007/05/harvard-business-ideacast-43-a.html.

Banaji, Mahzarin R., Max H. Bazerman, and Dolly Chugh. "How (Un)ethical Are You?" *Harvard Business Review*. December 2003. Accessed December 1, 2019. https://hbr.org/2003/12/how-unethical-are-you.

Barajas, Joshua. "Misty Copeland Makes History as American Ballet Theatre's First Black Principal Ballerina." *PBS News Hour,* June 30, 2015. Accessed December 26, 2019. http://www.pbs.org/newshour/rundown/misty-copeland-makes-history-first-female-african-american-principal-dancer/.

Barbulescu, Roxana, and Matthew Bidwell. "Do Women Choose Different Jobs from Men? Mechanisms of Application Segregation in the Market for Managerial Workers." *Organization Science* 24(3) (2012): 737–756.

Bargh, John A., Annette Lee-Chai, Kimberly Barndollar, Peter M. Gollwitzer, and Roman Trötschel. "The Automated Will: Nonconscious Activation and Pursuit of Behavioral Goals." *Journal of Personality and Social Psychology* 81(6) (2001): 1014–1027.

Bargh, John A., Mark Chen, and Lara Burrows. "Automaticity of Social Behavior: Direct Effects of Trait Construct and Stereotype Activation on Action." *Journal of Personality and Social Psychology* 71(2) (1996): 230–244.

Barker, Kim, and Ellen Gabler. "Charlie Rose Made Crude Sexual Advances, Multiple Women Say." *New York Times*, November 20, 2017. Accessed December 22, 2019. https://www.nytimes.com/2017/11/20/us/charlie-rose-women.html.

Barsh, Joanna, and Lareina Yee. "Unlocking the Full Potential of Women at Work." *McKinsey & Company*. Accessed December 26, 2019. https://www.mckinsey.com/business-functions/organization/our-insights/unlocking-the-full-potential-of-women-at-work.

Bartlett, Jamie. "The Trolling and Abuse of Women Rooted in Online Cultures." *Medium*, March 1, 2018. Accessed December 3, 2019. https://medium .com/@jamie.bartlett/the-trolling-and-abuse-of-women-rooted-in-online -cultures-667a54d4f88d.

BBC News. "US Election: Full Transcript of Donald Trump's Obscene Videotape." October 9, 2016. https://www.bbc.com/news/election-us-2016-37595321.

Beard, Mary. "The Public Voice of Women." *London Review of Books*, March 20, 2014. Accessed December 5, 2019. https://www.lrb.co.uk/v36/n06/mary -beard/the-public-voice-of-women.

Beilock, S. L., R. J. Rydell, and A. R. McConnell. "Stereotype Threat and Working Memory: Mechanisms, Alleviation, and Spillover." *Journal of Experimental Psychology: General* 136(2) (May 2007): 256–76. Accessed December 6, 2019. https://www.ncbi.nlm.nih.gov/pubmed/17500650.

Beinart, Peter. "Fear of a Female President." *Atlantic*, October 2016. Accessed December 22, 2019. https://www.theatlantic.com/magazine/archive/2016 /10/fear-of-a-female-president/497564/.

Bellstrom, Kristen. "Trump Supporters Are Selling 'Trump That Bitch' T-shirts Featuring Hillary Clinton." *Fortune*, April 25, 2016. Accessed December 22, 2019. https://fortune.com/2016/04/25/trump-clinton-misogynistic-merch/.

Bem, Sandra L. "The Measurement of Psychological Androgyny." *Journal of Consulting and Clinical Psychology* 42 (1981): 155–162.

Benard, Stephen, and Shelley J. Correll. "Normative Discrimination and the Motherhood Penalty." *Gender and Society* 24(5) (2010): 616–646.

Benenson, Joyce F. "The Development of Human Female Competition: Allies and Adversaries." *Philosophical Transactions of the Royal Society B: Biological Sciences* 368 (2013): 1–11. doi: 10.1098/rstb.2013.0079.

Bennett, Jessica. "I'm Not Mad. That's Just My RBF." *New York Times*, August 1, 2015. Accessed December 5, 2019. https://www.nytimes.com/2015/08/02 /fashion/im-not-mad-thats-just-my-resting-b-face.html.

Berenson, Tessa. "Watch Donald Trump Call Hillary Clinton a 'Nasty Woman.'" *Time*, October 19, 2016. Accessed December 22, 2019. https:// time.com/4537960/donald-trump-hillary-clinton-nasty-woman-debate/.

Bertrand, Marianne, Claudia Goldin, and Lawrence F. Katz. "Dynamics of the Gender Gap for Young Professionals in the Financial and Corporate Sectors." *American Economic Journal* 2(3) (2010): 228–255. doi: 10.1257 /app.2.3.228.

Biernat, Monica, M. J. Tocci, and Joan C. Williams. "The Language of Performance Evaluations: Gender-Based Shifts in Content and Consistency of

Judgment." *Social Psychology and Personality Science* 3(2) (2012): 186–192. doi: 10.1177/1948550611415693.

Brand, Billie. "Why It's Easier to Express Our Emotions in Emojis." *I-D Vice*, May 26, 2015. Accessed December 6, 2019. https://i-d.vice.com/en_us /article/xwxamz/why-its-easier-to-express-our-emotions-in-emojis.

Brescoll, Victoria L., and Eric Luis Uhlmann. "Can an Angry Woman Get Ahead? Status Conferral, Gender, and Expression of Emotion in the Workplace." *Psychological Science* 19(3) (2008): 268–275.

Brownmiller, Susan. *Against Our Will: Men, Women and Rape.* New York: Fawcett Books, 1975.

Bryant, Miranda. "More Fathers Are Taking Paternity Leave, but Others Are Still Doing all the Work." *The Guardian*, November 18, 2019. Accessed January 1, 2020. https://www.theguardian.com/money/2019/nov/17/more -fathers-are-taking-paternity-leave-but-mothers-are-still-doing-all-the -work.

Buchholz, Katharina. "In 2019, Global Emoji Count Is Growing to More than 3000." *Statista.com*, July 17, 2019. Accessed December 6, 2019. https://www .statista.com/chart/17275/number-of-emojis-from-1995-bis-2019/.

Burke, Garance. "AP: 'Apprentice' Cast and Crew Say Trump Was Lewd and Sexist." *AP News*, October 3, 2016. Accessed December 22, 2019. https:// apnews.com/2778a6ab72ea49558445337865289508.

Carli, Linda L., Suzanne J. LaFleur, and Christopher C. Loeber. "Nonverbal Behavior, Gender, and Influence." *Journal of Personality and Social Psychology* 68(6) (1995): 1030–1041.

Carlson, Nicholas. "Google Hiring Data Reveals Two Things Women Can Do to Get Hired and Promoted More." *Business Insider*, August 22, 2012. Accessed December 26, 2019. https://www.businessinsider.com /google-hiring-data-reveals-two-things-women-can-do-to-get-hired-and -promoted-more-2012-8.

Carney, Dana R., Amy J. C. Cuddy, and Andy J. Yap. "Power Posing: Brief Nonverbal Displays Affect Neuroendocrine Levels and Risk Tolerance." *Psychological Science* 21(10) (2010): 1363–1368.

Carney, Dana R., Judith A. Hall, and Lavonia S. LeBeau. "Beliefs about the Nonverbal Expression of Social Power." *Journal of Nonverbal Behavior* 29(2) (2005): 105–123.

Catalyst. "Quick Take: Women in the Workforce—United States." June 5, 2019. Accessed December 22, 2019. https://www.catalyst.org/research/women -in-the-workforce-united-states/.

Catalyst. "Report: The Myth of the Ideal Worker: Does Doing All the Right Things Really Get Women Ahead?" October 1, 2011. Accessed December 1, 2019. https://www.catalyst.org/research/the-myth-of-the-ideal-worker -does-doing-all-the-right-things-really-get-women-ahead/.

Catalyst. "Women 'Take Care,' Men 'Take Charge': Stereotyping of U.S. Business Leaders Exposed." Accessed December 19, 2019. http://www.catalyst.org /knowledge/women-take-care-men-take-charge-stereotyping-us-business -leaders-exposed.

Cerullo, Megan. "Harassment Allegations Slide Since Harvey Weinstein Accused." *MSN,* June 20, 2019. Accessed December 22, 2019. https://www .msn.com/en-us/money/companies/harassment-allegations-slide-since -harvey-weinstein-accused/ar-AAD7W3P?pfr=1.

Cerullo, Megan. "Sexual Harassment Allegations Are Down Sharply Since Harvey Weinstein First Accused." *CBS News,* June 19, 2019. Accessed December 22, 2019. https://www.cbsnews.com/news/metoo-index-shows -lowest-rate-of-accusations-since-harvey-weinstein/.

Chemaly, Soraya. "In Mixed Gender Groups, Can You Guess Who Talks the Most?' *Role Reboot,* October 22, 2018. Accessed December 26, 2019. http:// www.rolereboot.org/culture-and-politics/details/2015-10-in-mixed -gender-groups-can-you-guess-who-talks-the-most/.

Chesterman, Colleen, Anne Ross-Smith, and Margaret Peters. "The Gender Impact on Organizations of a Critical Mass of Women in Senior Management." *Policy and Society* 24(4) (2005).

Chozick, Amy. "Hillary Clinton Ignited a Feminist Movement. By Losing." *New York Times,* January 13, 2018.

Chung, YoonKyung, et al. "The Parental Gender Earnings Gap in the United States." US Census Bureau Department of Labor, November, 2017. Accessed January 1, 2020. https://www2.census.gov/ces/wp/2017/CES-WP-17-68.pdf.

Clear, James. "How to Be Confident and Reduce Stress in 2 Minutes per Day." Accessed November 23, 2019. https://jamesclear.com/body-language-how -to-be-confident.

Coleman, Nancy. "Ruling in Paul Haggis Case Gives Lift to #MeToo Lawsuits." *New York Times,* December 27, 2019. Accessed January 3, 2019. https://www.nytimes.com/2019/12/27/arts/paul-haggis-appeal-ruling.html.

Commission on Women in the Profession, American Bar Association. "The Grit Project: True Grit and a Growth Mindset." Accessed December 26, 2019. https://www.americanbar.org/groups/diversity/women/initiatives_awards /grit-project.

Connelly, Kathleen, and Martin Heesacker. "Why Is Benevolent Sexism Appealing? Associations with System Justification and Life Satisfaction." *Psychology of Women Quarterly* 36(4) (2012): 432–443.

Correll, Shelley J. "Minimizing the Motherhood Penalty." *Research Symposium, Gender and Work: Challenging Conventional Wisdom, Harvard Business School,* 2013. Accessed June 7, 2015. http://www.hbs.edu/faculty /conferences/2013-w50-research-symposium/Documents/correll.pdf.

Correll, Shelley J., and Stephen Benard. "Getting a Job: Is There a Motherhood Penalty?" *American Journal of Sociology* 112(5) (2007): 1297–1339. https:// doi.org/10.1086/511799.

Cortina, Lilia M. "Unseen Injustice: Incivility as Modern Discrimination in Organizations." *Academy of Management Review* 33(1) (January 2008) :55–75.

Crosby, Faye. "The Denial of Personal Discrimination." *American Behavioral Scientist* 27(3) (1984): 371–386.

Crosby, Faye. "Sex Discrimination, Personal Denial, and Collateral Damage." *Social Justice Research* 30(1) (2017): 89–105. doi:10.1007/s11211-017-0279-0.

Crusco, April H., and Christopher G. Wetzel. "The Midas Touch: The Effects of Interpersonal Touch on Restaurant Tipping." *Personality and Social Psychology Bulletin* 10(4) (1984): 512–517.

Cuddy, Amy. "Your Body Language Shapes Who You Are." *TED Global 2012,* June 2012. Accessed December 26, 2019. http://www.ted.com/talks/amy _cuddy_your_body_language_shapes_who_you_are.

Cuddy, Amy J., Matthew Kohut, and John Neffinger. "Connect, Then Lead." *Harvard Business Review* 91(7–8) (2013): 54–61. Accessed January 3, 2020. https://hbr.org/2013/07/connect-then-lead.

Cuddy, Amy J., S. Jack Schultz, and Nathan E. Fosse. "P-Curving a More Comprehensive Body of Research on Postural Feedback Reveals Clear Evidential Value for Power-Posing Effects: Reply to Simmons and Simonsohn (2017)." *Psychological Science* 29(4) (2018): 656–66. doi:10.1177/0956797617746749.

Cummings, Kelly. "Nonverbal Communication and First Impressions." Honors thesis, Kent State University. May 2011.

Cummins, Laura. "Modesty Holding Women Back at Work." *Female First.* Accessed December 31, 2019. http://www.femalefirst.co.uk/womens-issues /modesty-holding-women-back-at-work-543047.html.

The Cut. "The Meanie, the Lightweight, the Crazies, and the Angry, Dissembling Elitists." 2019. Accessed December 22, 2019. https://www.thecut .com/2019/11/lessons-from-six-women-running-for-president.html.

Dame Magazine. "What Happens When Women Don't Smile." May 31, 2018. Accessed December 5, 2019. https://www.damemagazine.com/2018/05/31 /what-happens-when-women-dont-smile/.

Dardenne, Benoit, Muriel Dumont, and Thierry Bonier. "Insidious Dangers of Benevolent Sexism: Consequences for Women's Performance." *Journal of Personality and Social Psychology* 93(5) (2007): 764–779.

De Pater, Irene E., Annelies E. M. Van Vianen, Agneta H. Fischer, and Wendy P. Van Ginkel. "Challenging Experiences: Gender Differences in Task Choice." *Journal of Managerial Psychology* 24(1) (2009): 4–28.

DeSilver, Drew. "Few Women Lead Large U.S. Companies, Despite Modest Gains Over Past Decade." *Pew Research Center.* Accessed December 1, 2019. https://www.pewresearch.org/facttank/2018/09/26/few-women-lead -large-u-s-companies-despite-modest-gains-over-pastdecade/.

Desvaux, Georges, Sandrine Devillard-Hoellinger, and Mary C. Meaney. "A Business Case for Women." *McKinsey Quarterly* (September 2008). Accessed December 17, 2019. http://www.rctaylor.com/Images/A_Business _Case_for_Women.pdf.

Diamond, Jeremy. "Trump Escalates Attacks on Clinton's Character." *CNN,* August 5, 2016. Accessed December 22, 2019. https://www.cnn.com/2016 /08/05/politics/donald-trump-hillary-clinton-unhinged-lock-her-up /index.html.

Dinolfo, Sarah, Christine Silva, and Nancy M. Carter. "High Potentials in the Pipeline: Leaders Pay It Forward." *Catalyst,* 2012. Accessed December 18, 2019. https://www.catalyst.org/research/high-potentials-in-the-pipeline -leaders-pay-it-forward/.

Donegan, Moira. "Half of White Women Continue to Vote Republican. What's Wrong with Them?" *The Guardian,* November 9, 2018. Accessed December 22, 2019. https://www.theguardian.com/commentisfree/2018 /nov/09/white-women-vote-republican-why.

Doyne, Shannon. "How Do You Feel about Being Told to Smile?" *New York Times,* April 23, 2018. Accessed December 5, 2019. https://www.nytimes .com/2018/04/23/learning/how-do-you-feel-about-being-told-to-smile .html.

Dubrin, Andrew J. *Impression Management in the Workplace: Research, Theory and Practice.* New York: Taylor & Francis, 2011.

Duller, David B., Beth A. LePoire, R. Kelly Aune, and Silvie V. Eloy. "Social Perceptions as Mediators of the Effect of Speech Rate." *Human Communication Research* 19(2) (1992): 286–311.

Duncan, Riana. "Excellent Suggestion, Miss Triggs." *Punch*, 1988.01.08.11.tif. Available at http://punch.photoshelter.

Dweck, Carol S. *Mindset: The New Psychology of Success*. New York: Ballantine Books, 2006.

Dworkin, Andrea. "Rape Atrocity and the Boy Next Door." In Johanna Fateman and Amy Scholder (eds.), *Last Days at Hot Slit: The Radical Feminism of Andrea Dworkin*. South Pasadena, CA: Semiotext(e), 2019.

Dworkin, Andrea. *The Complete Works of Andrea Dworkin*. RadFem Archive, January 29, 2012. Accessed January 3, 2020. http://radfem.org/dworkin/.

Eagly, Alice H., and Steven J. Karau. "Role Congruity Theory of Prejudice toward Female Leaders." *Psychological Review*, 2002. Accessed December 1, 2019. https://pdfs.semanticscholar.org/b00e/3ba04fc4b0f601b4db6f0386 d54abe710569.pdf?ga=2.132994830.1012640272.157 4119365-1576133896 .1516042834.

Eliot, Lise. "Hardwired for Combat? First Female Army Ranger Graduates Prove Grit Beats Gender in Military Training." *Huffington Post*, August 31, 2015. Accessed December 26, 2019. http://www.huffingtonpost.com/lise -eliot/hardwired-for-combat-first-female-army-ranger-graduates-prove -grit-beats-gender-in-military-training_b_8057094.html.

Ellemers, Naomi. "Gender Stereotypes." *Annual Review of Psychology* (January 2018). Accessed December 1, 2019. https://www.annualreviews.org/doi /full/10.1146/annurev-psych-122216-011719.

Ellison, Sarah. "Inside the Final Days of Roger Ailes's Reign at Fox News." *Vanity Fair*, September 22, 2016. Accessed December 22, 2019. https://www .vanityfair.com/news/2016/09/roger-ailes-fox-news-final-days.

Elsesser, Kim. "Power Posing Is Back: Amy Cuddy Successfully Refutes Criticism." *Forbes*, April 3, 2018. Accessed November 23, 2019. https://www .forbes.com/sites/kimelsesser/2018/04/03/power-posing-is-back-amy -cuddy-successfully-refutes-criticism/#347c016c3b8e.

Ennis, Linda Rose (ed.). *Intensive Mothering: The Cultural Contradictions of Modern Motherhood* (Demeter Press: 2014).

Farrow, Ronan. "From Aggressive Overtures to Sexual Assault: Harvey Weinstein's Accusers Tell Their Stories." *New Yorker*, October 23, 2017. Accessed December 22, 2019. https://www.newyorker.com/news/news -desk/from-aggressive-overtures-to-sexual-assault-harvey-weinsteins -accusers-tell-their-stories.

Fast, Nathanael J., Deborah H. Gruenfeld, Niro Sivanathan, and Adam D. Galinsky. "Illusory Control: A Generative Force Behind Power's Far-Reaching Effects." *Psychological Science* 20(4) (2009): 502–508.

Feldblum, Chai R., and Victoria A. Lipnic. "Breaking the Silence." *Harvard Business Review*, January 26, 2018. Accessed December 26, 2019. https://hbr.org/2018/01/breaking-the-silence.

Festinger, Leon. "A Theory of Social Comparison Processes." *Human Relations* 7(2) (1954): 117–140.

Fielding-Singh, Priya, Devon Magliozzi, and Swethaa Ballakrishnen. "Why Women Stay out of the Spotlight at Work." *Harvard Business Review*, August 28, 2018. Accessed December 26, 2019. https://hbr.org/2018/08/sgc-8-28-why-women-stay-out-of-the-spotlight-at-work.

Filipou, Pauline, Segal Mahajan, Allison Deal, et. al. "The Presence of Gender Bias in Letters of Recommendations Written for Urology Residency Applicants." *Urology* 134 (December 2019): 56–61. Accessed December 7, 2019. https://www.sciencedirect.com/science/article/pii/S0090429519307903.

Firestone, Shulamith. *The Dialectic of Sex: The Case For Feminist Revolution.* New York: Straus and Giroux, 2003.

Flynn, Francis J., and Daniel R. Ames. "What's Good for the Goose May Not Be As Good for the Gander: The Benefits of Self-Monitoring for Men and Women in Task Groups and Dyadic Conflicts." *Journal of Applied Psychology* 91(2) (2006): 272–281. https://doi.org/10.1037/0021-9010.91.2.272.

Fonseca, Todd A.. "Mirroring Body Language: 4 Steps to Successfully Mirror Others." *Science of People.* Accessed December 26, 2019. https://www.scienceofpeople.com/mirroring/.

Ford, Cecilia E. *Women Speaking Up: Getting and Using Turns in Workplace Meetings.* London: Palgrave Macmillan, 2008.

Ford, Thomas E., Mark A. Ferguson, Jenna L. Brooks, and Kate M. Hagadone. "Coping Sense of Humor Reduces Effects of Stereotype Threat on Women's Math Performance." *Personality and Social Psychology Bulletin* 30(5) (2004): 643–653.

Foster, Mindi D., and Micha Tsarfati. "The Effects of Meritocracy Beliefs on Women's Well-Being After First-Time Gender Discrimination." *Personality and Social Psychology Bulletin* 31(12) (2005): 1730–1738.

Fragale, Alison R.. "The Power of Powerless Speech: The Effects of Speech Style and Task Interdependence on Status Conferral." *Organizational Behavior and Human Decision Processes* 101 (2006): 243–261.

Franzin, Rachel. "'Lock Her Up' Chant Breaks Out at Trump Rally." *The Hill,* August 1, 2019. Accessed October 4, 2019. https://thehill.com/homenews/campaign/455874-lock-her-up-chant-breaks-out-at-trump-rally.

Gabler, Ellen, Jim Rutenberg, Michael M. Grynbaum, and Rachel P. Abrams, "NBC Fires Matt Lauer, the Face of 'Today.'" *New York Times*, November 9,

2017. Accessed December 22, 2019. https://www.nytimes.com/2017/11/29/business/media/nbc-matt-lauer.html.

Galinsky, Adam D., and Gavin J. Kilduff. "Be Seen As a Leader." *Harvard Business Review*, December 1, 2013. Accessed December 26, 2019. https://hbr.org/2013/12/be-seen-as-a-leader.

Gao, George, and Gretchen Livingston. "Working While Pregnant Is Much More Common than It Used to Be." *Pew Research Center*, March 31, 2015. Accessed January 1, 2020. http://www.pewresearch.org/fact-tank/2015/03/31/working-while-pregnant-is-much-more-common-than-it-used-to-be/.

Gawande, Atul. "Personal Best." *New Yorker*, October 3, 2011. Accessed November 21, 2019. http://www.newyorker.com/magazine/2011/10/03/personal-best.

Gawande, Atul. "Want to Get Great at Something? Get a Coach." *TED 2017*. Accessed November 23, 2019. https://www.ted.com/talks/atul_gawande_want_to_get_great_at_something_get_a_coach.

"Gender, Equity, and Human Rights." *World Health Organization*. Accessed December 30, 2019. https://www.who.int/gender-equity-rights/en/.

"Gender, Equity, and Human Rights: Gender." *World Health Organization*. Accessed December 30, 2019, https://www.who.int/gender-equity-rights/understanding/gender-definition/en/.

George, Bill. *Authentic Leadership: Rediscovering the Secrets to Creating Lasting Value*. Jossey-Bass: San Francisco, 2003.

George, Bill. *Discover Your True North: Becoming an Authentic Leader*. John Wiley & Sons, Inc.: Hoboken, New Jersey, 2015.

Gerdeman, Dina. "Kids of Working Moms Grow into Happy Adults." *HBS Working Knowledge*, July 16, 2018. Accessed January 2, 2020. https://hbswk.hbs.edu/item/kids-of-working-moms-grow-into-happy-adults.

Gibson, Donald E., and Ronda Callister. "Anger in Organizations: Review and Future Directions." Paper presented at the 22nd Annual International Association of Conflict Management Conference, Kyoto, Japan, June 15–18, 2009.

Gil, Natalie. "4 Women on Death Threats, Abuse Online & What They're Doing to Stop the Trolls." *Refinery29*, April 30, 2018. Accessed December 3, 2019. https://www.refinery29.com/en-gb/2018/04/196751/sexist-online-abuse-trolling.

Gladwell, Malcolm. *Outliers: The Story of Success*. New York: Little, Brown and Company, 2008.

Goffman, Erving. *The Presentation of Self in Everyday Life*. New York: Doubleday Anchor Books, 1959.

Goh, Angeline. "An Attributional Analysis of Counterproductive Work Behavior (CWB) in Response to Occupational Stress." Dissertation. University of South Florida, November 21, 2006. http://digital.lib.usf.edu/content/SF /S0/02/62/13/00001/E14-SFE0001895.pdf.

Goldberg, Michelle. "Not the Fun Kind of Feminist: How Trump Helped Make Andrea Dworkin Relevant Again." *New York Times*, February 23, 2019. Accessed December 22, 2019. https://www.nytimes.com/2019/02 /22/opinion/sunday/trump-feminismandreadworkin.html.

Goman, Carol Kinsey. "The Art and Science of Mirroring." *Forbes*, May 31, 2011. Accessed December 24, 2019. https://www.forbes.com/sites /carolkinseygoman/2011/05/31/the-art-and-science-of-mirroring/#6ac 663401318.

Gonzalez, Patricia M., Hart Blanton, and Kevin J. Williams. "The Effects of Stereotype Threat and Double-Minority Status on the Test Performance of Latino Women." *Personality and Social Psychology Bulletin*, May 1, 2002. Accessed December 6, 2019. https://journals.sagepub.com/doi/abs /10.1177/0146167202288010.

Green, Fiona Joy. "*Intensive Mothering*," in Andrea O'Reilly, editor, *Encyclopedia of Motherhood*. Sage Publications (April 2010).

Grose, Jessica. "It's Not Your Kids Holding Your Career Back. It's Your Husband." *Slate*, November 18, 2014. Accessed January 1, 2020. https://slate .com/human-interest/2014/11/harvard-business-school-study-it-s-not -kids-but-husbands-that-hold-women-s-careers-back.html.

Grossman, Joanna L. "The Culture of Compliance: The Final Triumph of Form over Substance in Sexual Harassment Law." *Harvard Women's Law Journal* 26 (2003): 49–63. https://ssrn.com/abstract=2865996.

Gruenfeld, Deborah. "Playing High, Playing Low and Playing It Straight." *YouTube*, September 24, 2013. Accessed November 23, 2019. https://www .youtube.com/watch?v=zbUX3BGXJlc&index=3&list=PL_I4p0xEPo8rXi Clf U9vYlqwp AY0MYt3-.

Grunspan, Daniel Z., Sarah L. Eddy, Sara E. Brownell, Benjamin L. Wiggins, Alison J. Crowe, and Steven M. Goodreau. "Males Under-Estimate Academic Performance of Their Female Peers in Undergraduate Biology Classrooms." *PLoS ONE* 11(2) (2016): https://journals.plos.org/plosone /article?id=10.1371/journal.pone.0148405.

Gupta, Prachi. "Trump Supporters Sell Truly Disgusting Shirts Outside a Rally for the Candidate." *Cosmopolitan*, April 19, 2019. Accessed December 22, 2019. https://www.cosmopolitan.com/politics/news/a57107/donald-trump -t-shirts-misogynistic/.

Hall, Judith A., Erik J. Coats, and Lavonia S. LeBeau. "Nonverbal Behavior and the Vertical Dimension of Social Relations: A Meta-Analysis." *Psychological Bulletin* 131(6) (2005): 898–924.

Hancock, Adrienne B., and Benjamin A. Rubin. "Influence of Communication Partner's Gender on Language." *Journal of Language and Social Psychology* 34(1) (2015): 46–64.

Hanna, Julia. "Power Posing: Fake It until You Make It." *Working Knowledge,* September 20, 2010. Accessed December 26, 2019. http://hbswk.hbs.edu /item/6461.html.

Hanson, Katherine. "The Opportunity Cost of Fertility under the Rhetoric of Choice." Northern Illinois University, November 15, 2018, unpublished study, Communications 498 Independent Study. Available from the author upon request.

Harris, Aisha. "She Founded MeToo. Now She Wants to Move Past the Trauma." *New York Times,* October 15, 2018. Accessed December 22, 2019. https:// www.nytimes.com/2018/10/15/arts/tarana-burke-metoo-anniversary.html.

Hartocollis, Anemona, and Yamiche Alcindor. "Women's March Highlights as Huge Crowds Protest Trump: 'We're Not Going Away.'" *New York Times,* January 21, 2017. Accessed December 22, 2019. https://www.nytimes .com/2017/01/21/us/womens-march.html.

Harvard Business School. "Life & Leadership Survey After HBS." May 2015. https://www.hbs.edu/women50/docs/L_and_L_Survey_2Findings_12final .pdf

Hayes, Sharon. *The Cultural Contradictions of Motherhood.* (Yale U. Press, 1998).

Heath, Kathryn, Jill Flynn, and Mary Davis Holt. "Women, Find Your Voice." *Harvard Business Review,* June 2014. Accessed January 2, 2019. https://hbr .org/2014/06/women-find-your-voice.

Hedenstierna-Jonson, Charlotte, Anna Kjellström, Torun Zachrisson, Maja Krzewińska, Veronica Sobrado, Neil Price, Torsten Günther, Mattias Jakobsson, and Jan Stora. "A Female Viking Warrior Confirmed by Genomics." *American Journal of Physical Anthropology* 164(4) (2017): 853–860. doi:10.1002/ajpa.23308.

Heilman, Madeline E. "Gender Stereotypes and Workplace Bias." *Research in Organizational Behavior* 32 (2012): 113–135. https://doi.org/10.1016/j .riob.2012.11.003.

Heilman, Madeline E., Aaron S. Wallon, Daniella Fuchs, and Melinda Mo Tamkins. "Penalties for Success: Reactions to Women Who Succeed at Male Gender-Typed Tasks." *Journal of Applied Psychology* 89(3) (2004): 416–427.

Hewlett, Sylvia Ann. "Executive Women and the Myth of Having It All." *Harvard Business Review*, April 2002. Accessed on December 29, 2019. http://hbr.org/2002/04/executive-women-and-the-myth-of-having-it-all.

Hinchliffe, Emma. "GM's Board Will Have More Women than Men. It's Not the Only One." *Fortune*, May 20, 2019. Accessed December 1, 2019. https://fortune.com/2019/05/20/women-boards-fortune-500-2019/.

Hirschman, Linda. *Reckoning: The Epic Battle against Sexual Abuse and Harassment*. Boston: Houghton Mifflin, 2019.

Hoffman, A., W. Grant, M. McCormick, E. Jezewski, P. Matemavi, and A. Langnas. "Gendered Differences in Letters of Recommendation for Transplant Surgery Fellowship Applications." *Journal of Surgical Education*, 76(2) (March-April 2019): 427-432. Accessed December 7, 2019. https://www.ncbi.nlm.nih.gov/pubmed/30266555.

A. Hogan, Milana L. "Non-Cognitive Traits That Impact Female Success in Big Law." PhD diss., University of Pennsylvania, 2013.

Homer. *The Odyssey*, Emily Wilson (translator). New York: W. W. Norton & Company, 2018.

Horowitz, Juliana Menasce. "Despite Challenges at Home and Work, Most Working Moms and Dads Say Being Employed Is What's Best for Them." *Pew Research Center*, September 12, 2019. Accessed January 1, 2020. https://www.pewresearch.org/fact-tank/2019/09/12/despite-challenges-at-home-and-work-most-working-moms-and-dads-say-being-employed-is-whats-best-for-them/.

Hubbard, Amy S., A. Allen Tsuji, Christine Williams, and Virgilio Seatriz, Jr. "Effects of Touch on Gratuities Received in Same-Gender and Cross-Gender Dyads." *Journal of Applied Social Psychology* 33(11) (2003): 2427–2438.

Hume, David. "Of the Standard of Taste." In *Essays Moral, Political, Literary*. Eugene F. Miller, rev. ed. Indianapolis: Liberty Fund, 1985, 239.

Hurt, Harry. "Donald Trump Gets Small." *Esquire Classic*, May 1, 1991, 27.

Hyde, Janet Sibley. "Gender Similarities and Differences." *Annual Review of Psychology*, 2014. Accessed December 1, 2019. https://www.annualreviews.org/doi/10.1146/annurev-psych-010213-115057.

Inzlicht, Michael, and Talia Ben-Zeev. "A Threatening Intellectual Environment: Why Females Are Susceptible to Experiencing Problem-Solving Deficits in the Presence of Males." *Psychological Science* 11(5) (2000): 365–371.

Jasmin, Ernest A.. "Don't Copycat an Unpopular Boss's Behavior, Study Reminds." *MSNBC*, August 1, 2011. Accessed December 26, 2019. https://

www.nbcnews.com/health/body-odd/dont-copycat-unpopular-bosss
-behavior-study-reminds-flna1C6437233.

Johns, Michael, Toni Schmader, and A. Martens. "Knowing Is Half the
Battle: Teaching Stereotype Threat as a Means of Improving Women's
Math Performance." *Psychological Science* 16(3) (March 2005): 175–9.
Accessed December 18, 2019. https://journals.sagepub.com/doi/abs/10.1111
/j.0956-7976.2005.00799.x.

Johns, Michael, Michael Inzlicht, and Toni Schmader. "Stereotype Threat
and Executive Resource Depletion: Examining the Influence of Emotion
Regulation." *Journal of Experimental Psychology: General* 137(4) (2008):
691–705.

Johnson, Andrea, Kathryn Menefee, and Ramya Sekaran. "Progress in Advancing MeToo Workplace Reforms in #20 States by 2020." *National Wom-
en's Law Center*, July 2019. Accessed December 22, 2019. https://nwlc
-ciw49tixgw5lbab.stackpathdns.com/wp-content/uploads/2019/07/20
-States-By-2020-report.pdf.

Johnson, Kim K. P., Jeong-Ju Yoo, Minjeong Kim, and Sharron J. Lennon.
"Dress and Human Behavior: A Review and Critique." *Clothing & Textiles
Research Journal* 26(1) (2008): 3–22.

Johnson, Stephanie K., Ksenia Keplinger, Jessica F. Kirk, and Liza Barnes.
"Has Sexual Harassment at Work Decreased Since #MeToo?" *Harvard
Business Review*, July 18, 2019. Accessed December 22, 2019. https://hbr
.org/2019/07/has-sexual-harassment-at-work-decreased-since-metoo.

Jolie, Angelina. "Angelina Jolie Speak[s] on World Refugee Day 2009." *United
Nations High Commissioner for Refugees*, June 20, 2009. Accessed December 27, 2019. https://www.youtube.com/watch?v=q6msUKyiYic.

Judge, Timothy A., Beth A. Livingston, and Charlice Hurst. "Do Nice Guys—
and Gals—Really Finish Last? The Joint Effect of Sex and Agreeableness on
Income." *Journal of Personality and Social Psychology* 102(2) (2012): 390–407.

Kantor, Jodi. "Harvard Business School Case Study: Gender Equity." *New
York Times*, September 7, 2013. Accessed December 20, 2019. http://www
.nytimes.com/2013/09/08/education/harvard-case-study-gender-equity
.html.

Kantor, Jodi, and Megan Twohey. "Harvey Weinstein Paid Off Sexual
Harassment Accusers for Decades." *New York Times*, October 5, 2017.
Accessed December 22, 2019. https://www.nytimes.com/2017/10/05/us
/harvey-weinstein-harassment-allegations.html.

Kantor, Jodi, and Megan Twohey. *She Said: Breaking the Sexual Harassment
Story That Helped Ignite a Movement*. London: Penguin Press, 2019.

Karpf, Anne. *The Human Voice: How This Extraordinary Instrument Reveals Essential Clues about Who We Are.* New York: Bloomsbury USA, 2006.

Karpowitz, Christopher F., and Tali Mendelberg. *The Silent Sex, Gender, Deliberation and Institutions.* Princeton: Princeton University Press, 2014.

Karpowitz, Christopher F., Tali Mendelberg, and Lee Shaker. "Gender Inequality in Deliberative Participation." *American Political Science Review* 106(3) (2012): 533–547.

Kelly, Bridget Turner. "Though More Women Are on College Campuses, Climbing the Professor Ladder Remains a Challenge." *The Brookings Institution.* March 29, 2019. Accessed December 1, 2019. https://www.brookings.edu /blog/brown-center-chalkboard/2019/03/29/though-more-women-are-on -college-campuses-climbing-the-professor-ladder-remains-a-challenge/.

Keplinger, Ksenia, Stephanie K. Johnson, Jessica F. Kirk, Liza Y. Barnes. "Women at Work: Changes in Sexual Harassment between September 2016 and September 2018." *PLoS ONE* 14(7): 2019. e0218313. https://doi .org/10.1371/journal.pone.0218313.

Kim, Catherine. "Twitter Bans Ilhan Omar's GOP Rival for Tweeting about Hanging the Congresswoman." *Vox*, November 30, 2019. Accessed December 5, 2019. https://www.vox.com/policy-and-politics/2019/11/30/20989348 /twitter-ban-danielle-stella-ilhan-tweeting-treason-hanged.

King, Eden B., Whitney Botsford, Michelle R. Hebl, Stephanie Kazama, Jeremy F. Dawson, and Andrew Perkins. "Benevolent Sexism at Work: General Differences in the Distribution of Challenging Developmental Experiences." *Journal of Management* 38(6) (2012): 1835–1866. doi:10.1177 /0149206310365902.

Kleinke, Chris L. "Compliance to Requests Made by Gazing and Touching Experimenters in Field Settings." *Journal of Experimental Social Psychology* 13(3) (1977): 218–223.

Kluch, Sofia, and Megan Brenan. "U.S. Women Feel Less Respected than European, Canadian Peers." *Gallup*, March 8, 2019. Accessed December 22, 2019. https://news.gallup.com/poll/247205/women-feel-less-respected -european-canadian-peers.aspx.

Koblin, John. "The Year of Reckoning at CBS: Sexual Harassment Allegations and Attempts to Cover Them Up." *New York Times*, updated December 17, 2018. Accessed December 22, 2019. https://www.nytimes.com/2018/12/14 /business/media/cbs-sexual-harassment-timeline.html.

Koenig, Anne M., and Alice H. Eagly. "Stereotype Threat in Men on a Test of Social Sensitivity." *Sex Roles* 52(7-8) (April 2005): 489–496. Accessed December 6, 2019. https:link.springer.com/article/10.1007/s11199-005-3714-x.

Kramer, Andrea S., and Alton B. Harris. "How Do Your Workers Feel about Harassment? Ask Them." *Harvard Business Review*, January 29, 2018. Accessed December 1,2019. https://hbr.org/2018/01/how-do-your-workers-feel-about-harassment-ask-them.

Kramer, Andrea S., and Alton B. Harris. *It's Not You, It's the Workplace: Women's Conflict at Work and the Bias that Built It*. Boston: Nicholas Brealey/Hachette, 2019.

Kray, Laura J., Leigh Thompson, and Adam Galinsky. "Battle of the Sexes: Gender Stereotype Confirmation and Reactance in Negotiations." *Journal of Personal Social Psychology* 80(6) (June 2001): 942–58. Accessed December 6, 2019, https://www.ncbi.nlm.nih.gov/pubmed/11414376.

Kray, Laura J., Adam D. Galinsky, and Leigh Thompson. "Reversing the Gender Gap in Negotiations: An Exploration of Stereotype Regeneration." *Organizational Behavior and Human Decision Processes* 87(2) (March 2002): 386–409. Accessed December 6, 2019. https://psycnet.apa.org/doi/10.1006/obhd.2001.2979.

Kreamer, Anne. *It's Always Personal: Navigating Emotion in the New Workplace*. New York: Penguin, 2013.

Kulik, Carol T., and Mana Olekalns. "Negotiating the Gender Divide: Lessons from the Negotiation and Organizational Behavior Literatures." *Journal of Management* 38(4) (2012): 1387–1415.

LaFrance, Adrienne. "The 'Undesirable Militants' behind the Nineteenth Amendment." *Atlantic*, December 5, 2019. Accessed January 3, 2020. https://www.theatlantic.com/politics/archive/2019/06/most-dangerous-women-american-politics/590959/.

Laing, Sarah. "Why Do Men Need Women to Smile?" *Flare*, July 25, 2018. Accessed December 7, 2019. https://www.flare.com/news/greg-rickford-marieke-walsh-smile-women/.

Lam, Bourree. "Yes, There Really Are More Pregnant Women in the Office." *Atlantic*, April 8, 2015. Accessed January 1, 2020. http://www.theatlantic.com/business/archive/2015/04/yes-there-really-are-more-pregnant-women-at-the-office/389763/.

Lammers, Joris, David Dubois, Derek D. Rucker, and Adam D. Galinsky. "Power Gets the Job: Priming Power Improves Interview Outcomes." *Journal of Experimental Social Psychology* 49(4) (2013): 776–779.

Lange, Jeva. "61 Things Donald Trump Has Said about Women." *The Week*, October 16, 2018. Accessed December 4, 2019. https://theweek.com/articles/655770/61-things-donald-trump-said-about-women.

Lauzen, Martha M. "Celluloid Ceiling: Behind-the-Scenes Employment of Women on the Top 100, 250, and 500 Films of 2017." *Center for the Study of Women in Television and Film*, 2018. Accessed December 1, 2019. https://womenintvfilm.sdsu.edu/wp-content/uploads/2018/01/2017_Celluloid_Ceiling_Report.pdf.

LeanIn and McKinsey & Co. "Women in the Workplace 2018." Accessed December 1, 2019. http://wiwreport.s3.amazonaws.com/Women_in_the_Workplace_2018.pdf.

LeanIn and McKinsey & Company. "Women in the Workplace 2019." Accessed December 1, 2019, https://womenintheworkplace.com/Women_in_the_Workplace_2019.pdf.

Leanse, Ellen Petry. "Google and Apple Alum Says Using This One Word Can Damage Your Credibility." *Business Insider,* June 25, 2015. Accessed December 27, 2019. http://www.businessinsider.com/former-google-exec-says-this-word-can-damage-your-credibility-2015-6.

Lefcourt, Herbert M. "Humor: The Psychology of Living Buoyantly." New York: Klewer Publishing, 2001. Accessed December 26, 2019. http://academic.csuohio.edu/neuendorf_ka/chs.pdf.

LeMoyne, Terri, and Tom Buchanan. "Does 'Hovering' Matter? Helicopter Parenting and Its Effect on Well-Being." *Sociological Spectrum* 31(4) (2011): 399–418. https://doi.org/10.1080/02732173.2011.574038.

Liebenberg, Roberta D., and Stephanie A. Scharf. "Walking Out the Door: The Facts, Figures and Future of Experienced Lawyers in Private Practice." American Bar Association 2019.

Lieberman, Marc. "Jill Abramson's Voice." *Language Log,* October 18, 2011. Accessed December 27, 2019. http://languagelog.ldc.upenn.edu/nll/?p=3504.

Lindeman, Megan I. H., Amanda M. Durik, and Maura Dooley. "Women and Self-Promotion: A Test of Three Theories." *Psychological Reports* 122(1) (February 2019): 219–230. Accessed December 7, 2019, https://journals.sagepub.com/doi/pdf/10.1177/0033294118755096.

Lythcott-Haims, Julie. *How to Raise an Adult: Break Free of the Overparenting Trap and Prepare Your Kid for Success.* New York: Henry Holt and Company, 2015.

Lythcott-Haims, Julie. "Kids of Helicopter Parents Are Sputtering Out." *Slate,* July 5, 2015. Accessed January 1, 2020. http://www.slate.com/articles/double_x/doublex/2015/07/helicopter_parenting_is_increasingly_correlated_with_college_age_depression.html.

Maass, Anne, Claudio D'Ettole, and Mara Cadinu. "Checkmate? The Role of Gender Stereotypes in the Ultimate Intellectual Sport." *European Journal of Social Psychology* 38(2) (May 2007). Accessed December 6, 2019. https:// onlinelibrary.wiley.com/doi/abs/10.1002/ejsp.440.

Madera, Juan M., Michelle R. Hebl, and Randi C. Martin. "Gender and Letters of Recommendation for Academia: Agentic and Communal Differences." *Journal of Applied Psychology* 94(6) (2009): 1591–1599. doi: 10.1037 /a0016539.

Madera, Juan M., Michelle R. Hebl, Heather Dial, et al. "Raising Doubts in Letters of Recommendation for Academia: Gender Differences and Their Impact" *Journal of Business and Psychology* 34(3) (June 2019): 287–303. Accessed December 7, 2019. https://link.springer.com/article/10.1007/s10869 -018-9541-1.

MacLellan, Lila. "70% of Top Male Earners in the US Have a Spouse Who Stays Home." *Quartz*, April 30, 2019. Accessed January 2, 2020. https://qz.com /work/1607995/most-men-in-the-top-1-of-us-earners-have-a-spouse-who -stays-home/.

McCarthy, Ellen. "She Famously Said that Women Can't Have it All. Now She Realizes that No One Can." *Washington Post*, August 26, 2016. Accessed January 1, 2020. https://www.washingtonpost.com/lifestyle/style/she -famously-said-that-women-cant-have-it-all-now-she-realizes-that-no-one -can/2016/08/26/889944e4-5bf3-11 e6-831d-0324760ca856_story.htm.

McCauliffe, Kathleen. "Gaslighting 101: Are You Being Manipulated at Work?" *Career Contessa*, February 21, 2019. Accessed December 7, 2019. https:// www.careercontessa.com/advice/gaslighting-in-the-office.

"Microaggression." *Merriam-Webster, s.v.* Accessed December 27, 2018. https:// www.Merriam-Webster.com/dictionary/microaggression.

Milkie, Melissa A., Kei A. Nomaguchi, and Kathleen E. Denny. "Does the Amount of Time Mothers Spend with Children or Adolescents Matter?" *Journal of Marriage and Family* 77(2) (2015): 355–372. doi: 10.1111/jomf .12170.

Miller, Claire Cain. "Even among Harvard Graduates, Women Fall Short of Their Work Expectations." *New York Times*, November 28, 2014. Accessed September 13, 2015. http://www.nytimes.com/2014/11/30/upshot/even -among-harvard-graduates-women-fall-short-of-their-work-expectations .html.

Miller, Claire Cain. "Is Blind Hiring the Best Hiring?" *New York Times Magazine*, February. 25, 2016. Accessed December 1, 2019. https://www.nytimes .com/2016/02/28/magazine/is-blind-hiring-the-best-hiring.html.

Miller, Claire Cain. "The Motherhood Penalty vs. the Fatherhood Bonus: A Child Helps Your Career, if You're a Man." *New York Times*, September 6, 2014. Accessed January 1, 2020. http://www.nytimes.com/2014/09/07 /upshot/a-child-helps-your-career-if-youre-a-man.html.

Miller, Claire Cain. "Even among Harvard Graduates, Women Fall Short of Their Work Expectations." *New York Times*, November 28, 2014. Accessed January 1, 2020. https://www.nytimes.com/2014/11/30/upshot/even -among-harvard-graduates-women-fall-short-of-their-work-expectations .html.

Millett, Kate. *Sexual Politics*. New York: Columbia University Press, 1969, 2016.

Mirkinson, Jack. "Donald Trump Writes Blistering Letter to Gail Collins, *New York Times* Columnist." *HuffPost*, June 9, 2011. https://www.huffpost.com /entry/donald-trump-gail-collins-new-york-times_n_847015.

Morin, Rebecca. "What We Know about the 'Send Her Back' Chants That Erupted at Trump's North Carolina Rally." *USA Today*, July 18, 2019. Accessed December 22, 2019. https://www.usatoday.com/story/news/politics /2019/07/18/what-we-know-send-her-back-chants-directed-ilhan-omar /1769042001/.

Moss-Racusin, Corinne A., John F. Dovidio, Victoria L. Brescoll, Mark J. Graham, and Jo Handelsman. "Science Faculty's Subtle Gender Biases Favor Male Students." *PNAS* 109(41) (2012): 16474–16479.

Mulac, Anthony, Karen T. Erlandson, W. Jeffrey Farrar, Jennifer S. Hallet, Jennifer L. Molloy, and Margaret Prescott. "Uh-huh. What's That All About? Differing Interpretations of Conversational Backchannels and Questions as Sources of Miscommunication across Gender Boundaries." *Communication Research* 25(6) (1998): 641–668.

National Association of Women Lawyers, "2019 Survey on Retention and Promotion of Women in Law Firms." Accessed January 3, 2020. https://www .nawl.org/p/cm/ld/fid=1163.

Nelson, Libby. "Donald Trump's History of Misogyny, Sexism, and Harassment: A Comprehensive Review." *Vox*, October 12, 2016. Accessed August 3, 2019. https://www.vox.com/2016/10/8/13110734/Donald-Trump-Leaked -Audio-Recording-billy-bush-sexism.

Nobel, Carmen. "Kids Benefit from Having a Working Mom." *Harvard Business Review Working Knowledge*, May 15, 2015. Accessed January 2, 2020. http://hbswk.hbs.edu/item/kids-benefit-from-having-a-working-mom.

Noonan, Peggy. Quote. Accessed December 26, 2019. https://www.quotetab .com/quote/by-peggy-noonan/humor-is-the-shock-absorber-of-life-it-helps -us-take-the-blows.

O'Brien, Katharine Ridgway. "Just Saying 'No': An Examination of Gender Differences in the Ability to Decline Requests in the Workplace." PhD diss., Rice University, 2014.

O'Grady, Kim. "How I Discovered Gender Discrimination." *What Would King Leonidas Do? Tumblr,* July 9, 2013. Accessed December 20, 2019. http://whatwouldkingleonidasdo.tumblr.com/post/54989171152/how-i -discovered-gender-discrimination.

Olsen, Stephanie. "How to Tell if They're Gaslighting You at Work." Inhersight .com. Accessed December 7, 2019. https://www.inhersight.com/blog/insight -commentary/gaslighting?_n=57725927.

O'Neill, Olivia, and Charles O'Reilly III. "Reducing the Backlash Effect: Self-Monitoring and Women's Promotion." *Journal of Occupational and Organizational Psychology* 84(4) (2010): 825–832.

Ordway, Denise-Marie. "What Research Says about the Kids of Working Moms." *Journalist's Resource,* August 13, 2018. Accessed January 1, 2020. https://journalistsresource.org/studies/economics/jobs/working-mother -employment-research/.

Parker, Kathleen. "What a Shame that Cruelty Isn't an Impeachable Offense." *Washington Post,* December 20, 2019. Accessed December 22, 2019. https://www.washingtonpost.com/opinions/what-a-shame-that-cruelty -isnt-an-impeachable-offense/2019/12/20/af94af66-2373-11ea-86f3-3b50 19d451db_story.html.

Parker, Kim, and Cary Funk. "Gender Discrimination Comes in Many Forms for Today's Working Women." *Pew Research Center,* November 15, 2019. Accessed December 1, 2019. https://www.pewresearch.org/fact-tank/2017/12/14/gender -discrimination-comes-in-many-forms-for-todays-working-women/.

Paturel, Amy. "Where Are All the Women Deans?" *Association of American Medical Colleges,* June 11, 2019. Accessed December 1, 2019. https://www .aamc.org/news-insights/where-are-all-women-deans.

Perlow, Leslie, and Stephanie Williams. "Is Silence Killing Your Company?" *Engineering Management Review* 31(4) (2003): 18–23.

Pershing LLC. "Americans Crave a New Kind of Leader—and Women Are Ready to Deliver." February 25, 2014. Accessed December 20, 2019. https:// www.pershing.com/our-thinking/thought-leadership/americans-crave-a -new-kind-of-leader-and-women-are-ready-to-deliver.

Pflum, Mary. "A Year Ago, Alyssa Milano Started a Conversation about #MeToo." *NBC News,* October 15, 2018. Accessed December 22, 2019. https://www.nbcnews.com/news/usnews/year-ago-alyssa-milano-started -conversation-about-me-too-these-women-n920246.

Phelan, Julie E., Corinne A. Moss-Racusin, and Laurie A. Rudman. "Competent Yet Out in the Cold: Shifting Criteria for Hiring Reflect Backlash Toward Agentic Women." *Psychology of Women Quarterly* 32(4) (2008): 406–413. https://doi.org/10.1111%2Fj.1471-6402.2008.00454.x.

Prentice, Deborah A., and Erica Carranza. "What Women and Men Should Be, Shouldn't Be, Are Allowed to Be, and Don't Have to Be: The Contents of Prescriptive Gender Stereotypes." *Psychology of Women Quarterly* 26(4) (2002): 279–280.

Preza, Elizabeth. "Howard Stern Says Trump's 'Misogynist, Sexist' Comments Are Exactly 'Who Trump Is.'" *Alternet*, October 27, 2016. Accessed December 22, 2019. https://www.alternet.org/2016/10/howard-stern-says-trumps -misogynist-sexist-comments-are-who-trump/.

Price, Neil, Charlotte Hedenstierna-Jonson, Torun Zachrisson, Anna Kjell- ström, Jan Storå, Maja Krzewińska, Torsten Günther, Verónica Sobrado, Mattias Jakobsson, and Anders Götherström. "Viking Warrior Women? Reassessing Birka Chamber Grave Bj 581." *Antiquity* 93(367) (2019): 181–198. doi:10.15184/aqy.2018.258.

Prime, Jeanine, and Corinne A. Moss-Racusin. "Engaging Men in Gen- der Initiatives: What Change Agents Need to Know." *Catalyst*, May 4, 2009. Accessed December 22, 2019. http://www.catalyst.org/knowledge /engaging-men-gender-initiatives-what-change-agents-need-know.

Quenqua, Douglas. "They're Like, Way Ahead of the Linguistic Currrrve." *New York Times*, February 27, 2012. Accessed December 27, 2019. https://www .nytimes.com/2012/02/28/science/young-women-often-trendsetters-in -vocal-patterns.html.

Reddit. "When Rude Customers Tell You to Smile…." Accessed December 5, 2019. https://www.reddit.com/r/TalesFromRetail/comments/agdduo/when _rude_customers_tell_you_to_smile/.

Reiman, Tonya. *The Power of Body Language*. New York: Pocket Books, 2007.

Reuben, Ernesto, Paolo Sapienza, and Luigi Zingales. "How Stereotypes Impair Women's Careers in Science." *PNAS*, March 10, 2014. Accessed December 1, 2019. https://www.pnas.org/content/early/2014/03/05/1314788111.

Rhode, Deborah. *What Women Want: An Agenda for the Women's Movement.* Oxford, UK: Oxford University Press, 2014.

Richardson, Hollie. "What Happened when I Was Gaslit by My Boss." *Refinery29*, September 15, 2019. Accessed December 7, 2019. https://www .refinery29.com/en-gb/gaslighting-at-work.

Roeters, Anne, and Kirsten van Houdt. "Parent-Child Activities, Paid Work Interference, and Child Mental Health." *Wiley Online Library, John Wiley*

& Sons, Ltd (10.1111), March 6, 2019. Accessed January 2, 2020. https://
onlinelibrary.wiley.com/doi/10.1111/fare.12355.

Rogers, Katie. "White Women Helped Elect Donald Trump." *New York Times*,
November 9, 2016. Accessed December 20, 2019. https://www.nytimes
.com/2016/12/01/us/politics/white-women-helped-elect-donald-trump
.html.

Rollings, Michaela. "You Might Be Surprised at the Three Most-Used Emojis
at Work." *Hive*, December 3, 2019. Accessed December 6, 2019. https://
hive.com/blog/most-used-emojis-work/.

Ross, Janell. "So Which Women Has Donald Trump called 'Dogs' and 'Fat
Pigs'?" *Washington Post*, August 8, 2015. Accessed December 22, 2019.
https://www.washingtonpost.com/news/the-fix/wp/2015/08/08/so-which
-women-has-donald-trump-called-dogs-and-fat-pigs.

Rowling, J. K. "The Fringe Benefits of Failure, and the Importance of Imagination." *Harvard Gazette,* June 5, 2008. Accessed December 26, 2019. http://
news.harvard.edu/gazette/story/2008/06/text-of-j-k-rowling-speech/.

Rudman, Laurie A., and Julie E. Phelan. "Backlash Effects for Disconfirming Gender Stereotypes in Organizations." *Research in Organizational
Behavior* vol. 28 (2008): 61–79. Accessed November 29, 2019. https://doi
.org/10.1016/j.riob.2008.04.003.

Rudman, Laurie A., and Peter Glick. "Feminized Management and Backlash
towards Agentic Women: The Hidden Costs to Women of a Kinder, Gentler
Image of Middle Managers." *Journal of Personality and Social Psychology*
77(5) (1999): 1004–1010.

Rudman, Laurie A., and Peter Glick. "Prescriptive Gender Stereotypes and
Backlash toward Agentic Women." *Journal of Social Issues* 57(4) (2001):
743–762. https://psycnet.apa.org/doi/10.1111/0022-4537.00239.

Sahadi, Jeanne. "Only 33 Women Now Lead Fortune 500 Companies. And
That's a Record High." *CNN*, May 16, 2019. Accessed December 1, 2019.
https://www.cnn.com/2019/05/16/success/women-ceos-fortune-500
/index.html.

Salem, Maya. "Does 'Having It All' Mean Doing It All?" *New York Times*. Accessed
December 30, 2019. https://www.nytimes.com/2018/12/07/business/michelle
-obama-women-having-it-all.html.

Samuelson, Kate. "Who Is Alicia Machado? She Says Donald Trump Called
Her 'Miss Piggy.'" *Time*, September 27, 2016. Accessed December 22, 2019.
https://time.com/4509243/donald-trump-miss-universe-alicia-machado
-piggy-housekeeping/.

Saul, Michael. "Caroline Kennedy No Whiz with Words." *New York Daily News,* December 29, 2008. Accessed December 27, 2019. http://www.nydailynews .com/news/politics/caroline-kennedy-no-whiz-words-article-1.355586.

Sayej, Nadja. "Alyssa Milano on the #MeToo Movement: 'We're Not Going to Stand For It Any More.'" *The Guardian,* December 1, 2017. Accessed October 4, 2019. https://www.theguardian.com/culture/2017/dec/01/alyssa -milano-mee-too-sexual-harassment-abuse.

Sayer, Liana, and Joanna R. Pepin. "Moms Spend Even More Time on House-work when a Man's in the House. Here's Why." *Washington Post,* May 8, 2019. Accessed January 1, 2020. https://www.washingtonpost.com /opinions/moms-spend-even-more-time-on-housework-when-a-mans-in -the-house-heres-why/2019/05/08/319da006-71ba-11e9-8be0-ca575670 e91c_story.html.

Scagell, Julie. "The Average Full-Time Working Woman Spends 21 Hours a Week on Housework." *Scary Mommy,* August 27, 2019. Accessed January 2, 2019. https://www.scarymommy.com/working-women-spend-21-hours-chores/.

Scarborough, William. "What the Data Says about Women in Management between 1980 and 2010." *Harvard Business Review,* February 23, 2018. Accessed December 1, 2019. https://hbr.org/2018/02/what-the-data-says -about-women-in-management-between-1980-and-2010.

Schaeffer, Katherine. "Among U.S. Couples, Women Do More Cooking and Grocery Shopping than Men." *Pew Research Center,* September 24, 2019. Accessed January 2, 2020. https://www.pewresearch.org/fact-tank /2019/09/24/among-u-s-couples-women-do-more-cooking-and-grocery -shopping-than-men/.

Schaffner, Brian F., Matthew MacWilliams, and Tatishe Nteta. "Understand-ing White Polarization in the 2016 Vote for President: The Sobering Role of Racism and Sexism." *Political Science Quarterly* 133(1) (Spring 2018): 9–34. https://onlinelibrary.wiley.com/doi/abs/10.1002/polg.12737.

Schifferin, Holly H., Miriam Liss, Haley Miles McLean, et al. "Helping or Hovering? The Effects of Helicopter Parenting on College Students' Well-Being." *Journal of Child and Family Studies* 23(3) (2014): 548–557. doi:10.1007/s10826-013-9716-3.

Schmader, Toni, and Alyssa Croft. "How Stereotypes Stifle Performance Poten-tial." *Social and Personality Psychology Compass* 5(10) (2011): 792–806.

Schneider, Andrea K., Catherine H. Tinsley, Sandra Cheldelin, and Emily T. Amanatullah. "Likeability v. Competence: The Impossible Choice Faced by Female Politicians, Attenuated by Lawyers." *Duke Journal of Gender*

Law and Policy 17 (2010): 363–384. https://scholarship.law.duke.edu/djglp/vol17/iss2/4.

Schumer, Amy. "I'm Sorry." Accessed December 27, 2019. https://vimeo.com/253499468.

Schweider, David. *The Psychology of Stereotyping*. New York: The Guilford Press, 2004.

Seck, Hope Hodge. "Controversy Surrounds Firing of Marines' Female Recruit Battalion CO." *Marine Times*, July 15, 2015. Accessed December 18, 2019. http://www.marinecorpstimes.com/story/military/2015/07/07/kate-germano-fired-marine-corps-female-recruit-unit-commander/29763371/.

Segrin, Chris, Alesia Woszidlo, Michelle Givertz, and Neil Montgomery. "Parent and Child Traits Associated with Overparenting." *Journal of Social and Clinical Psychology* 32(6) (2013): 569–595. doi: 10.1521/jscp.2013.32.6.569.

Seligson, Hannah. "Why the Sting of Layoffs Can Be Harder for Men." *New York Times*, January 31, 2009. Accessed January 1, 2020. http://www.nytimes.com/2009/02/01/jobs/01layoff.html.

Setzler, Mark, and Alixandra B. Yanus. "Why Did Women Vote for Donald Trump." *PS: Political Science & Politics* 51(3) (July 2018): 523–527. https://doi-org.proxy.lawrence.edu:2443/10.1017/S1049096518000355.

Shear, Michael D., and Eileen Sullivan. "'Horseface,' 'Lowlife,' 'Fat, Ugly': How the President Demeans Women." *New York Times*, October 16, 2018. Accessed December 22, 2019. https://www.nytimes.com/2018/10/16/us/politics/trump-women-insults.html.

Shear, Michael D., and Eileen Sullivan. "Trump Calls Omarosa Manigault Newman 'That Dog' in His Latest Insult." *New York Times*, August 14, 2018. Accessed December 22, 2019. https://www.nytimes.com/2018/08/14/us/politics/trump-omarosa-dog.html.

Shellenbarger, Sue. "Use Mirroring to Connect with Others: Adopting the Same Gestures, Posture, or Tone Can Enhance Bonding and Help with Networking or Negotiating—But be Subtle about It." *Wall Street Journal*, September 20, 2016. Accessed December 24, 2016. https://www.wsj.com/articles/use-mirroring-to-connect-with-others-1474394329.

Sherman, Gabriel. "The Revenge of Roger's Angels." *New York Magazine*, September 5, 2016. Accessed December 22, 2019. http://nymag.com/intelligencer/2016/09/how-fox-news-women-took-down-roger-ailes.html.

"Silencing Women's Public Voices, May 24, 2016. Accessed December 3, 2019. http://andieandal.com/silencing-womens-public-voices/.

Silva, Christine, Nancy M. Carter, and Anna Beninger. "Good Intentions, Imperfect Execution? Women Get Fewer of the 'Hot Jobs' Needed to

Advance." *Catalyst,* 2012. Accessed December 18, 2019. https://www
.catalyst.org/research/good-intentions-imperfect-execution-women
-get-fewer-of-the-hot-jobs-needed-to-advance/.

Simmons, Rachel. *The Curse of the Good Girl: Raising Authentic Girls with Courage and Confidence.* New York: Penguin, 2010.

Simon, George. "Gaslighting as a Manipulation Tactic: What It Is, Who Does It, and Why." Accessed December 30, 2019. https://counsellingresource.com
/features/2011/11/08/gaslighting/.

Singer, Jenny. "How Many Men at CBS Had Heard That Eliza Dushku Was Sexually Threatened On Tape?" *Forward, The Schmooze,* December 19, 2018. Accessed December 22, 2019. https://forward.com/schmooze/416342
/cbs-sexual-harassment-scandal-implicates-top-execs-showrunner
-actors-and/.

Singh, Val, Savita Kumra, and Susan Vinnicombe. "Gender and Impression Management: Playing the Promotion Game." *Journal of Business Ethics* 37(1) (2002): 77–89. www.jstor.org/stable/25074734.

Slaughter, Anne-Marie. *Unfinished Business: Women Men Work Family.* New York: Random House, 2015.

Slaughter, Anne-Marie. "Why Women Still Can't Have It All." *Atlantic,* July/August 2012. Accessed January 1, 2020. http://www.theatlantic.com
/magazine/archive/2012/07/why-women-still-cant-have-it-all/309020/.

Smith, Jessi, and Meghan Huntoon, "Women's Bragging Rights: Overcoming Modesty Norms to Facilitate Women's Self-Promotion." *Psychology of Women Quarterly* 38(4) (2013): 447–459. doi: 10.1177/0361684313515840.

Solnit, Rebecca. "A Nation Groomed and Battered." In *Nasty Women: Feminism, Resistance, and Revolution in Trump's America,* Samhita Mukhopadhyay and Kate Harding (eds.). New York: Picador, 2017.

Sparkes, Matthew. "Christine Lagarde: 'Women Can't Have It All.'" *Business Insider,* September 26, 2012. Accessed January 1, 2020. http://www
.businessinsider.com/christine-lagarde-women-cant-have-it-all-2012-9.

Sparks, John R., Charles S. Areni, and K. Chris Cox. "An Investigation of the Effects of Language Style and Communication Modality on Persuasion." *Communication Monographs* 65(2) (1998).

Stainback, Kevin, Sibyl Kleiner, and Sheryl Skaggs. "Women in Power: Undoing or Redoing the Gender Organization?" *Gender and Society* 30(1) (February 2016).

Stanberry, Lindsey. "Try This Experiment if You Say 'Sorry' Too Much." *Refinery29,* August 3, 2015. Accessed December 27, 2019. http://www.refinery29
.com/saying-sorry-at-work#.ozt2o1:J1f7.

Statista. "People Like Emojis at Work, but Feel Unsure at First." July 17, 2019. Accessed December 6, 2019. https://www.statista.com/chart/18717/emoji -use-at-work/.

Steel, Emily. "Fox Establishes Workplace Culture Panel after Harassment Scandal." *New York Times*, November 20, 2017. Accessed December 22, 2019. https://www.nytimes.com/2017/11/20/business/media/fox-news-sexual -harassment.html.

Steel, Emily. "How Bill O'Reilly Silenced His Accusers." *New York Times*, April 4, 2018. Accessed December 22, 2019. https://www.nytimes.com/2018/04/04 /business/media/how-bill-oreilly-silenced-his-accusers.html.

Steel, Emily, and Michael S. Schmidt. "Bill O'Reilly Thrives at Fox News, Even as Harassment Settlements Add Up." *New York Times*, April 1, 2017. Accessed December 22, 2019. https://www.nytimes.com/2017/04/business/media /bill-oreilly-sexual-harassment-fox-news.html.

Steele, Claude M., and Joshua Aronson. "Stereotype Threat and the Intellectual Test Performance of African Americans." *Journal of Personality and Social Psychology* 69(5) (1995): 797–811. Accessed December 18, 2019, 2019, doi: 10.1037//0022-3514.69.5.797.

Steinberg, Brian. "Fox News Fires Bill O'Reilly amid Sexual Harassment Storm." *Variety*, April 19, 2017. Accessed December 22, 2019. https://variety .com/2017/tv/news/bill-oreilly-fired-fox-newssexual-harassment-murdoch -1202044514/.

Stern, Howard. "Howard Stern." *Interview by CNN KFILE*, October 2016. https://soundcloud.com/user-704098053/howard-stern.

Stilwell, Victoria. "Fewer Millennial Moms Show U.S. Birth Rate Drop Lasting." *Bloomberg Business*, September 16, 2014. Accessed January 1, 2020. http://www.bloomberg.com/news/articles/2014-09-16/fewer-millennial -moms-show-u-s-birth-rate-drop-lasting.

Stop Street Harassment. "The Facts behind the #MeToo Movement." February 2018. http://www.stopstreetharassment.org/wp-content/uploads/2018/01 /Full-Report-2018-National-Study-on-Sexual-Harassment-and-Assault.pdf.

Strayed, Cheryl. "She Will." In *Nasty Woman: Feminism, Resistance and Revolution.* Samhita Mukhopadhyay and Kate Harding (eds.). New York: Picador, 2017.

Tambe, Ashwini. "Why #MeToo Happened in 2017." *National Public Radio*, February 7, 2018. http://www.npr.org/2018/02/07/583910310/why-metoo.

TeamPay. "Three Keys to Closing the Leadership Gap in Finance." March 22, 2019. Accessed December 1, 2019. https://www.teampay.co/insights/closing -the-finance-leadership-gap/.

"The Kardashians Talk Back to Tweets." *YouTube*, April 1, 2011. Accessed October 3, 2015. https://www.youtube.com/watch?v=d8jL8qz7dwM.

Thompson, Jeff. "Mimicry and Mirroring Can Be Good or Bad: Mirroring and Mimicry May Increase or Decrease Rapport and Liking," *Psychology Today*, September 9, 2012. Accessed December 26, 2019. https://www.psychologytoday.com/us/blog/beyond-words/201209/mimicry-and-mirroring-can-be-good-or-bad.

Thompson, Rachel. "The Most Harassed Women Online Share Why They're Not Logging Off." *Mashable*, 2018. Accessed December 5, 2019. https://mashable.com/2018/06/18/online-harassment-trolling-women/.

Thomson, Stephanie. "A Lack of Confidence Isn't What's Holding Back Working Women." *Atlantic*, September 20, 2018. Accessed December 7, 2019. https://www.theatlantic.com/family/archive/2018/09/women-workplace-confidence-gap/570772/.

Thorpe, J. R., "Why Do People Expect Women to Smile?" *Bustle*, July 6, 2017. Accessed December 7, 2019. https://www.bustle.com/p/why-do-people-expect-women-to-smile-67360.

Time. "Millennials: The Me Generation." May 20, 2013, accessed December 13, 2019. https://time.com/247/Millennials-the-me-me-me-generation/.

Tinsley, Catherine H., and Robin J. Ely. "What Most People Get Wrong about Men and Women." *Harvard Business Review*, May-June 2018. Accessed December 1, 2019. https://hbr.org/2018/05/what-most-people-get-wrong-about-men-and-women.

Torpey, Elka. "Women in Management." US Bureau of Labor Statistics, March 2017. https://www.bls.gov/careeroutlook/2017/data-on-display/women-managers.htm?view_full.

Tracy, Sarah J., and Kendra Dyanne Rivera. "Endorsing Equity and Applauding Stay at Home Moms: How Male Voices on Work-Life Reveal Aversive Sexism and Flickers of Transformation." *Management Communication Quarterly* 24(1) (2010): 3–43. https://doi.org/10.1177/0893318909352248.

Trix, Frances, and Carolyn Psenka. "Exploring the Color of Glass: Letters of Recommendation for Female and Male Medical Faculty." *Discourse & Society* 14(2) (2003): 191–220. https://doi.org/10.1177%2F0957926503014002277.

"Trump Calls Clinton 'Crooked,' Says She Lies about Him." *NBC News*, May 27, 2016. Accessed December 22, 2019. https://www.nbcnews.com/video/trump-calls-clinton-crooked-says-she-lies-about-him-6943344531972.

Trump, Donald (@realDonaldTrump). "@ariannahuff is unattractive both inside and out. I fully understand why her former husband left her for a man—he made a good decision." Tweet, August 28, 2012. Accessed December 22, 2019. https://twitter.com/realDonaldTrump/status/240462 265680289792.

Trump, Donald (@realDonaldTrump). "@BetteMidler talks about my hair but I'm not allowed to talk about her ugly face or body—so I won't. Is this a double standard?" Tweet, October 28, 2012. Accessed December 22, 2019. https://twitter.com/realDonaldTrump/status/262583859709882369.

Trump, Donald (@realDonaldTrump). "When you give a crazed, crying low-life a break, and give her a job at the White House, I guess it just didn't work out. Good work by General Kelly for quickly firing that dog!" Tweet, August 14, 2018. Accessed December 22, 2019. https://twitter.com/real DonaldTrump/status/1029329583672307712.

Tur, Katie. *Unbelievable: My Front-Row Seat to the Craziest Campaign in American History.* New York: HarperCollins Publishers, 2018.

Turner, Caroline. "Gender and Generational Differences: The Intersection." *Huffington Post,* updated December 6, 2017. Accessed January 6, 2020. https://www.huffpost.com/entry/gender-and-generational-d_b_5974624.

United States Census Bureau. "Women in the Workforce: 1940–2010." Accessed December 1, 2019. https://www2.census.gov/programs-surveys/sis/activities /history/hh-9_teacher.pdf.

Valentino, Nicholas A., Carly Wayne, and Marzia Oceno, "Mobilizing Sexism: The Interaction of Emotion and Gender Attitudes in the 2016 US Presidential Election." *Public Opinion Quarterly* 82(51) (2018).

Vanderkam, Laura. "What Does Authenticity Really Mean?" *Fast Company,* November 20, 2015. Accessed November 30, 2019. https://www.fastcompany .com/3053566/what-does-authenticity-really-mean.

Van Syckle, Katie. "Mila Kunis Says There's No Such Thing as Having It All." *The Cut.* Accessed January 2, 2020. https://www.thecut.com/2016/07/mila -kunis-bad-moms-having-it-all.html.

Vedantam, Shankar. "Salary, Gender, and the Social Cost of Haggling." *Washington Post,* July 30, 2007. Accessed January 1, 2020. http://www .washingtonpost.com/wp-dyn/content/article/2007/07/29/AR20070729 00827.html.

Waldman, Katy. "The Tyranny of the Smile: Why Does Everyone Expect Women to Smile All the Time?" *Slate,* June 18, 2013. Accessed December 7, 2019. https://slate.com/human-interest/2013/06/bitchy-resting-face-and -female-niceness-why-do-women-have-to-smile-more-than-men.html.

Warner, Judith, and Danielle Corley. "The Women's Leadership Gap," Center for American Progress, May 21, 2017. Accessed December 1, 2019. https://www.americanprogress.org/issues/women/reports/2017/05/21/432758/womens-leadership-gap/.

Warner, Judith, Nora Ellmann, and Diana Boesch. "The Women's Leadership Gap." Center for American Progress, November 20, 2018, Accessed December 1, 2019. https://www.americanprogress.org/issues/women/reports/2018/11/20/461273/womens-leadership-gap-2/.

Wayne, Sandy J., and Robert C. Liden. "Effects of Impression Management on Performance Ratings: A Longitudinal Study." *Academy of Management Journal* 38(1) (1995): 232–260. www.jstor.org/stable/256734.

Weeks, Holly. "Taking the Stress Out of Stressful Conversations." *Harvard Business Review*, July-August 2001. Accessed December 29, 2019. https://hbr.org/2001/07/taking-the-stress-out-of-stressful-conversations.

Wharton, Amy S. *Working in America: Continuity, Conflict, and Change in a New Economic Era.* 4th Ed. Routledge 2015.

Whiteman, Mauro. "PepsiCo CEO Indra Nooyi: 'I Don't Think Women Can Have It All Either,'" *Aspen Idea Blog,* July 1, 2014. Accessed January 1, 2020. http://www.aspeninstitute.org/about/blog/pepsico-ceo-indra-nooyi-i-don-t-think-women-can-have-it-all-either.

Williams, Joan C. "Hacking Tech's Diversity Problem." *Harvard Business Review,* October 2014. Accessed December 31, 2019. https://hbr.org/2014/10/hacking-techs-diversity-problem.

Williams, Joan C., Jodi Short, Margot Brooks, Hilary Hardcastle, Tiffanie Ellis, and Rayna Saron. "What's Reasonable Now? Sexual Harassment Law After the Norm Cascade." *Michigan State Law Review* (2019). https://digitalcommons.law.msu.edu/lr/vol2019/iss1/4/.

Winkielman, Piotr, Paula Niedenthal, Joseph Wielgosz, Jiska Eelen, and Liam C. Kavanagh. "Embodiment of Cognition and Emotion." *APA Handbook of Personality and Social Psychology: Vol. 1. Attitudes and Social Cognition* (2015): 151–175. American Psychological Association. http://dx.doi.org/10.1037/14341-004.

Winograd, Morley, and Michael D. Hais. "Race? No, Millennials Care More about Gender Equality." *Atlantic,* October 25, 2013. Accessed December 13, 2019. https://www.theatlantic.com/politics/archive/2013/10/race-no-millennials-care-most-about-gender-equality/430305/.

Workplace Bullying Institute. "2014 WBI U.S. Workplace Bullying Survey." 2014. Accessed December 17, 2019. https://workplacebullying.org/multi/pdf/2014-Survey-Flyer-B.pdf.

Young, Samantha. "Gaslighting at Work—When You Think You Are Going Crazy." Accessed December 30, 2019. https://www.linkedin.com/pulse /gaslighting-work-when-you-think-going-crazy-samantha-young.

Yovetich, Nancy A., T. Alexander Dale, and Mary A. Hudak. "Benefits of Humor in Reduction of Threat-Induced Anxiety." *Psychological Reports* 66(1) (1990): 51–58.

Zaleski, Katharine. "Female Company President: 'I'm Sorry to All the Mothers I Worked With.'" *Fortune*, March 3, 2015. Accessed January 1, 2020. http:// fortune.com/2015/03/03/female-company-president-im-sorry-to-all-the -mothers-i-used-to-work-with/.

INDEX

taking up space in, 175
verbal challenges and, 181–183
when to arrive and leave, 173–174
memory, stereotype threat and, 28–29
men, xxxi
characterization of, 5
mentoring, 11, 35, 74, 166, 198
meritocracy, 42–43
#MeToo movement, xxxii, 55–56, 58–59
Bill Cosby's sexual harassment of women, 58
Bill O'Reilly's sexual harassment of women, 56, 60
Harvey Weinstein's sexual predations, 56, 58, 60
Roger Ailes's sexual harassment of women, 57
microaggression, xxvii, 165
Midler, Bette, 51
Milano, Alyssa, 56
Millennials, gender bias among, 20–21
mind priming, 95–97
before meetings, 95
for self-promotion, 96
power posing and, 97
voice, 141
mirroring, 112–114
methods, 113–114
negative effects of, 113
research about, 112–113
misogynistic criticism of women, xxvii, xxxii
misogyny, xxvi–xxvii, xxxii, 48–55, 60
mixed-gender meetings, 172–173
airtime, 183–184
idea theft, 178–180
interruptions, 175–178
piling on, 180–181
postmeeting wrap-up, 174
premeeting meeting, 173–174
reaching consensus, 184–185
seat selection, 175
verbal challenges, 181–183
when to arrive and leave, 173–174
modesty stereotype, 43–45, 188–189, 191
Monroe, Marilyn, 124
Moonves, Les, 57, 60
motherhood
bias, xxv, 16–20
childcare, 215–216
fathers' responsibilities vs, 210, 221
having children, 212–216
household responsibilities, 216
maternity leave, 213–215

Muller-Lyer optical illusion, 7
myths
personal uniqueness, 40–42
work as meritocracy, 42–43

N
National Science Foundation, 203
negative bias, xxv–xxvi
negative gender bias, 11–14
aging out of, 20–24
negative gender stereotypes, 29
negative nonverbal behaviors, 106–108
appearing untrustworthy, 108
domineering behavior, 107–108
weak appearance, 106–107
neutrality, in feedback/criticism, 148
Newman, Omarosa Manigault, 51
nodding, 111–112
no impairment statement, 29–30
nonverbal communication, 79–80, 103–122
agentic, 104–106, 123
appearance, 119–122
communal, 104
dominance, 81, 116, 175
eye contact, 81–82
facial expressions, 80–81
hand gestures, 105–106, 109
handshakes, 115–117
head nodding, 82–83
hugs and kisses, 117–118
listening and nodding, 111–112
mirroring, 112–114
negative nonverbal behaviors, 106–108
positive nonverbal behaviors, 108–109
smiling, 82, 111
touching, 118–119
using hands and arms, 115
using space, 109–111
weakness shown by, 107
nonverbal cues, 27
Noonan, Peggy, 94
Nooyi, Indra, 217
normative discrimination at work, 19
"no," saying, 151–157

O
Obama, Barack, 53
Obama, Michelle, 217
occupational gender segregation, 32
O'Connor, Sandra Day, 48
O'Grady, Kim, 11

ABOUT THE AUTHORS

Andrea S. Kramer (Andie) and Alton B. Harris (Al) have been working for over 30 years to increase the gender diversity of senior leadership in all sorts of businesses and professional organizations. Their approach is to provide women with tools and techniques they can use to avoid or overcome gender bias, to make men aware of the serious career advancement obstacles women face and suggest steps men can take to become effective advocates for women, and to provide organizations with the guidance necessary to implement policies and procedures to ensure their career-affecting decisions are not influenced by gender stereotypes and bias.

Both Andie and Al have served in senior management positions and have in-depth experience with all aspects of personnel management, including recruiting, hiring, supervision of individuals and teams, evaluations, compensation, and promotion. They have written two books together about women, careers, and stereotypes and the bias that flows from them: *Breaking Through Bias: Communication Techniques for Women to Succeed at Work* (first edition, 2016) and *It's Not You, It's the Workplace: Women's Conflict at Work and the Bias That Built It* (2019). They have also written more than 200 professional and gender-related articles (including a number of articles in the *Harvard Business Review*) and blog posts. They collaborate in mentoring and coaching women, and they speak and conduct workshops separately and together about diversity, inclusion, bias, and communication skills. Their goal is to increase women's prospects for career advancement.

Andie is a nationally recognized authority on gender communication and gender bias. She is also a partner in an international law firm,

where she formed and chaired its Gender Diversity Committee and pre-
viously served on its Management Committee and Compensation Com-
mittee. Andie contributes to Forbes.com on the topic of women in the
workplace and is a coauthor of the American Bar Association's guide,
What You Need to Know about Negotiating Compensation. Some of
Andie's honors and accolades include being named one of the 50 Most
Influential Women Lawyers in America by the *National Law Journal;*
Gender Diversity Lawyer of the Year (ChambersUSA); Founder's Award
(Chicago Bar Association's Alliance for Women); and the "Woman with
Vision Award" and "Top Women Lawyers in Leadership Award" (Wom-
en's Bar Association of Illinois). For her sustained commitment to pro
bono work, she received the American Bar Association's Business Law
Section's National Public Service Award. *Chicago Lawyer* named her an
"Inspiring Innovator" for her efforts to promote gender equality, the *Chicago Tribune* identified her as a "Remarkable Woman," and *Crain's Chicago Business* recognized her as one of the Chicagoans best at mentoring
women.

Al was a founding partner of a midsized Chicago law firm that is
now part of a large national law firm. He served at various times as managing partner, Executive Committee and Compensation Committee
member, and head of the Corporate and Securities Practice Group. Al
served for over 20 years as an adjunct professor of law at Northwestern
University School of Law. Over the course of his career, Al has grown
increasingly concerned about the barriers and biases women face because
workplaces in traditionally male career fields are dominated by masculine norms, values, and expectations, and they are suffused with gender
stereotypes and biases. Al's extensive research, astute observations, and
pragmatic voice have made him a nationally recognized advocate for
women's career advancement. He focuses on the communication skills
women need to advance in their chosen fields despite the prevalence of
bias-driven career obstacles. A frequent lecturer and keynote speaker, Al
talks to women about what their male colleagues expect from them as
they seek to be recognized as leaders. He talks to men about why they
need to become allies and ways they can effectively advocate for women's

advancement. And he talks to organizations about the positive consequences of true gender diversity and practical steps to achieve it.

Andie and Al are married, have a daughter who is a medical doctor, and live in Chicago with four rescue dogs and four rescue cats.

*   *   *

We'd love to hear from you!
Please visit us at www.AndieandAl.com and sign up for our newsletter.
Follow us on Twitter @AndieandAl.
www.AndieandAl.com